The Deterioration of the
Mexican Presidency

Schmidt identifies the central feature of Mexico's political crisis as the deterioration of "presidentialism." It intensified, if it did not entirely originate, during the presidency of Luis Echeverría and has been worsening ever since. Schmidt believes that Echeverría came into office in 1970 determined to resolve this crisis. According to Schmidt, Echeverría began his term with three major goals: nationalism, anti-imperialism, and revitalization of the system. But because of personal flaws and the opposition of the bourgeoisie, he achieved only extended confrontation, destabilization of the economy, repressive pacification, and alienation of the regime's allies in all sectors of society. His personal failure contributed to the decline of the office of the presidency and a weakening of the Mexican regime.

Samuel Schmidt

The Deterioration of the Mexican Presidency: The Years of Luis Echeverría

Translated and Edited by
Dan A. Cothran

The University of Arizona Press
Tucson

F
1236
S3613
1991

THE UNIVERSITY OF ARIZONA PRESS

Copyright © 1991
Samuel Schmidt
All Rights Reserved

⊗ This book is printed on acid-free, archival-quality paper.
Manufactured in the United States of America.

96 95 94 93 92 91 6 5 4 3 2 1

LIBRARY OF CONGRESS CATALOGING-IN-PUBLICATION DATA

Schmidt, Samuel.
[Deterioro del presidencialismo mexicano. English]
The deterioration of the Mexican presidency : the years of Luis
Echeverría / Samuel Schmidt : translated and edited by Dan A.
Cothran.
p. cm.
Translation of: El deterioro del presidencialismo mexicano.
Includes bibliographical references (p.) and index.
ISBN 0-8165-1235-3 (cloth)
1. Mexico—Politics and government—1970–1981. 2. Echeverría,
Luis, 1922– . 3. Executive power—Mexico—History—20th century.
I. Title.
F1236.S35 1991
972.08'32'092—dc20   91-17540
                                                              CIP

British Library Cataloguing in Publication data are available.

To Adam and Noa

CONTENTS

ACKNOWLEDGMENTS

This book was developed in two stages. The first was a chronological study that was part of my investigative work in the Centro de Estudios Latinoamericanos of the Political and Social Sciences Faculty of the Autonomous National University of Mexico, or UNAM. Here I conceived the idea of comparing various sexennial regimes in hopes of understanding the particulars of political power and especially presidential power. CELA published one of the preliminary results of my investigation, the book entitled *La política de industrialización de Miguel Alemán*.

During this phase of my study I concluded that in the twentieth century, three periods stood out in which serious attempts were made to modernize the Mexican political system. The first was the administration of Lázaro Cárdenas (1934–40), who strengthened the presidency while he repressed efforts to unify the peasants and workers in a single organization. He also pressed the peasants and workers into following state leadership, at the same time politically co-opting and pointing the direction the dominant classes were to follow. The Miguel Alemán administration (1946–52) broadened the state's administrative apparatus, enlarging its sphere of action and influence while restricting the workers' ability to organize, submitting them to the designs of the dominant classes, who were to accumulate capital and bring about "progress." The third was the administration of Luis Echeverría (1970–76), who attempted to reconstruct the decaying state apparatus and the symbolic system, which were no longer functional instruments of sociopolitical control.

The support I received from my students in the Faculty of Political and Social Sciences provided me with the incentive to face the rigorous task of developing my framework and strengthening my analysis. Especially important were my associates at the Taller Autogestionario de Investigación Política.

The second part of the investigation consisted of a comprehensive theoretical framework developed in my doctoral thesis.[1] Later I continued this study as a postdoctoral student in history at the University of

California at Los Angeles (UCLA). Here I learned to work with statistics and derive meaning from cold data. I would like to recognize and express my gratitude to James W. Wilkie. He was not only a great teacher and colleague, but an excellent friend who, along with his wife, Edna Monzón de Wilkie, helped make my stay in California a pleasant and memorable occasion. The same should be said of the excellent treatment I received from the members of the Latin America Center at UCLA and the staff of the *Statistical Abstract of Latin America*.

I am also grateful for the financial support I received from the Fulbright Foundation and UNAM, which made my study at UCLA possible.

My special appreciation is extended to Martha Bonifaz, Alicia Carbajal, Esther Centeno, and Graciela Echaury, who helped me with the tedious task of typing the various manuscripts that developed into this book.

To translate a book implies not only a linguistic process, but also the adaptation of the book to another type of reader's mentality and the possibility of making corrections and improving the work. In this task Douglas Schubert, my student at San Diego State University, helped, but especially I want to express my deepest appreciation to Dan Cothran, political scientist at Northern Arizona University, because without his collaboration this English version would not be possible. His translation improved the book and made it available to the English-speaking reader.

Finally, I would like to recognize the efforts of Rosy, who accompanied me to California even though she had not yet become acclimated to Mexico City. She had to confront a new culture and to deal with the moods of an investigator who frequently was so occupied with his work that he had little time for anything else.

SAMUEL SCHMIDT

EDITOR'S INTRODUCTION
Pacification through Repression and Distribution: The Echeverría Years in Mexico

Dan A. Cothran

The Mexican political system is in a state of crisis. The nature and extent of that crisis, however, are a matter of considerable debate. Equally at issue are the origins of the crisis. Some see it as the failure of the political system to keep pace with the social and economic changes of the past fifty years. Others trace the origins to the poor economic performance of Mexico since the mid-1970s. Still others see it as a struggle within the political elite for control of the regime. The events of 1988, when the PRI nearly lost the presidency, indicate that the crisis is not over.

In the late 1970s and the 1980s a rash of books appeared in the United States on the political and economic crisis in Mexico. This type of book first appeared just after Echeverría's presidency, picked up momentum after López Portillo, and has continued unabated to the present. One of the earliest such books was *The Future of Mexico*. A veritable flood of studies appeared in the U.S. in the 1980s, with such titles as *Mexico's Political Stability*, *Mexico in Transition*, and *Mexico's Economic Crisis*.[1] Books also appeared in Mexico commenting on the crisis of the political system. In 1982 Juan Miguel de Mora published *Esto nos dió López Portillo*, and in 1986 Julio Scherer García published *Los presidentes*, a critical look at Díaz Ordaz, Echeverría, López Portillo, and de la Madrid.[2] One of the best at tracing the origins of the crisis is Samuel Schmidt's *El deterioro del presidencialismo mexicano: Los años de Luis Echeverría* (1986), here translated into English for the first time.

SCHMIDT AND THE DECLINE OF MEXICAN PRESIDENTIALISM

Schmidt believes that the central feature of the political crisis facing Mexico is the deterioration of "presidentialism," which intensified, if it did not entirely originate, during the presidency of Luis Echeverría and has been worsening ever since. He believes that Echeverría came into office in 1970 determined to resolve this crisis. According to Schmidt, Echeverría began his term with three major goals: nationalism, anti-imperialism, and revitalization of the system. But because of personal flaws and the opposition of the bourgeoisie, he achieved only extended confrontation, the destabilization of the economy, repressive pacification, and the alienation of the regime's allies in all sectors of society. His personal failure contributed to the decline of the office of the president and a weakening of the Mexican regime.

This book makes a contribution to our understanding of Mexican politics in several ways. First, it discusses in detail some revealing issues such as the Echeverría Letter, the anti-Zionist vote, the steroid controversy, and the guerrilla groups active in the 1970s. Schmidt believes that all these matters demonstrated Echeverría's ineptitude in handling Mexico's problems. The book also deals in a more explicit way than most with the issue of academic freedom in Mexico. Schmidt says in his Introduction that there is considerable academic and press freedom about most subjects, but not about the sacrosanct person of the president. As he puts it: "In Mexico, one can say anything about the president as long as it is not critical." The system of implicit censorship has made many Mexicans extremely skeptical; the regime is often suspected of skullduggery, and its claims of innocence are widely disbelieved.

Finally, this book helps to convey the important role of rumor and jokes in the Mexican political system, in which other means of criticism and communication are often stifled. Jokes, an omnipresent feature of the political scene, increase during times of discontent. A recounting of rumors and jokes gives a feel for how intensely Mexican society was polarized in the early 1970s. The vehemence and cruelty of much of the humor suggest that many people were committing "violence in their hearts" against the government, even if not yet translating their thoughts into actions. The jokes about Echeverría demonstrate just how low his political star had sunk and how much the office of the presidency itself was damaged. This pattern has continued, and political humor reached a fever pitch in Mexico during the 1988 election. Samuel Schmidt has become something of an expert on the subject and is currently at work on a book entitled *Humor and Politics*.

The modern Mexican political system was consolidated in the 1930s. In 1929 Plutarco Elías Calles created an umbrella political party within which all "revolutionary" forces could participate in politics. From 1935 to 1938 Lázaro Cárdenas restructured that party along corporatist lines by encouraging the creation of organizations representing some of the major social forces such as peasants, urban labor, and the middle classes and then bringing those groups formally into the party. This corporatist structure was a way of channeling and controlling demands, keeping the demands peaceful and at a level that the government could handle with limited resources. For decades, the regime enjoyed broad support from most groups in society as the economy grew and per capita income rose. Business had prospered during the years of import-substituting industrialization, in which the government provided conditions conducive to business profits, including tariff protection, subsidized credit, low taxes, tariff exemptions on imported machinery, and more.

By 1970, however, that political system was finding it difficult to deal successfully with new demands being placed on it. From the beginning of his term, Echeverría was confronted by a system in crisis. The student mobilization of the late 1960s had culminated in the massacre of demonstrators in Mexico City in October 1968. As minister of the interior, Echeverría had been intimately involved in the turmoil of the Díaz Ordaz years, in which hundreds died and thousands were jailed. The discontent that led to the confrontation between the regime and large segments of the population had many causes, but two important ones were a desire for greater political participation by the middle class and a desire to overcome the worst of the economic inequalities that had persisted during the years of the Mexican "economic miracle," from the 1940s through the 1960s. Although Mexico had experienced economic growth rates averaging at least 6 percent for many years, not all Mexicans had shared in the boom. Extreme inequalities of wealth had continued and in some ways had even increased.

Thus, by the late 1960s, significant indications of discontent began to appear. The economic growth during this period produced a much more complex society, especially a larger middle class. The turmoil of the 1960s and 1970s was led, and largely manned, by this new middle class. Although labor and the peasantry were less alienated from the regime by 1970 than was the middle class, these sectors also had become somewhat disenchanted. As industrialization proceeded, new unions emerged that the regime struggled to incorporate and control. As land available for redistribution became increasingly scarce, the regime found it more difficult to keep the peasants satisfied. Violence against the government was rare in the 1960s, but citizens found other ways to register their discontent. More and more of them abstained from voting. In the late 1960s growing numbers of students demonstrated against the government. The president even became an object of scorn to some people. In fact, Luis Javier Garrido says that Lopez Mateos "was the last chief executive to be able to attend public functions without eliciting jeers."[3] Popular vilification of the president was something relatively new in modern Mexican history and was no doubt partly responsible for the vehemence of the regime's response to mass demonstrations. The popular demonstration of August 27, 1968 was characterized by cries of "Death to the monkey Díaz Ordaz!" The massacre at Tlatelolco came just five weeks later.

As Schmidt points out, Echeverría recognized that significant changes had to be made. In terms of economic policy, he stepped up the distribution of benefits to various groups. He greatly increased government spending for programs ranging from increased social security to agricultural credit. The government took over failing firms, and thus the number of parastatal firms increased tenfold, from 84 in 1970 to 845 in 1976. One of the largest initiatives of the Echeverría administration was the increase in the activities of CONASUPO, the government network of stores providing basic necessities at subsidized prices. The parastatal firms were also used to bolster employment, especially of the young generation of recent graduates.

Echeverría's economic strategy was not limited to populist measures such as government employment and subsidized prices. It also pursued economic growth. One of the structural flaws of the Mexican economy was that the capacity for production had increased faster than purchasing power. The size of the internal market was held down by a rural peasantry that was virtually outside the cash economy and by a marginalized urban lower class that had little purchasing power. The Echeverría administration initiated some policies to stimulate demand, in an attempt to extend purchasing power to a wider population. That, in turn, was supposed to stimulate production. But Echeverría's economic policies were often confused, and when the opposing policies of distribution and growth conflicted, Echeverría chose distribution. Government expenditures increased far faster than government revenues, and business opposed the tax increases necessary to fund the new programs. The result was a large budget deficit and growing inflation. Some of Mexico's inflation in the 1970s was imported from the world economy, of course, but some was due to the government's fiscal policies. A second outcome was an increase in government debt, both domestic and foreign. The foreign debt was fueled by another of Echeverría's populist economic policies, which made it more difficult (and less attractive) for foreign firms to invest in Mexico. Thus as direct foreign investment declined, Mexico came to depend more and more on borrowing to sustain the economy.

Schmidt argues that Echeverría's policies were thwarted at every turn by the opposition of the capitalists themselves. His detailed account of the Mexican case adds to our understanding of an important and relatively common phenomenon—the conflict between business and a populist government. Obviously, the clash did not reach the level of intensity that it did in Chile during the same years nor did it have the same political outcome, but it did become vehement enough to fuel rumors of a coup d'etat toward the end of Echeverría's term.

From the beginning of his term, Echeverría tried to defuse the dissent by increasing the level of political participation. He opened the system to young people in various ways. The voting age was reduced to eighteen years. Many young university graduates were given jobs in government, especially in the new and expanded parastatal firms. This practice had always existed, but both the quantity of state employment and the quality changed. Not only did the bureaucracy grow rapidly and provide jobs for many more young people, but many of these young people were given mid-level positions much sooner in their careers than had previously been the case.

Echeverría did other things to try to put himself in front of the growing dissent in the country. He encouraged the creation of political parties, as long as they accepted PRI domination. He removed governors who were unpopular, seemed to encourage the creation of new peasant and labor organizations, and generally adopted a populist style of governing that was designed to place himself at the head of the movement for change. An important part of this strategy was his government's Third World "anti-imperialist" positions in foreign policy. In particular, Schmidt discusses the Echeverría Letter and Mexico's anti-Zionist UN vote in some detail. Although Schmidt sees them as symptomatic of the Echeverría administration's tendency to act in dramatic ways without fully calculating the consequences, they were aimed at enhancing the legitimacy of the regime in the eyes of its most active critics.

In the end these attempts at co-optation failed to achieve their main objective, which was to reduce dissent. Violent antiregime activity reached levels not seen in Mexico since the early 1930s. In both the cities and the countryside, guerrilla groups engaged in bank robbery, kidnapping, and occasionally murder. The regime's response was even more brutal. Under Echeverría, political arrests, torture, disappearances, and murder by government forces occurred at a rate highly unusual for Mexico.

The sides were becoming more polarized. Business blamed the president for fostering an antibusiness attitude that allegedly contributed to the willingness of dissidents to engage in violent antibusiness behavior. The most spectacular example was the kidnapping and murder of Eugenio Garza Sada, a leading Monterrey businessman. Business confidence in the government plummeted, contributing to capital flight, which in turn depressed economic growth. Schmidt argues that the bourgeoisie was economically astute but politically immature. It wanted government's help in all sorts of ways, and in fact, according to Schmidt, a "godfathered capitalism" (*el capitalismo apadrinado*) was created in Mexico. The government provided an infrastructure of protection that virtually guaranteed business its profits, rather than letting business be subjected to the rigors of market competition. Yet when government attempted to put limits on business or asked it to contribute more in taxes, the bourgeoisie struck back and sabotaged the government's efforts through criticism, opposition, capital flight, raising prices, and so on. Thus Schmidt sees big business as perhaps the chief despoiler of Echeverría's plans to resolve Mexico's problems.

It was against this background that business and the middle class engaged in a riot of rumor and humor. Rumors occur in all political systems, as Americans have witnessed recently in the cases of John Tower, Tom Foley, and others. But in Mexico rumors seem to have played a far larger role in destabilizing the political system. Schmidt contends that rumors flourish in inverse proportion to the openness and accuracy of the press. Not only do rumors abound in political systems where there are few other credible channels of information, but people seem to pay more attention to them in such systems. Schmidt recounts many rumors that made the rounds during Echeverría's presidency. Politically, the most significant was the rumor that a military coup might take place near the end of the sexenio. Rumormongers could not decide from which direction the coup would come, however. One version was that the army would set up a fascist regime to undo all of Echeverría's populist policies and prevent further movement to the left; another had it that Echeverría himself would lead a coup in order to remain in power.

Schmidt also argues that it is significant that every president since Echeverría has come to power through the bureaucracy, rather than through politics. Echeverría was the first of the bureaucratic presidents, and Schmidt believes that this trend has proved harmful to Mexico in a number of ways. First, he claims that bureaucratic presidents are not as politically effective as those who came up through the elective process. They are not as aware of the necessity of maintaining a balance in the coalition that sustains them nor are they as effective at doing the symbolic things that contribute to the system's political legitimacy. For example, technocratic presidents tend to fill their cabinets with other technocrats, rather than with appointments that achieve factional diversity. Schmidt argues in his Postscript that the political presidents used their cabinets to maintain a broad political coalition, but the technocratic presidents have appointed efficiency experts who do not necessarily represent large interests in society. Second, bureaucratic presidents are not as good at policy decision making. Schmidt likens Mexican presidents who rose only through the government bureaucracy to Lawrence Peter's automaton who knows only how to follow orders and not how to formulate policies. Such individuals continue to be promoted from positions in which they are competent until finally they reach a position where the demands are too much for them. The two shortcomings reinforce each other in that technocratic presidents might be more concerned with technical matters such as budget and trade deficits rather than with coordinating social peace, and the people with whom they surround themselves do little to broaden their vision. According to Schmidt, whatever the flaws of the pre-1964 Mexican political system, maintaining social peace and political legitimacy was what the regime did best. Recent presidents, he contends, have not been very good at this most important of political duties, and he believes that a primary reason is their bureaucratic background.

ECHEVERRÍA AND MEXICAN POLITICS

When Echeverría left office, he was extremely unpopular and was widely regarded as a failure, at least among the middle and upper classes. Is that assessment too negative? As indicated above, Echeverría had three main goals: nationalism, anti-imperialism, and revitalization of the political system. Leaving aside the first two, did he achieve the third? Did he succeed in reconsolidating the regime so that it had greater legitimate authority at the end of his term than at the beginning? What strategy did he use in the pursuit of this goal? In attempting to assess the Echeverría government, I would like to examine three questions. What role did the world context play in contributing to the turmoil of the Echeverría years? Has the bureaucratic background of recent Mexican presidents contributed to their failures? Were the failures of the Echeverría government due to the shortcomings of an individual or to the logic of the system?

To be fair, one should put Echeverría and Mexico into a larger world context. The causes of Mexico's economic problems are, of course, found partly in its position as a relatively poor country that is highly dependent on world capital and markets. That same position also constrains the Mexican government in the policies it can pursue in trying to achieve growth and distribution. Just as Canada will lose physicians to the United States if doctors' salaries are not reasonably close to those prevailing in the U.S., Mexico will lose domestic capital and not acquire needed foreign investment if the government too vigorously pursues policies that alarm those with capital to invest. Because Mexico is dependent on capital that can easily find outlets elsewhere, the smallest movement by the government toward positions that domestic and international capital consider unacceptable can lead to a sudden loss of needed investment. Thus it could be said that even if Echeverría's redistributive policies were not undesirable in themselves, capital in Mexico is so volatile than any Mexican government must be careful about frightening capitalists.

The world context contributed in another way to the problem faced by Echeverría. The late 1960s and early 1970s were a time of political turmoil throughout the world during which criticism of regimes reached levels not seen since the 1930s. Young people protested in country after country as a wave of political dissent swept through the industrialized world. This process by which events in one country influence events in other countries is called the "demonstration effect." Another aspect of the world context was the popularity of the Cuban revolution among those who favored radical change in Latin America.[4]

Governments in many countries overreacted, although the degree of overreaction was generally consonant with the traditions of the particular country. In the U.S. in July 1968, just three months before the October tragedy at Tlatelolco, the Chicago city government engaged in what would subsequently be called a "police riot" outside the Democratic Party National Convention. After Richard Nixon became president in 1969, his administration carried out a range of nefarious activities, including the one that would eventually be its undoing, the burglary and attempted wiretapping of the office of the Democratic National Committee. Thus, this was a time of intense political conflict in many countries, including even the "developed" ones. When seen in the perspective of what was happening in the world, therefore, events in Mexico do not seem so extreme. For example, it has been estimated that up to 400 people were murdered in Mexico for political reasons from 1970 to 1982. Contrast that figure with the 700 estimated political deaths in Chile from 1973 to 1986, almost twice as many deaths in a country with only one-seventh the population. Or more starkly, contrast it with Argentina, a country with one-third the population of Mexico, which suffered 20,000 political deaths in the "dirty war" of the late 1970s. Even one political death is too many, but all things considered, Mexico handled the turmoil with relatively little repression compared to some other Latin American countries.

Echeverría's government had very conflictual relations with business. Was some of the conflict due to Echeverría's personal style? Inflammatory words by the president can contribute to capital flight and noninvestment even if actual government policy toward business does not change. Conversely, it is possible that a political leader can accomplish considerable real reform behind the facade of gentle words and incremental actions. Echeverría's strong rhetoric repelled business while not accomplishing much in the way of increased popular support. Thus to a degree, the president's style, both in actions and in words, contributed to the failures of his term. As Judith Teichman says, "Echeverría's leftist rhetoric was no doubt also an important factor in the private sector's loss of confidence."[5] Echeverría had actually begun his term on positive terms with business. But the combination of his abrasive style and his actual economic policies had alienated much of business by 1973.[6] The importance of rhetoric should not be overstated, however. Neither Miguel

Ramírez nor Clark Reynolds attributes the tensions to presidential rhetoric.[7] At a minimum, it can be said that the role of rhetoric in contributing to tensions between government and major social forces is a subject deserving of further study.

Another possible explanation for the failures of Echeverría and subsequent presidents is that whatever their individual styles may have been, their fundamental debility was their lack of political skills. Schmidt makes much of the change from "political" presidents up to 1970 and the "bureaucrats" or "technocrats" (and, even more specifically, the "financiers") who have governed since then. He goes further and says they have not really governed, but only "administered." One way in which they have failed to take "politics" into account is in the makeup of their cabinets. In the Postscript, Schmidt implies that a contributing factor to the defection of Cuauhtémoc Cárdenas and other members of the "Democratic Current" from the PRI in 1988 was that the "politicians" had been frozen out of cabinet positions and out of a role in selecting the 1988 PRI candidate. As Schmidt says, "Where the cabinet had previously provided a space or forum for struggling 'institutionally' for power, with the coming of the bureaucrats the cabinet has become an instrument for paying off debts of loyalty and a medium of obedience where dissent is not allowed." Hence, "the president is bureaucratically strong but politically weak."

One would not want to exaggerate the significance of a succession of presidents who rose solely through appointive office. Nevertheless, it is possible that presidents are as subject to "trained incapacity" as the rest of us. An official like Echeverría, who rose through positions in which he specialized in pacification, might come to the presidency predisposed to see problems as being amenable to repressive solutions. Officials like de la Madrid, who had held mainly financial positions, might tend to see the problems facing them as essentially financial.

This argument could cut either way. One could reason that a fundamental strategy of the Mexican regime from at least 1940 has been to solve political problems through economic means, sometimes through distribution (Cárdenas, Echeverría, perhaps López Mateos) and sometimes through growth (all the other presidents). Thus all presidents have tried to use the economy to pacify the polity, technocratic presidents as well as "political" presidents. Or one could argue that the technocratic presidents, especially the "finance presidents" from López Portillo to Salinas, have intensified the proclivity of Mexican presidents to seek economic solutions to political problems. Thus technocrats might tend to define policy issues mainly in technical terms, such as budget deficits and foreign debt, rather than seeing them in a broader way that includes other values, including social peace and popular support for the regime. Whereas prior presidents might have paid more attention to coalition building, recent presidents may have focused more of their efforts on managing the economy. This is not to deny the importance of economic effectiveness as a key criterion by which citizens evaluate their government. The problem is that recent Mexican governments have delivered neither economic nor political effectiveness.

On the other hand, to draw such a distinction between the withdrawn and inelegant "politician" Díaz Ordaz and the gregarious, politically sensitive "bureaucrat" Echeverría is perhaps to emphasize an irrelevancy. It is possible that, on average, the "bureaucrats" are not as effective at manipulation of political symbols as the "politicians." For example, Miguel de le Madrid's lack of public activity in the first hours after the devastating October 1985 earthquake was a major symbolic failure. As a good technocrat, he may have been quite active behind the scenes in mobilizing relief efforts, but his activity was not seen publicly. Yet it is difficult to see how the other bureaucratic presidents were any less skillful or interested in symbolic politics than the "politicians."

Moreover, it can be argued that in Mexico there is little difference between politics and bureaucracy. In Mexico's semiauthoritarian institutionalized system, politics are highly bureaucratized in the sense that advancement does not come primarily from popularity with voters, but from satisfying one's superiors in the system. Conversely, the bureaucracy is highly politicized in the sense that nearly the entire public work force is subject to political rather than merit-based appointment. Thus a bureaucrat's promotion depends heavily on his political skill in, among other things, picking winners among his superiors.

It seems, therefore, that there has been little difference between "political" and "bureaucratic" presidents as far as their predilections and skills are concerned. All have tried to solve the political problems of legitimacy and participation through economic means, whether primarily from growth or from distribution. More importantly, their success or lack of it has been similar, no matter what their career trajectories. Both types of president have been unable to resolve key issues of public policy emanating from the limits of the Mexican economic model. These limits were becoming obvious by the time of Díaz Ordaz and contributed mightily to his regime's turmoil and loss of legitimacy. This view is analogous to the conclusion that Malloy and others have reached with regard to the relative effectiveness of civilian democratic versus military regimes in Latin America. Most studies have discovered little significant difference between the types of regimes in either encouraging economic growth or achieving distribution.[8] Likewise, in Mexico "political" and "technocratic" presidents have had about equal success in dealing with problems of political legitimacy and economic well-being in recent years.

In addition to personal style and presidential background, a third possible explanation for the conflict of the Echeverría years is the inherent logic of government-business relations in a capitalist society. It seems likely that just about any president who attempted Echeverría's reforms would have encountered serious opposition. His efforts at tax reform, land distribution, social welfare policies, and the like threatened the economic interests of business and the wealthy too much to go unchallenged. It is notable that a supposedly authoritarian regime such as Mexico's had such difficulty in carrying out reforms that more democratic governments enact routinely. Government and business in capitalist societies are caught in an existential relationship in which a certain amount of conflict between them is inevitable. Business seeks to maximize its profits, often through the pursuit of special privileges from government that allow unusually high profits (what Buchanan and others call rent seeking).[9] On its side, government tries to take advantage of the productive virtues of capitalism to achieve economic growth while mitigating the worst excesses of private enterprise. Thus conflict between the two occurs in every capitalist society. But in Mexico the potential conflict is particularly intense. Both business and labor in Mexico are so intent on achieving and maintaining their special privileges that they make government's task very difficult. Like Cárdenas in the 1930s, Echeverría was caught between populist demands and business resistance. The volatility of capital was a major source of this difficulty.

Governments that pursue redistribution may face this problem in any capitalist system, but some face it in a stronger form than do others. Hamilton says that "dominant classes and foreign groups have obvious means at their disposal to prevent the state from substantially threatening their interests, as indicated during the Echeverría regime (1970–1976)."[10] Hellman argues that "the Echeverría administration had demonstrated the limits of reform. It indicated that a basic reorientation of the course of Mexican development in the direction of greater 'distributive justice' could not be carried out because of the intransigence of bourgeois interests." Regarding Echeverría's reforms, she says "The reforms did not work because they could not work, given the structure of power, the impotence of peasants' and workers' organizations, the intransigence of the conservative bourgeoisie, the opposition of foreign capital, and the general alignment of political forces in Mexico."[11]

Even if conflict between government and business is integral to the political economy of capitalism, some governments are obviously able to regulate and tax business quite severely. The governments of northern and western Europe, and to a lesser degree that of the United States, have done exactly that for decades. Even if capitalist states are faced with "limits to autonomy," that does not necessarily mean that all capitalist governments are paralyzed in the face of business opposition. Why are some governments able to control business more than others? A common answer for Latin America is dependency. Presumably, the smaller and more dependent a country is on the world economy, the weaker its government is relative to business. Nevertheless, many small and export-oriented societies such as Sweden, Denmark, New Zealand, and others have achieved a high degree of "social democracy," which includes a significant amount of government control over business. I will not try to answer the question of why a welfare state emerged in certain countries over the past century. I merely point out that it is possible for governments in capitalist societies to pursue redistributive policies despite the active opposition of business.[12]

For Mexico, an additional question is why a supposedly "authoritarian" regime was unable to force its policies on business. One possible answer is that "the Mexican state is not truly authoritarian because it is often flexible in its response to different group interests."[13] Thus the regime bases its control not only on coercion but also on the legitimacy derived from attending to a multiplicity of interests. The Mexican regime is especially solicitous of the interests of business. In fact, as Reyna wrote toward the end of the Echeverría years, "it is difficult to find a case in Latin America where the state has so favored the bourgeoisie."[14] This does not mean that the Mexican regime is dominated by business, however. Thus Camp argues that the Mexican state is guided by a particular development model, not dominated by any single social group. Sometimes this model leads to conflict with business and sometimes to cooperation. Nevertheless, that tension did contribute mightily to the conflict between government and business in Mexico during the Echeverría years because of the government's policy goals.

Thus during Echeverría's term Mexico experienced conflict that was largely a result of the inherent tension between capitalism and a populist government. The tension was intensified, however, by the demonstration effect of political dissent in other countries and the attractiveness of the Cuban revolution for Mexican radicals. Moreover, it is possible that Echeverría's bureaucratic background and his dramatic antibusiness rhetoric contributed to the high level of tension. Whatever the causes of the conflict and the loss of legitimacy by the regime, what strategy did Echeverría employ to try to counteract the damage and reconsolidate the regime?

A ruler has a portfolio of methods for attempting to establish the authority of a regime. Broadly speaking, those methods can be categorized as political and economic. In terms of his "political" strategy, Echeverría used both repression and participation. Although the Mexican regime used less violent repression than did several other large Latin American countries at about the same time, it still employed a considerable amount, and that amount was inversely linked to its unwillingness to expand political participation in any meaningful way, such as allowing free elections.

As it turned out, the trend in Latin America (and the world) was in the direction of more liberal, democratic political systems over the next twenty years. Echeverría was well poised to be a leader in that trend, but he chose not to be. He expanded the participation of young people in the bureaucracies of government and party, and eight new political parties emerged during his term.[15] But he did not come to grips with the fundamental political problem of the Mexican state—that it is a one-party, semiauthoritarian regime in a world and in a country in which that form of government is increasingly anachronistic. His political reforms were extremely limited and did not move Mexico toward a resolution of its basic political problem: how to maintain or restore its legitimacy, its right to rule, in the eyes of most Mexicans. In the 1990s Mexico is still trying to come to grips with the problem of one-party rule.

Political legitimacy is strongly affected, of course, by a regime's effectiveness in managing the economy. However much participation or repression a regime practices, its legitimacy will be greater the more prosperous the society is and the more just the economic distribution is seen to be. With regard to the available economic strategies, Echeverría pursued distribution in hopes that it would lead to growth and to enhanced political legitimacy. Some reasonable degree of distribution of the existing economic wealth is necessary and desirable, and the experience of numerous countries suggests that distribution can contribute to growth. Some countries, however, such as Uruguay and Argentina, have over several decades tried to distribute more than they had, in the sense that their governments spent more than they taxed and their societies consumed more than they produced (not unlike the United States in the 1980s). The inevitable result is ballooning government deficits and national trade deficits. Mexico had already started down this road before Echeverría, but the trend gathered powerful momentum during his term. In his desire to distribute in order to enhance social justice and therefore regime legitimacy, he led Mexico down a path from which it is still trying to escape. As Luis Rubio and Roberto Blum note:

> The changes made by Echeverría (and later by José López Portillo) demonstrated a precise and unequivocal reading of the situation. Realizing that Mexico was facing a challenge that was largely political, these two presidents resorted to government spending as a means of appeasing political conflict. In the short term, their actions increased economic growth and appeared to diminish conflict. As a long-term policy, however, it was a disaster because

it subordinated the up-to-then extremely successful economic policy to short-term political gain.[16]

Another aspect of Echeverría's economic policies was equally damaging to the welfare of the country in the long run. Protectionism can be a rational long-term strategy for a nation that uses the time well. Behind the protective walls provided by government, a country can build up its domestic industry so that eventually it can enter the world market and compete in at least a few goods. Numerous countries have effectively used such a strategy, not least the United States and Japan. But Mexico seems not to have used the four decades of protection to prepare itself to compete in the world market. Its business became comfortable with the guaranteed profits provided by a captive market, high subsidies, and low taxes. Echeverría tried to correct some of the negative effects of the Mexican economic model, such as highly unequal income, but he made others worse by frightening domestic capital and discouraging foreign investment.

One could say that even if Echeverría did not make the political system more stable and legitimate, his policies did not necessarily make it any less so either. In this regard, it is revealing that in the United States Richard Nixon was driven from office, more than thirty of his advisers and aides eventually went to jail, and his party was defeated by the voters in the next election. In Mexico, by contrast, Echeverría finished his term, selected his successor, and was appointed ambassador to France. His choice of López Portillo seemed reasonable, and the presidential succession in 1976 was welcomed by most Mexicans. Relations between government and business improved immediately and dramatically under the new president, suggesting that Echeverría had not done any irreparable damage to the political system.

Nevertheless, by greatly increasing the size and presence of government in the economy, Echeverría made Mexico's fundamental economic flaw even worse and set the country up for the fall that would come in the 1980s. In fairness to Echeverría, it should be noted that an equally serious economic error was López Portillo's mismanagement of the oil wealth over the next six years, although perhaps no president could have withstood the pressure to use this wealth for immediate benefits. Like many countries in the past twenty years, Mexico has been overwhelmed by the impact of a changing world economy characterized by increased competition, volatility of energy prices, huge debt, and slow economic growth. Mexico did things that made the problems worse, but to a large extent the world economy imposed harsh conditions on Mexico, and perhaps no president could have done much better.

What about the other questions posed by Schmidt's book? Has Mexican "presidentialism" deteriorated? If so, did that decline begin with Echeverría? What are the implications of such a decline?

By *presidentialism* most observers mean a political system in which the president is extremely powerful, perhaps far more powerful than all other political institutions combined.[17] Presidentialism has declined in Mexico in the sense that the president and his decisions have been called into question far more in recent years than previously was the case. A powerful presidency is, however, only one component—although perhaps the most important one—in a larger "regime," or ongoing set of political rules, rulers, and political relationships. The regime includes the government, party, parastatal agencies, state and local institutions, and in Mexico even the labor and farmer confederations. The decline of legitimacy of the Mexican regime began before Echeverría became president. The most dramatic political incident of the modern period—the massacre at Tlatelolco—occurred under Díaz Ordaz, although of course Echeverría, as minister of the interior, must bear considerable responsibility for that action.

In a sense, presidentialism began to decline under Díaz Ordaz and continued to suffer diminished public respect and allegiance under Echeverría, López Portillo, and de la Madrid. But the broader point is that the entire regime itself suffered a loss of legitimacy during this same time. Carlos Salinas has restored a good deal of respect for the presidency; in early 1990, polls showed that about 75 percent of voters approved of his performance as president. But the regime is still being called into question; that same poll indicated that more than half of the voters doubted that Salinas had actually won the 1988 election. Polls also indicate that a majority of Mexicans would like fair elections, which in themselves would produce a new "regime" in which one party does not completely dominate the political system.

A wave of liberal democratization has swept the globe in recent years. In an unintended way, if Echeverría and others contributed to the decline of respect and power of the presidency, perhaps they unknowingly promoted the development of Mexican democracy. The term of each president since Díaz Ordaz has been flawed by one or more qualities that have contributed to his unpopularity: Díaz Ordaz and repression, Echeverría and strident populism, López Portillo and corruption, and de la Madrid and economic stagnation. Even if Salinas brings the economy around, the pressure for a more liberal, multiparty democracy will not necessarily disappear. In a perverse way, then, the "decline of presidentialism" may be the prelude to democracy.

Since 1920 Mexican presidentialism has changed in fundamental ways about every twenty-five years. Without claiming that this pattern is a fixed law of political development, I believe it is provocative that from 1920 to

1946 (26 years) every full-term president was a general; from 1946 to 1970 (24 years) every president was a nongeneral with a background of elective office; from 1970 to 1994 (24 years) every president had a background as a civilian bureaucrat. Is it possible that in 1994 Mexico will enter a new phase in the history of presidential selection? Perhaps that year will bring a new era of freely elected presidents in a multiparty system.

GLOSSARY

BANRURAL. Banco Nacional de Crédito Rural (National Bank of Rural Credit)

CANACO. Camára Nacional de Comercio (National Chamber of Commerce)

CCI. Central Campesina Independiente (Independent Peasant Center)

CIA. Central Intelligence Agency

CNC. Confederación Nacional Campesina (National Peasant Confederation)

CODISUPO. Compañía Distribuidora de Subsistencias Populares (Staple Products Distribution Corporation, CONASUPO's marketing branch)

CONACYT. Consejo Nacional de Ciencia y Tecnología (National Council for Science and Technology)

CONASUPO. Compañía Nacional de Subsistencias Populares (National Staple Products Corporation)

CONCAMIN. Confederación Nacional de Cámaras Industriales (National Confederation of Chambers of Industry)

CONCANACO. Confederación Nacional de Cámaras de Comercio (National Confederation of Chambers of Commerce)

COPARMEX. Confederación Patronal de la República Mexicana (Employers' Confederation)

COR. Confederación Obrera Revolucionaria (Revolutionary Labor Confederation)

CROM. Confederación Regional de Obreros Mexicanos (Regional Mexican Workers' Confederation)

CTM. Confederación de Trabajadores de México (Mexican Labor Confederation)

FONACOT. Fondo Nacional para el Consumo de los Trabajadores (National Fund for Workers' Consumption)

FIDEURBE. Fideicomiso para el Desarrollo Urbano (Trust Fund for Urban Development)

FOVISSTE. Fondo de Vivienda del Instituto de Seguridad Social al Servicio de los Trabajadores del Estado (Housing Fund of the ISSSTE)

FEG. Federación de Estudiantes de Guadalajara (Student Federation of Guadalajara)

FEJ. Federación de Estudiantes de Jalisco (Student Federation of Jalisco)

INMECAFE. Instituto Mexicano del Café (Mexican Institute of Coffee)

IMPI. Instituto Mexicano de Protección a la Infancia (Mexican Institute for Infant Protection)

INFONAVIT. Instituto Nacional del Fondo para la Vivienda de los Trabajadores (National Institute of the Workers' Housing Fund)

IMCE. Instituto Mexicano de Comercio Exterior (Mexican Institute of Foreign Commerce)

ISSSTE. Instituto de Seguridad Social al Servicio de los Trabajadores del Estado (Institute of Social Security and Services for Public Employees)

IMF. International Monetary Fund.

OPEC. Organization of Petroleum Exporting Countries.

PRI. Partido Revolucionario Institucional (Institutional Revolutionary Party)

PEMEX. Petróleos Mexicanos (Mexican Petroleum Company)

PROQUIVEMEX. Productos Químicos Vegetales Mexicanos (Mexican Vegetable Chemical Products)

PMT. Partido Mexicano de los Trabajadores (Mexican Workers Party)

PRT. Partido Revolucionario de los Trabajadores (Revolutionary Workers Party)

PNR. Partido Nacional Revolucionario (Revolutionary National Party)

PRM. Partido de la Revolución Mexicana (Party of the Mexican Revolution)

PPM. Partido Popular Mexicano (Mexican Popular Party)

PLO. Palestine Liberation Organization

PAN. Partido de Acción Nacional (National Action Party)

SUTERM. Sindicato Unico de Trabajadores Eléctricos de la República Mexicana (Sole Union of Electric Workers of the Mexican Republic)

SOMEX. An investment bank.

TABAMEX. Tabacos Mexicanos (Mexican Tobacco)

UGOCM. Unión General de Obreros y Campesinos de México (General Union of Workers and Peasants of Mexico)

UNAM. Universidad Nacional Autónoma de México (National Autonomous University of Mexico)

UN. United Nations.

UNCTAD. United Nations Conference on Trade and Development

The Deterioration of
the Mexican Presidency

AUTHOR'S INTRODUCTION

In Mexico it is common to read political commentaries, usually in the press, that give the impression of political analysis. Yet the differences between commentary and analysis are more important than is apparent. *Political commentary* is the appraisal of a political event developed out of the author's store of knowledge, generally at the time of the event. *Political analysis*, on the other hand, is the study of political events viewed from a broader perspective that throws light on relationships among the fundamental factors in the system. It is obvious that to write commentary one needs to have a general knowledge of the issues. But commentary differs from analysis in the amplitude, depth, and scope of the arguments. This is the reason why commentary is found in the press and analysis is sought in academia.

All scientific work faces the problem of lack of information and availability of data. This situation has led to an unproductive polemic stating that the social sciences lack scientific rigor, for they cannot count on quantitative data to justify their argument, nor can they use mathematics to verify their analytical conclusions. This argument confuses the law of gravity with political events. That is, social and political phenomena may not repeat themselves with the same regularity and predictability as physical phenomena. Therefore, we must consider alternative methods for studying social phenomena. Even though we may lack adequate data series on political events, it is still of utmost importance to attempt to gather whatever relevant information we can. One such method is to compare past, present, and future. If quantitative information is available, it should be used to test certain types of hypotheses and to analyze long periods of time, but it may not be useful for short periods.[1] Some hypotheses are simply not amenable to quantitative analysis.

On the other hand, the information that is most useful in some of the social sciences is derived from participants' testimony, yet even that is limited in scope for it would be necessary to interview all factions participating in a political event to arrive at a totally clear picture of the situation. Even if we could overcome this obstacle, we would still be faced with the fact that living political actors almost always retain their political interests, reason enough for them to keep silent. Thus one is forced to examine the archives of the dead. Archives of prominent people such as former presidents are important, but one must go beyond even these to get a balanced picture of reality.

To resolve some of these difficulties, I decided to use an analysis of the correlation of forces.[2] When analyzing the correlation of forces, one identifies the historical forces that are significant for the political system that is being studied. The correlation is the way in which these social forces interact in the pursuit of their interests, using all the resources at their command. Thus one must consider the moment in which social classes develop certain organizational or political practices. Each force seeks to impose its goals and values on all the others. Such imposition is what is usually meant by the exercise of "power." If a single force imposes its will on the rest of society, that force can be said to have hegemony.[3]

Quantitative methods for measuring the dimensions of power may answer such questions as the following: How many workers were there? How many unions? How many strikes were held? Independent of such quantitative methods is the more important qualitative perspective that examines the level and character of the struggle. For example, one would interpret the strike of one electricians' central labor federation much differently from the strike of, say, fifty small, independent locals. A nationwide strike of a single large union could paralyze the entire country, but strikes by fifty local textile unions may have much less effect because retail stores may have ample inventory of the product for a long period of time.

At this point I would like to address one of the most sensitive aspects of the analysis of the correlation of forces: the issue of subjectivity. The investigator should keep in mind that in pursuing its interests, each force within a society expresses itself, exerts pressure, and makes requests and demands, trying to gain concessions and to increase its power within the political system. The analyst must take into consideration the various factors that are truly important within the economic, social, and political contexts. It is quite likely, however, that the analyst will sympathize with one particular group more than others. Yet he must try to be as objective as possible, trying to describe reality in an honest way and to avoid distortion in the analysis.[4]

There is a good deal of stability in most political systems over time. The political situation in a given system does not change so rapidly that the forces of yesterday necessarily disappear. They may no longer carry as much weight as before, and some of them may indeed be on the verge of disappearing, but these old forces, and their specific role in modern society, must also be part of the investigation. [Because of the degree to which the U.S. is a "modern" society, North Americans may have difficulty understanding the extent to which old social forces such as large landowners still play an important political role in Latin America.—Ed.]

In this context it is important to be able to discern the level at which these forces express themselves. The microlevel implications of an event would not necessarily be the same as the macro implications for the entire system, and vice versa. A micro level event such as a strike may not have an impact at the macro level, such as the overall balance of power within the system. But a political action at the micro level, such as land invasions, may have a consequence at the macro level, such as the fall of a governor. Both the micro and macro levels of analysis must be observed, because a political measure may have relevance at one level of analysis and not at the other. On the other hand, a political measure planned at one level may have implications not calculated at other levels, creating causal relationships that are complex and potentially uncontrollable. In most cases a political action at the macro level will have an effect at the micro level.

The sociopolitical struggle is not necessarily a zero-sum game in which the gain of power or other resources by one social group implies an equivalent loss by another. A political or social system may experience an increase or decrease in the total amount of power or other resource such as wealth. The political process is complex and not a simple matter of adding and subtracting. The analyst must try to find at any moment all forces competing in every one of the important political processes or arenas. In addition, various forces will not have the same social, economic, and political impact in all situations and historical moments, especially when the structure is being transformed; on the contrary, all have their unique characteristics, actors, and specific practices, and their importance will vary by situation. Moreover, not all social forces are involved in all conflicts, and conflicts do not affect all social forces equally. For example, bankers may stay out of an agrarian problem.

The correlation of forces changes over time. Usually, it changes slowly, but sometimes one can identify a turning point after which conditions change significantly. The turning point is nothing but a moment in time in which something significant occurs that affects the rest of the system.[5] Determining the turning point, or "juncture" [*coyuntura* in Spanish], can be arbitrary on the part of the investigator, depending on the importance he assigns to the events being studied. For example, some authors have seen the strikes at Cananea and Río Blanco as the turning point of the Porfirian dictatorship, since they represented serious challenges to that regime. Others consider the economic crisis of 1905 as more significant. Such junctures may vary in duration and in importance, depending on the systemic and contextual implications of the events.

In the Mexican political system the transition from one sexenio (six-year presidential term) to another often marks a turning point in the system. Each president's term tends to impose a particular stamp on the composition of the state and on its activities and functions with regard to civil society. These characteristics acquire significance because they remain in the structure to become the new reality for the presidents that follow. Methodologically, the sexenio can be a useful instrument for analyzing the modern history of state intervention in Mexico, and it can indicate where such intervention stops being merely a problem of pure government and becomes a picture of a state in constant and dynamic transformation.

The popular notion is that Mexican politics are transformed more as the product of the will of an individual than as the result of complex social, economic, and political relations. Even if it cannot be denied that the actions of the president and his team are powerful in defining political decisions, the explanation of government action cannot be reduced to the simplistic one in which things occur merely because the president wants them to occur. It is a mistake to think that the decision-making process is a matter only of presidential will, unaffected by the other social forces that pursue their interests. Even if presidential will is taken as the determining factor in politics in some situations, it is still necessary to investigate and to understand on what basis this powerful position is acquired and how this will is formed.

The Mexican president is at the apex of power, at the peak of the decision-making process.[6] Even if he inherits a system influenced by his predecessors, he still has considerable latitude to impose both positive and negative, or veto, decisions on the system. The form in which he exercises his power within the system that is given to him becomes his personal style of governing, and that personal style may become a significant variable.[7]

This location of the president at the apex of the system has confused many investigators, creating the myth of an all-powerful president. I would like to propose an alternative perspective. The Mexican president is like Lawrence Peter's professional automaton, who has little capacity for independent judgment; he always obeys, never decides. From the point of view of the hierarchy, this behavior is competence, and so Peter's automaton is a candidate for promotion. He will continue to be promoted until fate puts him into a position in which he has to make decisions. Then he will encounter the level of his own incompetence. During the entire time, he "no longer sees himself as the instrument of public service. He sees the public as the raw material to maintain him, the system, and the hierarchy."[8]

In the words of Luis Echeverría: "I dedicated myself to working with enthusiasm in all tasks that the party and my bosses gave to me, with loyalty, with a spirit of discipline, with dedication, and promotions came one after another. My career was in reality very rapid because having joined the party in 1946, I became the candidate for president of the republic in 1969, just 23 years later."[9]

Luis Echeverría Alvarez began his political career at 23 years of age when he married the daughter of Guadalupe Zuno Hernández, a powerful politician and former governor of Jalisco. From that point on he was impelled ever upward until he reached the pinnacle of power. One year after his marriage Echeverría joined the ruling party (PRI, the Partido Revolucionario Institucional) and began his attachment to General Rodolfo Sánchez Taboada, to whom he was private secretary. Echeverría became press secretary to the PRI National Committee while the general was president of PRI from 1946 to 1952. In 1952, when the general became secretary of the Navy, Echeverría was director of accounts for the Secretariat of the Navy. In 1954 he was the chief of staff (*oficial mayor*) of the Department of Public Education and in 1957 the *oficial mayor* of PRI. In 1958 he became undersecretary of *gobernación*, or interior; in 1964 he became secretary; and in 1970, of course, he became president of the republic. Echeverría's rise to the presidency was very fast and entirely through government and party bureaucracies, rather than elected office.[10]

Although many may have thought that Echeverría was an obscure politician before his rise to the presidency, he actually had a long record in the control of social conflict. According to Judith Hellman, as an official of the Department of Public Education he helped to arrange the military occupation of the National Polytechnic Institute in 1956; as an undersecretary of the ministry of government he played a leading role in the suppression of the railroad workers' union in 1958. He was also active in the collection of intelligence material on leftist Castroite movements. As secretary of government when Díaz Ordaz was named presidential candidate, he was responsible for managing PRI victories at the local, state, and national levels and acquired notoriety for his tireless efforts in the persecution of Communist organizations, the destruction of some leftist publications, and the imposition of an official script on radio and television. Finally, according to Hellman, "he was the non-military official most closely associated in the public mind with the policy of repression of the students in 1968."[11]

It is clear that Echeverría, as part of the generation of youth that rushed to the coattails of General Rodolfo Sánchez Taboada, followed a political career that carried him through the labyrinthine bureaucracy to important posts. The fact that he never had been elected to office did not make him obscure. Rather, it demonstrates that there were many roads to the presidency of Mexico and that it is dangerous to claim that there was only one formula or career path for reaching that position.

Numerous scholars have argued that a pendulum effect determines presidential succession in Mexico,[12] in which the political system adapts to pressures by selecting a new president from the opposite side of the political spectrum from the previous one.[13] But Echeverría showed that, at least in his case, other factors can explain the rise of a person to the highest office:

> In a political-administrative hierarchy, I considered it my duty always to cooperate with the greatest discretion with my superiors. I believe that it is not a violation of Social Law with regard to the tasks of high officials to keep those charged with responsibility well-informed, and that one's opinions should go through proper channels. For me, it was always a principle to inform my superiors, and I consider this to be a healthy administrative practice. In my successive responsibilities, I did not have any reason to doubt the idea that I should keep my superiors informed. That just seems an obvious conclusion for anyone who works in a hierarchy.[14]

Echeverría's conception of hierarchy and discipline is fundamental for explaining many of his actions during his presidency. In particular, he made a large number of declarations, which diminished his capacity for maneuver because a public declaration commits a president to a particular course of action. It was difficult for him to contradict a presidential declaration, and when he tried, the results were disastrous. I return to this subject later with some examples, of which the most spectacular and the most damaging was the Mexican government's anti-Zionist policy.

Echeverría's conception of hierarchy and discipline in itself was the origin of some of the events that occurred during his term. If it is true, as he said, that he was accustomed to receiving orders and transmitting them down a bureaucratic chain, what happened when he only gave the orders and then became aware that not all bureaucrats were adequate for carrying out those orders? It is common to hear among Mexican politicians that Echeverría was not well informed about what happened with his orders. This claim is, of course, the favorite pretext of modern bureaucracy for disguising its inefficiency.

One can maintain that Echeverría was very competent in executing orders or transmitting them to others, but when he had to originate them, he felt vulnerable because he did not know if they would be carried out and he was now responsible for them. The same can be said of his declarations. Possibly, he did not feel that he had sufficient social and political support to achieve some of the great measures that he wanted to achieve. In this way, for example, his confrontations with the bourgeoisie, in matters of social and economic justice, lost their real content and were often converted into simple fits of temper that enraged the ruling class but did not really affect it.

I do not doubt that Echeverría tried to change radically some of the characteristics of Mexican politics and that this effort provoked much fear and mistrust. For example, he attempted to overcome the great isolation of Mexican presidents. For that purpose, he tried to carry out the demands of the people, and if his presidential campaign was dynamic, his presidential period was even more so. I have the impression that his campaign lasted seven years, but more in the sense of making himself the receptacle of the people's demands than in trying to perpetuate himself in power; some people, however, did talk of his trying to perpetuate a "*minimato*," similar to Calles's "*maximato*" from 1928 to 1934.

When Suárez asked Echeverría what sorts of petitions he received during the campaign, he answered:

> It is a tradition. The people complain of abuses, of injustices; they ask for things. I read many of the requests and I decided. Others followed their course through government agencies. Even though the state is becoming modern, we must not throw away this type of communication. The people feel that they have placed their problems in the hands of the president and therefore they have hope. Besides, it is a way for the president to find out about many things that in other ways perhaps will not come to his attention.[15]

As clear as this statement is, it should be noted that, if to many people this practice was a symbol of his populism, it was actually an attempt to revive a hope that was lost in the failure of a social revolution now living only in the demagoguery of the politicians. It was symbolically very clever for the state to offer what it could not give. Echeverría continued with the practice of making promises, knowing that he also could not deliver on them. But he apparently felt that it was the only way to regain the lost legitimacy, and he put forth a great deal of effort in that direction.

Echeverría opened the doors of Los Pinos, the presidential residence, and held numerous meetings with groups of various sizes. Even though this practice annoyed some intellectuals,[16] it was another useful mechanism for broadening the contacts between the state and the masses. It was also a way to make contact with society's dissident elements.

Echeverría governed during a tumultuous period of economic-political development in which conflicts acquired an unusually vehement form of expression (see Chapter 1). Still, it must be remembered that the period 1970–76 was a continuation of the Mexican political system and not a completely new era.

According to Shmuel Eisenstadt,[17] societies in the process of transformation must acquire the capacity for adaptation, especially on the part of the government. As the economy changes, so must the government change. It is along these lines that we can trace not only the evolution of bureaucracies, but also the decisions of government and the behavior of social forces, generating a complex interaction that emerges in a process of modernization.[18]

Echeverría's term can be seen in the context of modernization. From 1940 to 1970 Mexican society experienced profound economic and social changes, but the political structure did not change to the same degree. Much of the behavior of Echeverría and his government can be interpreted as an effort to adapt the political system to the economic and social changes that had occurred up to that time.

Policy making is the essence of government behavior. By *policy making*[19] we mean the process in which policies (courses of political action) are analyzed, designed, elaborated, and implemented. We should not confuse this process with the moment in which decisions are made, for ultimately the decision in itself is only the synthesis of the factors that influence the process. In itself, the decision does not show the process that led to it. Besides, not all the factors are influential at every step in the process; the specific weight of the factors will vary according to the stage of the decision making. Decisions are made at many stages, a fact that greatly increases the complexity of analysis.

If we relate the policy-making approach to the analysis of correlation of forces, we should be able to recognize the forces that influence government decisions, why those forces are important, and how the president affects the process. This investigation is part of the purpose of this book. Certain variables can have greater weight than others at certain stages, but those variables can virtually disappear at other stages. Take, for example, "*el coyote*," an eternal factor in the Mexican system that can help resolve problems in such a way that the demands that are unsatisfied do not become problems throughout the system. A *coyote* is someone with personal contacts who can "arrange" procedures such as licenses or permits without all the normal requirements. The *coyote* "helps" the administration to be "efficient," thus diminishing the pressure on the government and helping to eliminate the demands for change, because, in a sense, the system works. Such special treatment therefore serves to alleviate pressure on the system as a whole and to reduce the need for fundamental change.

In the perspective I present here, I have made use of some sources that are relatively unusual in Mexican political science. In some sections, I make considerable use of quantitative data to support the argument, especially the economic analysis, which without statistical support loses analytical relevance. By contrast, I decided to use rumors and political humor to show the temper of the times, which is very important for an understanding of this period. Although jokes about presidents are not new and some are even taken from one context to another by merely changing the name of the leader, in the case of Echeverría they acquired very clear political-symbolic importance.[20]

Among my sources of information, newspapers were important, especially those of the U.S. To review the North American press gave me a distinct view of the Mexican situation. In a sense, the fact that the news transcended national borders showed how important these events were. This source also helped me overcome some of my Mexican biases. In addition, I reviewed the Mexican press to gain a more detailed treatment of the events.[21]

Political analysis is a kind of academic work relatively rare in Mexico, given the caution of a large part of the academic community which sees its life in the university as a stairway to the political system.[22] The academic is very careful not to "touch live interests" that could serve him later in his striving for promotion. Whoever does not play by these rules can run a number of risks: (a) His work may not be published or he may have to finance the publication, something not so easy given the low salaries in the universities.[23] This book was rejected by four publishers. One of them said, "It is a good book, but I don't like it." Another one rejected the book because the editor, who was related to Echeverría, said, "I don't agree with what you say about foreign policy." (b) The scholar may see his efforts at academic promotion—and, of course, his salary—obstructed. (c) A third risk, which some scholars do not find offensive, is to be co-opted by the PRI political system.[24]

Since I have already written the book and want to continue being cautious, I include some provisos about my purposes below. The political analyst in Mexico sails in difficult waters. Although truth, objectivity, and freedom should go together in science, they often do not coexist in political reality. According to some authors,[25] to lie is an endemic condition of Mexican politics.

In Mexico the writer is free to say whatever he wants until censorship commands the opposite, and censorship appears in many forms. My first encounter with censorship came in 1976–77 when I wrote for *Diorama de Excelsior*, the Sunday cultural magazine of the newspaper *Excélsior* in Mexico City. The title of my article for the last week of January 1977 was "Mexican Federalism: Quo Vadis?" in which I discussed José López Portillo's federalist conception. When I received the newspaper on Sunday morning, I read my article carefully and noticed that a full page was missing in the conclusion where I criticized the president's federalist notions. A couple of days later I asked the magazine editor why she took

the page out of the article, and she answered that it was to accommodate
a picture on that page. I said that if that was the reason, why did she
include a picture of Vicente Guerrero, the first president of Mexico, who
had nothing to do with the article? She responded: "Well, he was very
cute." Nonetheless, in Mexico an author can evade censorship and write
pretty much what he wants until he touches the sacrosanct image of the
president.

Juan Miguel de Mora is a renowned Sanskrit scholar. He is vice-pres-
ident of the International Association of Sanskrit Studies (the presidency
is reserved for an Indian Sanskritist), and has been guest professor in
Sanskrit at Delhi University. He has published books and articles on
Sanskrit topics[26] and is very well known in India[27] but totally ignored in
Mexico by government orders. De Mora is also a journalist, a theater
critic, and a novelist, and in his free time he writes books on Mexican
presidential administrations. But in 1988, by government order, he was
not allowed to publish articles in defense of the National Autonomous
University of Mexico (UNAM) in the daily Mexico City paper, *Excélsior*.

De Mora's books are based on an excellent organization of information
from newspapers and magazines and have an impressive impact. After
his editor refused to bow to government pressure against publishing it,
his book on the 1968 student uprising sold more than 100,000 copies in
22 editions over the 16 years following its initial appearance.[28] His
subsequent books[29] criticizing the Mexican government and various
presidents appeared while those presidents were still in office, an unusual
practice in Mexico. The government unsuccessfully tried to stop the selling
of his 1985 book, *Ni renovación, ni moral*.

The limits to de Mora's freedom became apparent in the 1970s when,
after a few attempts to corrupt him by buying him off, it was indirectly
suggested that he leave the country to stay alive. While he was driving
south in Mexico, after two overnight stops, strange things began to
happen: all the nuts in one wheel came loose at one time, and his trailer
inexplicably became unhooked from his car while on a difficult mountain
road.

I always thought that de Mora's international and national reputation
would protect him from repression, but that does not seem to be the case.
Neither is it the case for the dozens of journalists assassinated in Mexico
during 1988 or the civilians who have simply disappeared.[30] Juan Miguel
de Mora has been lucky, or the attempts against him have been clumsy.[31]
But others were not as lucky, such as Carlos Loret de Mola, former
governor of Yucatán, journalist, and writer, who was killed under very
strange circumstances.[32]

The image and private life of the Mexican president seem to represent
the limits of freedom and, of course, the limits of truth. In Mexico one

can say anything about the president as long as it is not critical. At the moment the writer attempts to criticize the president, the stop signal lights up in front of his eyes.

My most recent encounter with this stoplight suggests that Mexican presidential power can extend even beyond the borders of the country. After I was interviewed in 1988 by the Los Angeles Spanish-language newspaper *La Opinión* on my political humor research, the editor suggested that I write a series of short, humorous articles. I undertook the project with great feeling since it was the first time I had attempted actually to write political humor and not merely to analyze it. But after glancing at the first article entitled "The Presidential Succession," the director rejected it because it lacked the appropriate accent marks. I concluded that the omission of accent marks was a more serious lapse for an editor than I had realized, so I corrected them and mailed them back to the director of the newspaper. But then I noticed that the same editor had allowed the *Los Angeles Times* to print his name without the proper tilde.[33] At that point I realized that the problem was not the accent marks, but the criticism. Some time later, I learned that the director of *La Opinión* was invited as a special guest to the inauguration of Carlos Salinas de Gortari.

Since I still had the four articles in hand, I decided to try elsewhere, so I talked to a friend with good press contacts in Mexico and asked him to help me publish the articles. When we talked on the telephone, he was obviously embarrassed and told me that, according to his point of view, to publish the articles would be difficult because I was criticizing the person (the president) whom one does not criticize.

Afterward I had an interview with the director of the Tijuana weekly *Zeta* and gave him six articles—the original four slightly revised and two more with a strong moral message about the Mexican political system. Without notifying me, *Zeta* began to publish the articles. In a second interview we reached an agreement to publish an article weekly, and to have a permanent column, and we set payment at 50,000 pesos (U.S. $22) per article. But the director gave me back the article "The Presidential Succession" and told me, "Some of your articles were written a long time ago and are no longer current." I revised the piece and mailed it back to him with a new title, "Advice for the President." Three weeks later I received a money order, the article, and a letter in which the editor said that because of "space" reasons, he had decided to stop publication of my articles. His explanation was as follows: "Enclosed you have your recent article, which we did not publish since it refers to an event treated enough in books and publications. It is very common to find references to this event in recent times." This reasoning was a bit confusing: if talking about the presidential succession was common, why censor the article? If he didn't want to publish that particular article, why terminate our collaboration altogether? Perhaps my insistence irritated him. I don't know the answer, but I include here the article censored by *Zeta*, a magazine that claims to be free of government pressure. The reader can judge the limits of press freedom in Mexico.[34]

The Presidential Succession (first title)

Advice for the President (second title)

No doubt the change from one president to another worries the people. I cannot explain this preoccupation, unless it is mere selfishness. I think the fears are baseless, because, after all, the president tries with great devotion to improve the lot of the people. So let us think positively for a moment and stop being selfish.

Remember that the president is also concerned. He has a job that nobody else wants, a job that came suddenly to him as a great surprise. Even though he knows he is the best man for the job, the best qualified, the most intelligent, the handsomest, the brightest star in the sky, etc., he doesn't know if all the people know that he has these qualities.

During the transition period, the new president is the man with the most companions, but he is also the loneliest because everyone surrounding him is interested in a reward. Therefore, although many people want to advise the president, he cannot accept their advice because he knows that it comes with compromises he cannot accept. So the president has to ignore most of this advice since much of it would harm him. This brings an extra burden to a job that is already very heavy.

But, of course, one person whom the new president can trust is the outgoing president, Miguel de la Madrid. People "in the know" say that the outgoing president met with the new president, Carlos Salinas, and gave him the following advice.

When I came to the presidency, my predecessor gave me three envelopes and told me to open them when I got into political difficulties. Two years passed, the debt problem got worse, economic conditions deteriorated further, and the people began to complain loudly. So I opened the first envelope and read the advice from the former president:

"MAKE CHANGES IN THE CABINET."

I completely reorganized my cabinet, and the situation improved greatly. But two years later corruption became notorious, the economic situation became disastrous again, and the government bungled its handling of an earthquake. So I opened the second envelope and read its message:

"MAKE AN IMPORTANT ANNOUNCEMENT."
I did so. This diverted people's attention from the problems, and
things calmed down. But two years later the debt problem, the
economic situation, and corruption all reached overwhelming propor-
tions. So I opened the third envelope and read the final message:
"MAKE THREE MORE ENVELOPES."
So, my dear Carlos, here are your three envelopes.

I don't know if Salinas accepted the advice, and it is probably
too early to judge. But I think the advice was very valuable.

For two reasons, this work is not intended to be a biography. First,
for a biography, Echeverría himself would have to be interviewed and he
wasn't, although some of his supporters were. Although interviewing his
supporters gives important insight into the thinking of Echeverría himself,
it does not guarantee that their representations will faithfully mirror his
thought. Second, I try to analyze a system and not an individual.
Repeatedly, I claim that the Mexican political system is much more than
the will of an individual president, even though his will has great weight
since the president is positioned at the pinnacle of the political system.[35]
The president has the capacity to impose immediately his stamp on
politics, and on occasion this power reaches even to the dress of officials.
Recall that with Echeverría the *guayabera* [a loose-fitting Mexican shirt
that originated in Yucatán] became the style to the point that
Echeverristas were identifiable by this particular item of clothing.

To recognize this personal influence, however, is to run the risk of
exaggerating the biographical and anecdotal, even though in certain cases
these elements are useful to illustrate important points. And even if
political psychology can explain much about the management of power,
here I intend to analyze the system, without reducing myself to seeing the
role of an individual in it as the fundamental factor or most important
cause. It is in this way that the analysis of conditions, processes, and
political conflicts during the period will reveal more about the character
of Mexican politics than would holding fast to dogmatic versions of an
omnipotent president and a society subject to his designs.

This essay also does not intend to construct a historical judgment of
the presidential actions of Luis Echeverría. I am not for or against
Echeverría. I am not interested in taking part in the world of passions
where the struggle for power takes place. Even though I am aware that
these pages abound with sensitive points regarding such matters, my
approach is that of a scholar and not a politician.

I do not pretend to offer myself as a psychological judge of Echeverría
as an individual, because for most readers that would put me automati-
cally for or against him. There are those who think that Echeverría was

crazy and that all that he did was a result of his madness. That type of reader will seek in this book the arguments that appear to reinforce his opposition, and if perhaps he finds them, he will applaud enthusiastically. I neither seek nor want such applause. On the other hand, there will be those who will seek to glorify the former president, and if they find such arguments they will applaud. I do not want a job in the Mexican government. My intention is to analyze the Mexican system and to contribute to its understanding. If I achieve this objective, I will consider myself rewarded.

Nevertheless, the work is not a detailed account of all that happened during the sexenio. It is a selection of the events that I consider significant for their political, economic, and social importance.

The book is divided into three sections. The first section analyzes the conditions that the country faced at the beginning of the Echeverría presidency, conditions of systemic decline. The second part examines the series of measures that Echeverría offered to neutralize the decline. The third part investigates the most important conflicts that occurred in the country as a result of the measures adopted by the government. This section examines the confrontation between business and government and the confrontation with the United States and concludes with a discussion of the possibility of a coup d'etat at the end of the term.

Some of the claims and conclusions should be seen as hypotheses until they can be tested by more data. Some of the actors directly involved may be persuaded by historians to do an oral history. Some may publish their memoirs, although these should be read with caution. Someday archives with confidential information may be opened. But even with all this information, probably only the margin of error will diminish, and the complete truth about the era may never be known.

This is my honest position, since I refuse to assume a paradigmatic posture that pretends to give definitive answers. I believe that in political analysis there are possible explanations[36] and ideal explanations. The former depend on the available information, since there is a certain correlation between correct information and valid analysis. The ideal explanation, for its part, can exist only in the moment that one can count on practically exact information. This leaves open a double task and necessity to try to elaborate a system of information that approximates reality. Meanwhile, scholars must continue to elaborate possible explanations that in turn feed back to the system of information.

I want to end this introduction with two references to the search for truth, one from a philosopher and one from a writer:

> Let's accept . . . the destruction of the belief in truth in all its forms. The matter is serious for those of us who claim to be not

only intellectuals, but also leftists, which means that we are responsible for [telling] the truth. This effort demands at least that we
abandon our faith in the value of our own discourse, of theoretical
discourse, [and recognize that] the function of real discourse [is to
give] glances of the truth.[37]

Nietzsche understood that none of these acts of understanding, none
of those forms of possession, are true possession or genuine understanding, and that truth, really, never allows itself to be possessed by anybody:
"Whoever thinks he possesses the truth, how much escapes him!"[38]

PART I

Echeverría Confronts Decline

There is nothing so bad that it couldn't be worse.
—GEORGE BERNARD SHAW
(ECONOMISTS WOULD CALL THIS "MURPHY'S LAW.")

CHAPTER 1

The Problems Facing Mexico at the Beginning of the 1970s

THE END OF THE MEXICAN MIRACLE

During the decade of the sixties several authors sought to demonstrate that in reality the "Mexican Miracle" had been only a manipulation of statistics. Discussions centered on the fact that government spokesmen called "development" what critics considered only growth. Even though statistical growth was undeniable, the argument hinged on the distinction between qualitative and quantitative development.[1]

Without entering into that argument, we must recognize that immediately preceding the Echeverría presidency Mexico did experience high economic growth rates. They gave the appearance of a healthy and robust capitalism with miraculous qualities, especially considering Mexico's location in the dominated and backward part of the world. Even if their religious character induced the Mexican people to see this phase as an economic "miracle," it was becoming apparent that the bottlenecks that economists had detected at the end of the miracle were arriving much more rapidly than scholars had predicted.[2]

DISTRIBUTION OF INCOME AND THE MARKET

Those who discussed the miracle recognized that Mexican capitalism was far from being a just economic system and noted that this characteristic would strongly impede its future progress. Thus one of the aspects that received the most emphasis in the controversy was the maldistribution of income. In 1950 the poorest 50 percent of the population received 19 percent of the national income. Their relative position continued to deteriorate, and in the period between 1963 and 1969 the same 50 percent controlled only 15.7 percent of the income with an average wage of 825 pesos, or U.S. $66, per month. [The peso was valued at 8 U.S. cents from 1954 to 1976.—Ed.] By this measure, economic growth seemed to be working against the poor.

On the other hand, the 20 percent in the highest strata steadily increased their share of the national income from 60 percent in 1950, to 62.6 percent in 1963, and to 64 percent in 1969. Their median income was 13,000 pesos, or U.S. $1,040, per month. In the period between 1963 and 1969 there was a redistribution of income that benefited even more the top 5 percent of the population and hurt the lower 70 percent. The maldistribution of income was also notable between the rural and urban sectors, with the rural sector at a considerable income disadvantage.[3]

To look at the problem from another point of view, let us examine the peasant sector. This sector can be divided into two major categories: (a) The "peasant" economic sector of family type units. These are mostly subsistence farms and include communal *ejidos*, agrarian communities, and private properties smaller than 5 hectares. This category includes 86 percent of the country's total farming plots, which encompass 58 percent of the arable land, 38 percent of the pasture land, 67 percent of the forests, 62 percent of the irrigable surface, and 52 percent of the agricultural, ranching, and commercial forest value. It accounted for 80 percent of all agricultural labor and had a productivity per worker of 2,661 pesos, or U.S. $213. (b) At the other extreme are the commercial or capitalist enterprises of various sizes which employ salaried laborers, are capital intensive, and reach levels of productivity as high as 9,863 pesos per worker (U.S. $789), with a median productivity of 4,370 pesos (U.S. $350). The productivity of the rest of the economy is 29,000 pesos,[4] or U.S. $2,300.

With regard to salaries, of the 6.3 million people not working in the agricultural sector in 1965, only 2.4 million, or 38 percent, enjoyed an income higher than the legal minimum wage; 1.7 million, or 27 percent, received the minimum wage; and 2.2 million, or 35 percent, received salaries lower than the minimum wage.[5]

On the other hand, the real industrial wage began to decline in 1963,[6] while the minimum nominal salary in the countryside grew sluggishly, from 11 pesos (U.S. $.88) per day in 1963 to 21 pesos (U.S. $1.69) in 1970. Deflated by the Mexico City consumer price index, wages went from 13.31 pesos (U.S. $1.06) to 20.38 pesos (U.S. $1.63) during the same years.[7]

In another comparison general wages declined from 34 percent of the gross national product in 1950 to only 28 percent in 1958.[8]

In terms of employment, the situation was no better. In 1960 there were 506,000 unemployed, a sum that rose to 2,464,000 by 1970, an increase of 487 percent. By 1973 the situation had grown even worse: "Of the 15 million people who made up the labor force in the country, 7 million (47 percent) lacked jobs or were underemployed, and of the 8 million who did work, half were earning the minimum wage or less."[9]

The principal reason for this situation was the slow creation of new jobs at the same time that high population growth led to an excess of laborers. Because of union corruption and labor laws that constrained enterprises, many firms preferred to deposit their profits in financial institutions or to buy urban real estate rather than to invest in expansion or diversification. This way they could avoid additional legal or labor problems.

The large cities, strong magnets of immigration, were unable to absorb the great army of unemployed. Thus the employment rates were low, maintaining a level of about 45 percent in 1979.[10] All this helps us understand who was paying the high price for the rapid growth that the Mexican government was so proud of in the 1960s. In the words of Casio Luiselli: "We did not expect to leave by the wayside of modernization 20 million marginalized people, not only because it is a question of justice, but also . . . because there is a need for an increase in the internal market."[11] Even though these words were written in 1980, they still demonstrate the acuteness of a situation that had been deteriorating since the 1960s, and the efforts of the 1970s neither mitigated nor corrected the problem.

It is clear that the actions of the state in the 1970s were mainly guided not by humanistic considerations, but by a capitalist logic which was signaling the need for an expansion of internal markets as a necessary condition for future development.[12] Because capitalism cannot exist without growth and expansion, the state had to seek out means of internal expansion, since external means of expanding were not available (a subject I return to later). The state had to take this step if it expected to achieve a growing economy that would allow the maintenance of social tranquility and to nip the budding dissident movements that had shown extreme violence in the 1960s. These groups translated the message of impatience into popular violence as they confronted a dying revolution that had not fulfilled its promises. Thus, development of the market could be seen as the main economic solution to the deterioration the Mexican economy had suffered during the years in which the "miracle" was supposed to have taken place.

GODFATHERED CAPITALISM

The Mexican state decided to take seriously its self-assigned task of creating the conditions for the advancement of capitalism. However, these same actions of the state, in the context of market conditions, led to the development of an economy that depended in great measure on the production, expenditures, and capital investments of the state. That is why I call it "godfathered capitalism" (*el capitalismo apadrinado*), in the sense that a godfather is responsible for the protection of his godson, no matter what problems he might have. He is a second father, but without the authority implied in a paternal relationship.

It was natural for Mexican politicians to favor a paternalistic state since their professional relations are generally of this type. The godfather relationship includes the protection and promotion of the godson, activities in which Mexican politicians are very skilled, since they usually advance only with the assistance and protection of a sponsor. Therefore, the Mexican bourgeoisie decided to follow this practice, which had brought about such "good" results for politicians.[13]

Such relationships are reciprocal. As the godson advances, the godfather is strengthened, thus creating a symbiotic relationship that reaches the point where one cannot exist without the other. Mexican capitalism follows this pattern. To the extent that capitalism advances, the state has a greater reason for existing and becomes a stronger state, with greater capabilities for protecting or imposing the conditions for that capitalism to reproduce itself. Only at certain moments, when dark clouds loom on the horizon, when godfather and godson have frictions and clash, do they have problems. But this does not mean that the two will try to destroy each other; they will only reorient their relationship and the terms in which protection, support, and submission will be given in the future. The Mexican state protected its godchild for many years, and everything went well while the godchild grew fast and apparently strong. Nevertheless, when symptoms of illness began to emerge, the godfather tried to impose a little order so the illness would not be serious. But this subject is material for the following chapter.

As the state fostered business, it necessarily fostered a business class, or bourgeoisie. There were many ways in which the state decisively supported the development of the Mexican bourgeoisie, even to the extent that the state was given sole credit for the creation of this class.[14] Among the instruments to foster capitalist development were laws that protected the creation of industries.[15] The support of import-substitution industries through high tariffs and other measures put Mexican industry in a highly

Table 1.1
Relationship of Taxes to Gross National Product, 1971

Nation	Taxes as % of GNP	Nation	Taxes as % of GNP
Germany	37.9	Canada	15.4
Britain	34.4	Kenya	14.7
Denmark	28.2	Peru	14.4
Finland	26.3	South Africa	14.4
Australia	23.9	Turkey	13.7
Austria	23.6	Spain	12.7
Belgium	23.5	Colombia	12.3
United States	22.5	Uganda	11.4
Sweden	22.0	Japan	10.9
Venezuela	21.3	Ecuador	9.5
France	17.3	Brazil	9.0
Italy	16.9	Mexico	7.2

SOURCE: Carlos Tello, *La política económica en México, 1970–1976. (México: Ed. Siglo XXI, 1980), 45.*

protected situation where it could produce merchandise of poor quality and still maintain its largely captive market. The state assisted the bourgeoisie in various other ways: it dispensed cheap credit, provided tax exemptions for the importation of machinery, and implemented loose and tolerant tax policies.

The secretary of natural resources during Echeverría's term wrote: "The federal government should not charge high taxes, as long as it can meet its financial needs. The parastatal firms and state enterprises should subsidize industrial enterprises without worrying about their own expenditures, and finally, the public sector should not 'disloyally' compete with the private sector for internal markets or developmental investment funds."[16] In other words, the godfather should not obstruct the road for the godson.

Mexico has some of the lowest taxes in the world, especially taxes on capital. Between 1940 and 1969 the percentage that taxes comprised of the gross national product (GNP) was less in Mexico than in almost any other Latin American country (Table 1.1).

If taxes as a share of GNP have risen in recent years, it is because the taxes on wages, rather than capital, have increased. Mexico has an inequitable tax system whose regressive structure is based on indirect taxes.[17] It is the salaried workers who pay these taxes, even though they already pay the consumer sales tax (see Table 1.2).

Another major problem with the Mexican fiscal system is tax evasion. In 1962 President López Mateos announced that only 2 percent of the population paid taxes.[18] He said that with tax reform this number might reach 20 percent. Even that change would render Mexico's fiscal system able to collect only 10 percent of personal income, compared to 7 percent in 1971 (see Table 1.1).

Although the fiscal system was supposed to function as a tool for redistribution, it succeeded only in becoming an instrument for supporting the accumulation and concentration of capital. Though the tax system was supposed to endow the state with the resources to achieve its self-assigned goals, it managed only to increase the load on the most disadvantaged sectors in the population, thus worsening an already bad income distribution. That helped to restrict a small market even further by taking income from the potential consumers who could least afford to lose it. In addition, because the overall tax burden was so low, it forced the government to increase its external borrowing to pay for the services it was providing and then to pay the interest that the debt itself required.[19]

Table 1.2
Gross Tax Collections on Capital, 1970–82
(In Millions of Pesos)

Year	No. of Enterprises	Rate of Increase (%)	No. of Persons	Rate of Increase (%)
1970	9,180		6,298	
1971	9,211	0.3	7,631	21.2
1972	11,112	20.6	9,706	27.2
1973	13,470	21.2	11,770	21.3
1974	20,409	51.5	14,915	26.7
1975	26,656	30.6	21,710	45.6
1976	33,068	24.1	32,062	47.7
1977	46,378	40.3	46,131	43.9
1978	66,410	43.3	64,532	39.9
1979	97,177	46.3	74,550	15.5
1980	142,844	47.0	103,215	38.5
1981	194,405	36.1	135,855	31.6
1982	218,562	12.4	243,118	79.0
Total % Increase For The Period:		2,381		3,861

SOURCES: 1970–72 in JLP A-EH, 1979; 1973–82 in *Secretaría de Hacienda y Crédito Público, Indicadores tributarios*, 1983.
NOTE: JLP A-EH assigns its series of data a slightly higher percentage. SHCP series data was used because it is more up-to-date.

As if these fiscal supports were not enough, the government created a state-owned economic sector that served two fundamental purposes. First, it covered those areas in the economy that private capital did not, either because those industries provided low profit yields or carried a high risk, or because those areas required high amounts of investment capital and provided low profit returns. This process included buying those enterprises that found themselves in economic difficulties. Using state capital to socialize the losses from nonprofitable industries gave private investors the opportunity to invest in enterprises yielding higher profits, while the state and the taxpayers took the risks and the losses. Here again we see how the godfather does not let the godson taste defeat. The sponsor will always protect his protege, so that he may savor the sweetness of triumph and fortune.

A second purpose served by state enterprises was to be a constant source of support for private capital. The state finances, buys, and sells, and if a business goes sour for the investor, the state buys it back at a very good price. A major justification for this practice is to ensure that the working class remains employed. Thus in protecting employment, the state protects the bourgeoisie. And when the bourgeoisie is unable to invest in the creation of new jobs, the state does so to prevent the market from collapsing, even if it means putting the country further in debt.[20]

Finally, the state has created large irrigation districts for the production of foodstuffs.[21] Such a large-scale subsidy of agriculture has contributed to the policies that allow low salaries for both rural and urban workers. All these protectionist measures have caused economic and social distortions that the state has been unable to correct over time.

According to Luiselli, the turning over of land to the livestock industry since the 1960s has provoked "The Crisis" in Mexican agriculture.[22] Other authors argue that it was created by the decapitalization of the countryside in favor of the cities.[23] The truth is that historically neither the Mexican capitalists nor the state saw the peasants or the working class as consumers; rather, they saw them only as producers of surplus. This view created an important slowdown in the expansion of the market and an even more significant deterioration in the reproduction of the system. The state tried to stop the contraction of the market by generating state employment, but it lacked adequate financial resources to do so.

The impulse toward industrialization at all costs created a large industrial capacity that was underutilized and consequently resulted in high unemployment. Therefore, the major effect of the fiscal stimulus and the import-substitution tariffs was a technological framework for a large-scale economy, but since the internal market was restricted (with less than 20 percent of the population participating in it), the demand simply did not exist for all the supply that could be produced. The result was a large number of weak firms that continued to require state aid to survive or, in extreme cases, had to be taken over by the state.

During the 1960s the economy grew at a rapid pace, but by the 1970s the effects of industrialization had become practically the opposite. Most enterprises could not afford to expand, because the market for the output of many industries was only about 50 percent of capacity. This situation led to an increase in the costs of production, which was forcefully translated into inflation. That explains in part the failure of several enterprises that the state was forced to buy out in order to hide the shaky nature of the economy and to avoid an even larger increase in unemployment. Yet because the state could not prop up every ailing firm, many went bankrupt, unemployment rose, and popular discontent increased. The godfather understood that his efforts to make the godson grow healthily created only an appearance of good health which hid some of the symptoms of the illness.

POLITICAL DISCONTENT

The great legacy of Lázaro Cárdenas to the Mexican political system, besides a strengthened presidency, was the destruction of the union of the peasants and the workers and the integration of the leaders of these classes into the state apparatus. From then on, the state was able to carry on a semiauthoritarian corporatist system and to achieve relative social tranquility.

The dominated classes—the workers and peasants—did not exactly achieve peaceful coexistence with the state and with the dominant class; they were somewhat restless during the 1950s and 1960s. But even the great movements such as those of the railroad workers in 1958, the teachers in 1964, and the doctors a year later did not present a serious threat to the political and economic regime. On the contrary, and paradoxically, these popular mobilizations permitted the state to experiment with and refine various forms of control and repression.

The years of the Mexican Miracle were a period in which the state experimented with diverse forms of control to repress the otherwise uncontrollable dissident expressions of the dominated classes. The state practiced various forms of social pacification, ranging from co-optation to corruption, torture, and assassination.[24] The widespread social discontent began to appear even among members of the middle class, because they felt most intensely the restriction of economic and social mobility. In addition, since the political system was limited to members of the revolutionary family, most people were shut out of meaningful political activity as well.

This was a case not just of the mass movements mentioned before, but also of the revival of a university, which brought back memories of the struggles of the 1920s, when the autonomy of the university was won[25] and in which several of today's leading politicians participated. The fuse began to burn in 1966 when UNAM rector Ignacio Chávez fell.[26] Demands were made to rid the campus of university police and the regulations that accompanied them. The university students also sought to appeal to the preparatory students by advocating that they be given automatic entrance into the university. [Attached to UNAM is a preparatory high school. To enter this school, and therefore greatly improve their chances of later entering UNAM, students must pass a general examination. Before 1966, the students then needed to pass another exam before entering a professional school at UNAM. By asking that this exam be dropped, the students were saying that they wanted to enter directly into professional school without an exam, on the basis of gradepoint average alone.] Not until the university students made this demand did the preparatory students begin to support their movement.

It was said in government circles that the student movement was provoked by President Gustavo Díaz Ordaz, because the rector, Ignacio Chávez, a distinguished cardiologist, wanted to use his position to launch his presidential candidacy. But another hypothesis also was ventured. Apparently, there existed a medical group that was close to the López Mateos government when Chávez was rector of the university. This group lost its connections when engineer Javier Barros Sierra assumed the rectorship in 1966 and adopted a position contrary to that of President Díaz Ordaz. Barros Sierra was then replaced by the sociologist Pablo González Casanova, who was not far from the Echeverrista positions. The medical group regained its power when Dr. Guillermo Soberón (married to Chávez's niece) assumed the rectorship during Echeverría's presidency. Therefore, the removal of Chávez meant that this group temporarily lost much of its power.

In light of the fact that the rector is designated with at least the consent of the Mexican president, it can be seen that the fall of Rector Chávez was a skirmish over the direction the presidential succession would take. (It should be noted that Echeverría's most important contender for the presidency was Emilio Martínez Manautou, also a physician.) None of this is to deny the genuine discontent among students over the possibilities for social and employment mobility for university graduates. The economic "miracle" seemed relatively unmiraculous to this group.

In 1967 in Morelia the representatives of the polytechnical students, who traditionally were aligned with the state, were denied recognition by the students themselves. The reason for the denial was apparently that these students were strong supporters of Carlos Madrazo, a president of PRI who tried to reform and democratize the party in the 1960s.

Finally, in 1968, with strong support from the Communist and Maoist groups in UNAM and the National Polytechnic Institute (IPN), a movement was initiated that was in great part provoked by the police, who used unusually violent means to put down a fight among students in Mexico City. This action inflated the conflict, whose participants were military groups, hired thugs, and idealistic students; many times the students did not know who was manipulating them.[27] Without going into the analysis of the student movement, which is far from the purpose of this work, we can see that one of its great unexpected contributions was to demonstrate how far the tolerance of the system could be pushed. Those limits appeared to be relatively narrow.

Although the system was able to finish with a single blow the guerrillas who emerged with the Spartacist movement in 1967, it was not capable of co-opting or corrupting a much broader movement that succeeded in bringing more than one hundred thousand protesters to the streets. The regime chose instead to use military violence to end the movement. I do not believe that the government in 1968 understood the causes and the purposes of the student movement. This is not to say that society in general was any better prepared to do so. Another factor was that since the country was on the eve of the 1970 elections, many people saw the skirmishes of the summer of 1968 as part of the preliminary campaign for the presidential succession. For that reason, many politicians chose to stay outside the events so as not to get burned. This episode showed very clearly how Mexican democracy works.

The student unrest gave an unexpected opportunity for Luis Echeverría, secretary of government (or interior), to demonstrate his political virtues. Some believed that Echeverría won the presidential nomination because he was the official with the greatest quickness, intelligence, and loyalty who stood by Díaz Ordaz during these difficult times. I believe this argument should not be discarded, since it is part of the explanation of the presidential succession during that period.

The events of 1968 were mostly a middle-class expression. Reinforcing that argument is the explanation of Rosenstein Rodán,[28] who believed that the political pressures in the 1970s and 1980s would originate in the middle sectors, whom he called the "intelligentsia." Kenneth Johnson claimed that the PRI had no plan to get closer to these middle classes in 1968, even though they represented 30 percent of the population.[29] It was from this group that the leadership of the opposition movements came.

What is certain is that the PRI was greatly worried by the fact that not only were the middle classes distancing themselves from the party, but they were becoming radicalized and more inclined toward antisystem adventures. The guerrilla movement that resurged in the 1970s in Mexico was more a response to the discontent and desperation of the middle classes than it was an example of the Guevarista *foco* movement that swept across Latin America during the 1960s. The ideological proletarianization and fixed wage scales suffered by the middle classes in the 1970s, by-products of an economy increasingly characterized by the tertiary or service sector, led them to identify themselves more as working class and to begin embracing labor unions and other party platforms on a scale not seen in the past.

Significantly, the PRI dedicated an issue of its magazine *Línea* to a study of the middle class. From it I extract two quotations:

> If the Mexican middle class has not adopted the position of vanguard in the popular alliance that backs the actions of the government of the republic, and if there have been ideological deviations that could hinder the march of the country, it is due in great part to its relative lack of means of organization and expression. That is why it is necessary constantly to revise the methods and the policies our party follows in its relations with this important sector.[30]

> Francisco López Cámara affirms that the middle class is favored in every way. At the top, it is rapidly climbing the stairway leading to its integration with the new Mexican bourgeoisie. Below, it receives the firm support of the popular classes to convey its demands in a way that will attend to and consolidate its situation as a privileged sector.[31]

Here we see the great importance of the middle class in the Mexican political system. The state is deeply worried about losing its influence on this sector. It should be added that the previously strong control of the PRI over the workers and peasants was also dissipating rapidly.

TOWARD A NEW WORKERS' UNION

For decades Fidel Velázquez has reigned over the Mexican working class through the leadership of the Mexican Workers' Confederation (Confederación de Trabajadores Mexicanos, or CTM), but not without problems. The CTM has lost control of the major national industrial unions that arose in the country as a result of the rapid economic development of recent decades. These unions, many times in strategic industries belonging to the state, saw no point in entering the CTM, since joining and negotiating through the large labor central would have meant losing the advantages of independence.[32]

The question of labor independence arises because the state controls certain areas of the economy that are considered strategic. The government seeks to avoid uncontrollable factors that will unbalance its ability to handle the strength of labor. Therefore, the unions are taken into the state by giving them seats in the Senate and the Chamber of Deputies and even an occasional governorship. This tactic politically co-opts the union leaders and ensures that they will pursue a policy of collaboration, rather than confrontation, with the state. With labor leadership thereby tamed, the government can experiment with various forms of control over the working class.[33] In an authoritarian regime tight control of labor is necessary because the huge size of this class potentially gives it great political and economic power. For this reason, the regime allows political practices by union leaders, such as reelection, that it does not tolerate even in politicians. Union leaders are thus allowed to dominate the unions so that they can be kept under proper control for the regime.

Nevertheless, even if the state could more or less control the working masses through their co-opted union leaders known as "*charros*,"[34] more demands would still emerge from the unions than the government could handle. That was why the government originally wanted a single voice for labor, and the CTM was created in the 1930s for that purpose. But new, independent unions grew up during the 1950s and 1960s, the period of most rapid industrialization. Then, in 1966, the large independent unions and the national industrial syndicates were united in the Workers' Congress (El Congreso del Trabajo, or CT). Here all the separate unions were supposed to maintain their capacity to negotiate, and yet the government could count on a great labor central that would legitimate and support its labor policies. The CTM, however, remained the major entity in the new organization. The other purpose of the CTM was to control the political activities of the Workers' Congress, while the other centrals and unions would maintain their capacity for negotiating for sinecures, such as positions in state legislatures and the federal Congress. Finally, though the intent in creating the new labor central was to weaken the CTM and its leadership, the result was the exact opposite, which would be clearly seen during the 1970s.

THE PEASANT UNIONS

By the 1960s the state had decided that land distribution could not continue;[35] there was not enough land to give to everyone demanding it and it made no sense to continue parceling it out in small endowments. The Confederación Nacional Campesina (CNC), the largest and most important peasant union, began to support the government's new position. In doing so, however, it lost the little support it still had in the countryside, since one of its main objects had been to defend agrarian land distribution. Its principal actions had been to organize peasants so they could acquire land and to continue the process of calling for more land distribution. Once the CNC abandoned that call, it abandoned the cause that justified its existence.

As Bartra says:

> In that way, the CNC gave up its ability to manipulate the illusions of the peasants and lost what little was left of its already declining effectiveness as an organism of control. Precisely at the time when the need for land was the greatest, the official organisms of control and mediation refused to deal with those demands, and the results were explosive. The peasant saw himself being forced more and more to assert his legal right by other avenues, and thus independent organization was seen as the only alternative left.[36]

The peasant unions' characteristic form of action had been to request land. When the unions lost their power to manipulate, control, and mediate peasant actions, the state saw those expressions of discontent multiply and become violent. And in Mexico the armed conflict of 1910, with all its bloodshed, was an ever-present image. Seeing the situation, Díaz Ordaz reversed the trend in land distribution and executed even more presidential declarations of land reform than were published, or publicly announced. This distinction is important but often confusing. The government first publishes a presidential resolution granting land to the peasants and later, often years later, executes the resolution in order actually to give the peasants possession of the land. So in talking about "land distribution," one must distinguish between published resolutions (*resoluciones publicadas*) and executed resolutions (*resoluciones ejecutadas*) (see Appendix H).

Díaz Ordaz's step-up in land distribution made the situation worse for the official unions, because the peasants saw that land was still given out but that their unions had very little to do with it. In addition, the great geographical distances involved made it difficult for the unions to control the peasants efficiently. These factors allowed the emergence of local political alternatives, which later began communicating with other regions, increasing their effectiveness.

By the 1970s it was evident that the policy toward the countryside had to be reoriented, and not only in agrarian actions executed directly by the state. If the regime was to maintain control of the situation, it had to reinforce the instruments and mechanisms of control over the masses.

VOTER ABSTENTION

The refusal to vote is one of the most obvious signs of the deterioration of the state's image in the eyes of the citizenry, for it implies a high level of discontent regarding governmental policies, or even disapproval of a regime in general. Even though the state may be able to count on forms of private support that might carry more weight than the vote, such forms have less of a propaganda impact.

In Mexico voter abstention began to increase, depriving the state of the only real mechanism by which it could publicly show that it continued to enjoy the support of the majority of the people. According to Cosío Villegas in 1976, the number of Mexicans who were not interested in the identity of the next *"tapado"* [PRI-selected candidate for president] was between 7 and 9 million.[37] The abstention rate in the presidential election of 1964 was 39 percent, but Echeverría was elected in 1970 with the abstention of 58 percent,[38] or with a vote of 21 percent of all eligible voters. Thus it was clear that he was the president of a minority, and his skillful and dynamic campaign did not result in the electoral success that was expected.

The memory of the Mexican people was awakened; not only did they remember the elite selection and imposition of candidates, but they felt a lethargy toward government policies in general, provoked by the behavior of *caciques* [local bosses] who hid behind the tricolor emblem of the PRI. (The PRI emblem is the Mexican flag without the national seal. Thus for many years the party convinced some of the ignorant segments of society that to vote for the PRI was to vote for the nation.) In the city they remembered the outward display every three years which fleetingly showed them a deputy whom they would never see again. Everywhere, people felt the repression of a governing elite that manipulated the dominated classes with revolutionary imagery while it associated with the dominant economic classes to carry out lucrative deals. Elections ceased to have significance for the masses, and the 20 million marginal Mexicans Luiselli talks about were not worried about who would be the next deputy or senator. Nonetheless, people might try to get close to a governor with their demands, but he would have difficulty listening, since the elites are not accustomed to paying attention to the people.

One hypothesis about abstention is that the vote had ceased to have significance as a means to influence the government, if indeed it had ever had such significance.[39] It also was no longer seen by the voter as a legitimating instrument. The question, then, is whether the voter saw abstention as a delegitimating instrument. If legitimacy is the open and constant acceptance of a system, it will be seen in various forms of reaffirmation; that is what we can call a lively and legitimate democracy. But if the people distance themselves from the ballot boxes, democracy dies and legitimacy thereby dissipates.

Nevertheless, legitimacy is not expressed uniformly. While the masses express themselves through voting, the minority, especially the dominant class, expresses itself by accepting or at least not opposing the state. The state seeks and assures itself of this support (or lack of opposition) when it succeeds in having the economy rest on its shoulders. This responsibility becomes not only support for development, but also self-promotion by the state, with an apparatus that includes regulation of money and finance and a series of business supports and subsidies. Mexico's liberalism is *sui generis*, where all is done under the vigilant eye of the protective godfather.

In the face of this panorama of systemic deterioration, Luis Echeverría took the reins of the federal executive power with the intention of guiding the "social and economic transformation of the state."[40] But reality forced the state and government to try to stop the systemic deterioration. The first years of the 1970–76 presidential term were dedicated to this effort, as we see in Part II.

PART II

Echeverría Battles the Decline

To abolish private property would be contrary to the principles contained in our social pact. Some businessmen suffer a certain amount of political illiteracy.

—FAUSTO ZAPATA, DEPUTY SECRETARY OF
THE PRESIDENCY UNDER LUIS ECHEVERRÍA

To say that the private capitalist economy cannot ensure the stability and the rhythm of economic expansion is not an argument in favor of socialism, but simply one favoring the increased intervention of the state in economic life.

—CORNELIUS CASTORIADIS

CHAPTER 2

Management of the Economy

The years between 1940 and 1970 demonstrated a miraculous situation of constant deterioration, notwithstanding (or perhaps because of) the high degree of state intervention in the economy. The end of the first stage of import-substituting industrialization, principally in consumer goods, was translated into a natural deceleration when the market became saturated. This result was in part because modernization eliminated certain artisan activities and in part because the Mexican bourgeoisie did not see the working class or the peasants as potential consumers. The business class was dedicated to extracting economic surpluses from these groups without giving them purchasing power.

The most dynamic sectors of industry were in the hands of foreign enterprises, a fact that led to national decapitalization when these firms practiced overbilling and exported most of their profits. Internal technological development was halted by the importation of technology, which was, however, developed for a much larger market than Mexico. Industrial production was distorted when it sought profits through manipulating supply rather than through improvements in productivity.

Mexico was not able to enter the international manufacturing market and remained weak in a world market of raw materials controlled by the centers of international domination. Even when the Mexican economy ceased to be dominated by a few products, diversification produced few positive results. The early exhaustion of agricultural production and the extension of cattle raising—whether for export to the U.S. or to change eating habits in the rapidly growing cities—led to a significant reduction in agricultural production and thus to the end of cheap foodstuffs produced for an urban labor force at low prices. This development also freed the rural workforce, which migrated to the cities, where excess laborers caused the depression of wages, but did not facilitate the growth of markets. For the state, these trends created strong pressure to provide more infrastructure and services, provoking serious fiscal and ecological problems. (For the growth of the cities, see Appendix I.)

On the part of capital, this situation also provoked migration from one sector to another. Part of the profits acquired in the primary sector were transferred to the tertiary, but not necessarily to the same geographic area from which they had been extracted. The construction and real estate industries became the major speculative activities for capital accumulated in the primary and secondary sectors. In other words, capital was leaving rural areas and concentrating in cities.

For Fitzgerald, these were the causes that explained state intervention.[1] But as was explained earlier, they were also the consequences that led to a "godfathered capitalism" encompassing all of civil society, placing it under official control, and keeping it from moving. This state sponsorship was part of the economic panorama that greeted Luis Echeverría in December 1970 and from which he would have to pursue a new economic logic. Some Marxist economists considered it to be the new model of capital accumulation. Though not a completely new phenomenon, Echeverría's economic policy would largely reformulate the ways the state intervened in the economy.

Echeverría initiated a new and much-needed economic discourse about development. The government recognized that the so-called stabilizing development begun by López Mateos had accentuated social inequality, and therefore the regime had to "abandon the declaration that economic growth will be the only, or principal, objective for the development of the country. The new government emphasized the importance of an increase in employment and the improvement of income distribution, the quality of life, and the reduction of external dependence."[2] The state's new political program sought to fulfill the promises of the fifty-three years of revolutionary regimes.

Unfortunately, the Mexican economic situation and international economic conditions were both so frail in 1970 that Mexico could no longer engage in economic experimentation without running the risk of suffering almost catastrophic consequences. To modify the economic model in a period of strong global imbalances, the state would have to make a series of major policy responses at a crucial time, yet this very fact put it at a distinct economic disadvantage. As it turned out, what should have been a series of well-thought-out, mature, planned political decisions became instead a string of erratic measures based on last-minute evaluations which did not achieve their objectives. Although the policies were meant to have overall and long-term effects, they responded mainly to the pressures of the moment.

According to a high public official, the state intended to

> support economic growth through stimulation of internal demand and increased productivity, transfer the effects of modernization to the rural sector while distributing more equitably the infrastructure for internal development, and stimulate the creation of new sources of rural employment. It also intended to promote the intensive exploitation of natural resources, open the economy of semidesert areas, decentralize industrial activities, tighten the relationship between manufacturing and human resources, and relocate fiscal stimulants from the production of consumer goods to the processes of industrial integration. Other goals were to generate abundant employment by strategically selected public and private investment, promote the intensive training of labor, strengthen savings in the public sector, increase welfare services substantially, increase the efficiency of the education system, and strongly promote scientific and technological research.[3]

But if these were the goals of the state, it was difficult to find concrete results of all these proposals. Moreover, they were implemented in a piecemeal fashion, rather than as an integrated program.

Unfortunately, the evaluation of a political system is not based on its proposals, even when they are interesting. Rather, a system must be evaluated in terms of its results. Frequently, one errs in considering the promises of politicians as though they were measures carefully calculated and well thought out, taking into account time, space, and cost, without considering that the promises might have solely a demagogic purpose to appease demands and revive aspirations. The proposals enunciated above by a high government official should be taken as indicators of political intention, but their results should be measured in the middle and long term. Success resides not in the intentions or proposals themselves, but in the performance of other factors, such as the training of labor and the improvements in education or scientific research. Yet we must also analyze the political effects of these statements, since some political actors will feel threatened by their application.

Let us now see how the state managed some of its resources to achieve the desired effects, and let us also see what the effects were in the short run.

Table 2.1
Projected and Actual Federal Expenditures in
Mexico (1935–76), in Percent

President	Economic		Social		Administrative	
	Projected	Actual	Projected	Actual	Projected	Actual
Cárdenas 1935–40	30.5	37.6	23.0	18.3	46.5	44.1
Avila Camacho 1941–46	30.7	39.2	23.5	16.5	45.8	44.3
Alemán Valdés 1947–52	39.2	51.9	18.6	13.3	42.2	34.8
Ruiz Cortines 1953–58	43.8	52.7	20.4	14.4	35.8	32.9
López Mateos 1959–64	38.9	39.1	31.6	19.5	29.5	41.4
Díaz Ordaz 1965–70	38.0	40.6	37.5	21.0	24.5	38.4
Echeverría Alvarez 1971–76	39.1	45.3	27.6	23.5	33.4	31.2

SOURCE: J. Wilkie, *La revolución mexicana*, 66, 111, 116, 118, 119, 124, 322, 354, 358, 454.
NOTE: Includes the federal government.

EXPENDITURES AND INVESTMENTS

Public expenditure and investment are major instruments for state intervention, especially for economic development. The first analysis of public spending should be sought in historical comparison, by looking at the trends evident in periods of strong presidential governments, from Cárdenas forward (see Table 2.1).

In the case of federal spending, what stands out first is the great difference between projected and actual expenditures (see Table 2.2). The great gap between what Congress appropriates at the beginning of the fiscal year and what the government eventually spends demonstrates a number of important qualities of the Mexican political system. Perhaps the most important is the considerable degree to which the Mexican president is free from control by Congress.

One scholar has divided Mexican government spending into three categories: economic, social, and administrative.[4] For economic spending, or spending for economic development, the variation between projected and actual expenditures from Cárdenas to Ruiz Cortines is a 26 percent increase. That is, about one-fourth more was actually spent for economic

Table 2.2
Difference between Projected and Actual Federal Expenditures in Mexico, 1934–76, in Percent

President	Economic	Social	Administrative
Cárdenas	+23.3	-20.4	-4.9
Avila Camacho	+27.7	-29.8	-3.3
Alemán Valdés	+32.4	-28.1	-17.5
Ruiz Cortines	+20.3	-29.4	-8.4
López Mateos	+0.8	-38.3	+40.4
Díaz Ordaz	+6.6	-43.9	+56.7
Echeverría Alvarez	+15.9	-14.9	-6.3

SOURCE: Calculated from data in Table 2.1.
NOTE: The percentage of variation is calculated with respect to the previous presidential term in each case.

purposes than was projected in the initial budget presented by the president to Congress at the beginning of the fiscal year. By contrast, in every presidential term a smaller share of the budget was spent for social programs than was projected (27 percent less, on average). The third category, administration, got just about what was projected (actually, 8 percent less). During the administrations of López Mateos and Díaz Ordaz the pattern changed, and actual spending for economic development programs was only 4 percent greater than projected. Actual social spending, however, was 41 percent less than projected, while administrative spending was almost 49 percent greater than projected.

It should be noted that social spending is the only category that lost consistently with respect to what was projected, while administrative spending gained considerably. (Much of the overrun for administration was for debt service, which actually went to all parts of the budget.) Actual spending for the economic sector was never less than projected, although the difference was not as great from 1959 to 1970 as it had been from 1947 to 1952 (51 percent of total expenditures) or from 1953 to 1958 (53 percent of the total).

The analysis of the disparities between projected and actual spending reveals the difference between what the state intends or claims to do and what it actually succeeds in accomplishing or, at least, what it succeeds in allocating money for. Wilkie suggests that this flexibility in the deployment of resources gives the president latitude in the face of changing conditions and opportunities.[5] The suggested explanation is a good one. [For a detailed analysis of Mexican government expenditures from 1935 to 1982 and some possible reasons for the yawning gap between projected and actual spending, see Cothran and Cothran, "Mexican Presidents," 1988.—Ed.]

The increasing importance placed by the Mexican government on economic development can be seen in the share of the total budget made up by economic spending. It increased from 38 percent of actual spending under Cárdenas and 39 percent under Avila Camacho to 52 percent under Alemán and 53 percent under Ruiz Cortines. It then declined to 39 percent of the budget under López Mateos and 41 percent under Díaz Ordaz.

On the other hand, social spending lost ground, from 18 percent of total spending under Cárdenas to 14 percent under Ruiz Cortines. It then increased again to almost 20 percent under López Mateos and was maintained at that level under Diaz Ordaz (21 percent).

Administrative expenditure was maintained by Cárdenas and Avila Camacho at 44 percent, dropped under Alemán (35 percent) and Ruiz Cortines (33 percent), rose under López Mateos (41 percent) and dropped once again under Díaz Ordaz (38 percent).

With Echeverría these tendencies appeared to vary once again, both in the gap between projected and actual expenditures and in the actual share that each category comprised of the total. Echeverría actually spent 16 percent more on economic programs than he projected, while Díaz Ordaz had spent only 6.6 percent more (Table 2.2). The gap between projected and actual spending for social programs was much smaller under Echeverría (15 percent) than under Díaz Ordaz (44 percent). The gap for administration was almost nonexistent under Echeverría (6 percent) but was very large under Díaz Ordaz (57 percent).

Echeverría's budgeting, therefore, represented a new direction. Under

Table 2.3
Federal Public Spending, 1971–76

Year	Total (millions of pesos)	Central Government (%)	Parastatal (%)
1971	109,269	46.3	53.7
1972	135,505	51.8	48.2
1973	188,272	50.1	49.9
1974	255,642	49.1	50.9
1975	373,277	50.0	50.0
1976	444,896	49.3	50.7

SOURCE: Table 2.1 and Samuel Schmidt, "Las distintas caras de la deuda del sector público mexicano, 1970–76," in James W. Wilkie and Stephen Haber, eds. *Statistical Abstract of Latin America,* vol. 22 (Los Angeles: UCLA Latin American Center Publications, 1982).

Table 2.4
Mexico's Actual Federal Public Expenditures in Current Prices
and in Constant Pesos per Capita, 1971–76

Year	Actual Expenditures (millions of current pesos)	Actual Expenditures per Capita[a] (current pesos)	Actual Expenditures[b] (millions of constant pesos)	Actual Expenditures per Capita[a] (constant pesos)
1971	109,269	2,083.3	95,348	1,817.9
1972	135,505	2,496.9	112,639	2,075.5
1973	188,272	3,352.4	139,667	2,486.9
1974	255,642	4,398.5	153,263	2,637.0
1975	373,277	6,205.8	194,618	3,235.5
1976	444,896	7,137.8	200,313	3,213.7
Increase	307.2%	242.6%	110.1%	76.8%

SOURCE: Table 2.3.
[a] According to population figures in International Monetary Fund, *International Financial Statistics Yearbook* (New York, 1976).
[b] Deflated according to the index in Appendix A.

Echeverría, economic expenditures increased to 45 percent of the total. Social spending increased to 23.5 percent of the budget, the highest percentage in the entire period from 1934 to 1976. Spending for administration decreased to 31 percent of the total federal budget, the lowest share for the entire period.

We should look more closely at the expenditures to understand their importance. In the first place, Wilkie's analysis covers only the expenditures of the central government, because it was by far the most significant component of total government spending until 1970. Under Echeverría, the parastatal sector grew rapidly, with the number of parastatal entities increasing from 84 in 1970 to 845 by 1976.[6] Because central government expenditures also increased rapidly at the same time, however, their shares of the total federal budget remained roughly equal at about 50 percent each (see Table 2.3).

The expenditures of the central government sector include fund transfers and subsidies to the parastatal sector, and this category of spending is what fundamentally changed. To the extent that the central government spends its money on salaries, the increase in public employment gives an indication of where much of the money went. Of the 488,400 jobs created in the public sector from 1970 to 1976, 74 percent, or 365,323 positions, were absorbed by the federal government. Of these, 249,084 went to the Department of Public Education.[7] Thus 68 percent of the new jobs went to education and all of the other jobs for the central government combined amounted to fewer positions than the jobs created in the parastatal sector.

The parastatal entities absorbed 122,900 new employees, about 25 percent of the state total, of which the Institute of Social Security absorbed 15 percent, or 72,283 persons. In addition, 41,000 employees were absorbed by three agencies: PEMEX (3.4 percent of the total), the electrical sector (4.0 percent), and railroads (1.0 percent). Thus the burgeoning parastatal sector represented a major concentration of state employment.

Public spending rose in similar proportions, from 109 billion pesos (U.S. $8.74 billion) in 1971 to 445 billion pesos (U.S. $35.6 billion) by 1976. These figures represent an increase of 307 percent in current pesos during Echeverría's term. (see Table 2.4). But if we adjust for inflation, we find 95 billion pesos in 1971 (U.S. $7.63 billion) compared to 200 billion pesos (U.S. $16 billion) in 1976, or an increase of 110 percent in real terms.

Total state spending per capita grew from 20,833 pesos (U.S. $1,667) in 1971 to 71,378 pesos (U.S. $5,710) in 1976, an increase of 242 percent in current pesos. The deflated per capita expenditures for the same period are 1,818 pesos (U.S. $145) in 1971 to 3,214 pesos (U.S. $257) in 1976; that is only a 77 percent increase for the same period. The national index of consumer prices went from 108.7 to 222.1, an increase of 204 percent (see Appendix A). Seen from this perspective, real public spending remained lower than inflation, which was perhaps the central problem with state spending. Instead of having a regulatory effect, it was heavily involved in the market game. That is, instead of correcting such economic problems as inflation, the government simply contributed to them.

In a circular way, as inflation increased the costs for the state, the growth in state expenditures caused even greater inflation. The pattern was self-reinforcing, as severe cuts in expenditures or investment would have led to a fall in demand, producing a deep recession.[8] If a cut in expenditures was ever considered, it seems that the government discarded the idea rapidly. In the end the problem came to be seen as a result of poor presidential decisions instead of the product of the interaction of complex internal and external forces. As Whitehead wrote:

> On the domestic front the administration sought to reduce external dependency and therefore decided to suspend foreign credit, reduce the deficit in the balance of payments, and avoid the devaluation of the peso, reducing Mexico's inflation rate below that of the United States. . . . Indeed, inflation and the deficit in the balance of payments declined, but per capita income stood still and unemployment increased. . . . From then on, Echeverría evidently decided

Table 2.5

Public Revenues and Expenditures (In Millions of Pesos) and Rate of Annual Increase

Year	Gross Revenues	Increase (%)	Effective Revenues	Increase (%)	Effective Tax Revenues	Increase (%)	Total Authorized Expenditures[a]	Increase (%)	Total Actual Expenditures	Increase (%)
1969	36,144	n.d.	30,212	n.d.	26,718	n.d.	107,942	n.d.	98,001	n.d.
1970	41,367	14.5	33,868	12.1	29,792	11.5	119,631	10.8	109,238	11.5
1971	44,655	7.9	36,530	7.9	32,554	9.3	130,023	8.7	121,331	11.1
1972	54,470	22.6	42,336	15.9	37,836	16.2	157,782	21.3	148,768	22.6
1973	70,134	28.1	53,822	27.1	47,979	26.8	215,074	36.3	204,033	37.1
1974	96,977	38.3	72,893	35.4	67,224	40.1	288,693	34.2	276,483	35.5
1975	133,358	37.5	103,551	42.1	95,022	41.4	416,811	44.4	400,650	44.9
1976	167,110	25.3	136,612	31.9	124,500	31.0	522,007	25.2	483,798	20.8

SOURCE: JLP A-EH, 1973.
[a]Includes central government and parastatal sector.

Table 2.6
Revenues and Expenditures of the Mexican Federal Government, 1971–76 (In Millions of Pesos)

CATEGORY	1971	1972	% Change	1973	% Change	1974	% Change	1975	% Change	1976	% Change
Total revenues	36,530	42,336	15.9	53,822	27.1	72,893	35.4	103,078	42.1	135,616	31.0
Current revenues	35,745	41,665	16.6	52,217	25.3	71,995	37.9	102,591	42.1	134,082	31.1
Capital revenues	785	671	-14.5	1,605	139.2	898	-44.0	1,252	39.4	1,534	22.5
Total spending	41,317	59,061	42.9	81,237	37.5	104,130	28.2	145,126	39.4	191,593	32.0
Current spending	28,947	37,998	31.3	50,010	31.6	70,670	41.3	95,800	35.6	129,289	35.0
Capital spending	12,370	21,063	70.3	31,227	48.3	33,460	7.2	49,326	47.4	63,304	26.3
Budget deficit	4,787	16,725	249.4	27,415	63.9	31,237	13.9	41,754	33.1	55,977	34.6
Savings on current account	6,798	3,667	-46.1	2,207	-39.8	1,325	-40.0	6,500	390.6	4,793	26.3
Deficit on capital account	11,585	20,392	76.0	29,622	45.3	32,562	9.9	48,074	47.6	60,770	26.4

SOURCE: L. Angeles, *Crisis y coyuntura*, Apéndice Estadístico, Table 17.

that the administration of the economy was a matter much too important to leave in the hands of the technicians.[9]

Reinforcing the image that everything depended on the will of the president, Whitehead concluded that "toward the end of 1972 the only one who could decide whether or not to continue forward was the president. The only limitations were those derived from the consequences of continuing forward, and the only way to exercise pressure was to take complaints directly to President Echeverría in person."[10] Even though Whitehead's study is very well done, he could not avoid accepting the myth of presidentialism, and he failed to take into consideration all the factors involved in political decisions.

In this context we must recognize what seems to be a tradition in Mexico of economic contraction during the first and last years of the sexenio. Notwithstanding Whitehead's argument that the president's main goal was to limit indebtedness and equalize the balance of payments, the primary intent was to cover the necessary governmental financing by increasing both taxes and public spending. But in the end it was revealed that the state was working with a budget based on imponderables, which meant that the entire political economy was functioning without a sound financial base.

The financing of the budget provides a good example of this lack of soundness. The primary source for financing should be tax revenues, which represented around 70 percent of gross revenues. The government proposed fiscal reform to permit an increase in revenues relative to expenditures; however, it seems that revenues and expenditures were considered independently of one another. In 1972, 1973, and 1975 the rate of growth in authorized (projected) spending was greater than the rate of increase in revenue collection. Actual spending also increased faster than did revenue collection in 1971, 1972, 1973, and 1975 (see Tables 2.5 and 2.6).

By such mismanagement the deficit increased and indebtedness continued to grow. The printing of paper money to cover the deficit caused greater inflation, especially since it occurred during a time of international financial disequilibrium, characterized especially by a fall in the dollar. This type of contradiction in the handling of public finances was an important reason for the recession called economic debility (*atonía economica*).[11]

The allocation of resources in this sexenio seemed to be very erratic; instead of demonstrating balanced planning, the government merely responded to market disequilibria. As can be seen in Tables 2.5 and 2.6, from 1970 to 1971 spending increased moderately (11 percent); from 1971 to 1972 spending increased by 23 percent; and in 1973 by 37 percent. By

Table 2.7
Actual Public Spending by Sector, 1971–76
(In Millions of Pesos)

Year	Total	Energy		Communications		Social Development		Industry		Commerce		Agriculture, Fisheries		Administration, Defense		Tourism	
		Amount	%	Amount	%	Amount	%	Amount	%	Amount	%	Amount	%	Amount	%	Amount	%
1971	121,331	38,634	31.8	14,614	12.8	30,022	24.7	7,464	6.2	4,350	3.6	5,725	4.7	21,175	17.5	208	0.2
1972	148,971	43,782	29.4	18,161	12.2	37,837	25.4	8,906	6.0	4,660	3.1	10,161	6.8	24,806	16.7	658	0.4
1973	204,173	55,283	27.1	23,616	11.6	44,674	21.9	18,384	9.0	8,242	4.0	16,926	8.3	36,425	17.8	621	0.3
1974	276,608	69,592	25.2	26,178	9.5	64,132	23.2	29,948	10.8	14,253	5.2	23,294	8.4	48,435	17.5	776	0.3
1975	400,832	108,383	27.0	33,355	8.8	85,241	21.3	41,952	10.5	22,083	5.5	39,918	10.0	66,441	16.6	1,457	0.4
1976	484,073	128,470	26.5	42,852	8.9	113,722	23.5	42,990	8.9	24,863	5.1	36,106	7.5	93,656	19.3	1,864	0.4

SOURCE: JLP A-EH, 1979, pp. 85–98.
NOTE: Includes central government and parastatal sector.

1974 the increase had declined to 5.5 percent; it went up again to 45 percent in 1975 and then drastically slowed to 21 percent in 1976.[12] It was obvious that the ultimate effect of these fluctuations was great confusion in the business sector. It could not plan its investments, but it did understand that the period was ripe for speculation.

The difficulty in reducing public spending is not solely economic, but political and social as well. Even if present overspending would cause future problems of inflation and high interest rates, the government felt obliged to respond to the urgent needs of society. That is why the social sector was the one that lost the least (see Table 2.7). Yet social spending contributed to the constantly increasing deficit. It was not as though the economy was suffering a prolonged recession and for that reason the state could not cover its budgetary needs. On the contrary, the economy was booming: "while profits increased 110 percent in two years (1972 to 1974), sales went up 74 percent."[13] The question is, Where did the profits go?

Although in the beginning the state found it impossible to enforce savings through taxation, it achieved this goal later by increasing the percentage of deposits that commercial banks had to maintain in the Central Bank. The only difference is that tax revenue is free for the state, but financing through bonds and other borrowing involves interest charges that create an important financial burden for the government. Luis Angeles calculated that before the devaluation in 1976, 84 percent of the deficit was financed from internal credit and 16 percent from foreign sources.[14]

To curb inflation without having to cut programs, the government began to reduce the money supply and interest rates to force the banks to lend more. In 1973 the ability of the banking system to attract funds was weakened, and in 1974 government action was required to adjust internal interest rates in relation to external interest rates to avoid capital flight. That was accomplished by an increase in the margin requirement, or percentage of their funds that banks had to deposit in the Bank of Mexico.

By 1975 all these actions had produced a widespread recession, an increase in inflation, and bankruptcies in the small business sector,[15] forcing the government, as the determining sector of the economy, to go rapidly into greater foreign debt. This measure reinforced the "dollarization" of the economy and in the final analysis was one more factor that provoked the devaluation of the peso in 1976.

In its eagerness to comply at least minimally with its revolutionary rhetoric and without wanting to affect the immediate interests of business, the government restricted credit and generated more economic pressures on workers and on its own economic policy with regard to inflation.

Table 2.8
Public Investment in Current Prices, 1971–76
(In millions of pesos)

Year	Total	Central Government		Parastatal Sector	
		Amount	%	Amount	%
1971	22,392.7	6,815.7	30.4	15,577.0	69.6
1972	33,297.9	11,630.3	34.8	21,694.4	65.2
1973	49,778.4	16,871.3	33.9	32,907.1	66.1
1974	64,817.3	19,701.9	36.4	45,115.4	69.6
1975	95,766.7	27,521.9	28.7	68,244.8	71.3
1976	115,610.3	35,038.7	30.3	80,571.6	69.1

SOURCE: JLP A-EH, 1979, pp. 110, 112.

Public investment, for its part, had gone from 22 billion pesos in 1971 to 116 billion by 1976, an increase of 516 percent. Even when inflation is taken into account, this figure still meant an increase of 266 percent in the six years (see Table 2.8).

Spending for industry and for social development was very important,[16] and the agricultural and fishing sectors received great attention as well (Table 2.9).

The priorities of public spending may have had a logical relationship to meeting the objectives of capitalist development, but the way in which they were handled did not have any relationship to the reality that existed at the time. It seems that the state did not understand the fundamental fact that the Mexican economy was intimately related to the economic cycle of the United States. In addition, it failed to understand that economic conditions did not permit a timid adjustment to satisfy salary demands. Moreover, the government did not have the necessary political courage to state its goals firmly without demagoguery, with its destabilizing effects.

Monetary measures clashed with credit policies, and expenditure policies contradicted financing policies.[17] It seemed that the state was acting in desperation and had lost control of events. The devaluation of 1976 appeared to be more the decision of the López Portillo government, which was coming in, than of the Echeverría government, which was by now in a hurry to leave.[18]

In any case the economy rested so much on the back of the state that two major errors in economic management—the failure of tax policy and the poor control of spending—had catastrophic consequences. This outcome was compounded by the economic myopia of the dominant

Table 2.9
Actual Public Investment, 1971–76, in Percent

Sector	1971	1972	1973	1974	1975	1976	Distribution of increase 1971–76
Total	100.0	100.0	100.0	100.0	100.0	100.0	100.0
INDUSTRY	41.6	34.5	32.6	36.0	41.5	46.0	47.0
Oil/Petrochemicals	23.6	18.8	15.5	15.7	15.3	19.5	18.4
Electricity	14.1	11.7	11.7	11.2	13.0	14.3	14.3
Steel	1.9	1.1	2.1	5.5	8.7	7.1	8.4
Other	2.9	2.9	3.3	3.6	4.5	5.1	5.9
SOCIAL WELFARE	21.7	23.1	25.8	20.8	16.5	14.5	12.6
Urban and rural services	13.4	12.5	4.4	4.7	4.8	3.3	2.8
Construction of schools	5.5	6.1	14.5	11.6	7.8	6.3	4.4
Hospitals	2.7	4.2	6.6	4.3	3.6	3.3	3.4
Other	0.1	0.3	0.2	0.2	0.3	1.6	2.0
TRANSPORT AND COMMUNICATIONS	20.5	23.7	25.4	24.0	20.7	19.2	18.8
Roads	2.1	14.8	12.3	8.8	7.2	7.3	6.0
Railroads	4.1	3.4	4.3	5.1	5.2	4.5	4.6
Shipping	1.8	1.6	2.0	1.8	1.6	0.4	—
Air	0.8	2.0	0.6	1.9	1.1	0.8	0.8
Telecommunications	1.7	1.8	6.2	6.4	5.6	6.2	7.4
AGRICULTURE	14.6	14.8	14.1	16.9	18.1	14.7	15.0
Agriculture	12.9	13.3	11.3	14.0	13.8	11.1	10.7
Livestock	0.3	0.2	0.5	0.4	0.3	0.7	0.9
Forests	0.2	0.1	0.4	0.3	0.5	0.3	0.4
Fisheries	1.2	1.2	0.6	0.5	0.7	0.9	0.8
Rural development	—	—	1.3	1.7	2.3	1.7	2.2
TOURISM	0.2	0.4	0.4	0.6	1.1	1.3	1.6
ADMINISTRATION AND DEFENSE	1.4	3.5	1.7	1.7	2.1	4.3	5.0

SOURCE: *Secretaría de Programación y Presupuesto Información Económica.* 1 (March 1978):114–17, cited in Tello, *La política económica,* 195.

bourgeoisie, which was preoccupied more with increasing its immediate economic earnings than with achieving a smoothly functioning economy. The situation worsened to the point that the crisis was taken seriously even within the government.

PARASTATAL ENTERPRISES

Using supports, stimulants, and subsidies to achieve a certain balance, the state assured capitalists that the economic cycle would not be too volatile. One important instrument for this purpose was the parastatal enterprise. Traditionally, the parastatal enterprises have played two fundamental roles: (a) to produce cheap goods and services; and (b) to buy expensively (i.e. ensure certain prices to producers).

The impact of the state on the economy was undeniable. Not only was public investment increasing, but in certain years it grew more than the average for the economy as a whole. Furthermore, between 1971 and 1973 private investment decreased, while public investment increased. I would argue that public investment increased in those years precisely *because* private investment was not increasing (Table 2.10).

The same can be said with respect to consumption. While during the entire sexenio private consumption decreased, public consumption increased (Tables 2.11 and 2.12)

If we take the year 1975 as an example, we see that of the 109 billion pesos expended on the public sector, almost 90 percent went to 36 entities. Of these, PEMEX absorbed 15.3 percent; CONASUPO, 11.3 percent; the Federal Electricity Commission, 10.3 percent; and the Las Truchas Iron-works, 9.3 percent. That means that four entities representing a wide range of products took 46 percent of all funds, as can be seen in Appendix C.

In the six years of Echeverría's term the parastatal sector grew much more rapidly than the rest of the economy. From 1970 to 1975 the parastatal sector's contribution to the GDP grew by an average annual rate of 26 percent, while the contribution of the rest of the economy grew by about 18 percent.[19] The parastatal sector increased its contribution to tax revenues, employment growth, and imports and exports.

Table 2.10
Gross Fixed Investment in Relation to GNP, 1971–1976
(Percentage Rate of Increase)

Sector	1971	1972	1973	1974	1975	1976
Total	18.2	18.9	20.4	20.6	21.2	20.1
Public	5.4	7.1	8.8	8.2	9.6	8.7
Private[a]	12.8	11.8	11.6	12.4	11.6	11.4

SOURCE: Tello, *La política económica*, 194.
NOTE: GNP in 1970 prices.
[a] National and foreign.

But in the five years from 1970 to 1975 the government deficit increased to an annual rate of 37 percent while the rest of the economy was at 31 percent.[20] Thus although the size of the parastatal sector constantly increased, especially when petroleum production recovered,[21] its mismanagement made it a burden on the economy.

With a system of prices and tariffs that were not adjusted with the necessary flexibility to meet the inflationary conditions of the national economy, the decapitalization of certain industries became worse. By 1976 the federal government had to grant a subsidy of 10 billion pesos and a contribution of 175 billion pesos. It should be noted that the adjustment of prices and tariffs was not possible, because of the fierce opposition of the bourgeoisie, which "did not understand that counting on parastatal enterprises to function rationally from an economic point of view could result in the medium and long term in better prices and services, even though the costs would momentarily be much higher."[22] In this way the Mexican bourgeoisie demonstrated once again its economic myopia and its voracious appetite for profits, even at the cost of its own development in the long run.

Historically, decentralized parastatal enterprises had played an important role in the support of capital, and during Echeverría's term this role diversified and increased. The enterprises or decentralized agencies were sufficiently malleable instruments because they "did not require the approval of Congress to establish new programs, activities or organizational units. They were free of an annual audit conducted by the Congress and they had the right to determine the use of the income generated by their own activities."[23]

Table 2.11
Consumption in Mexico, 1970–76
(In Millions of Pesos of 1960)

Year	1. Internal Spending	2. Federal Consumption Spending	3. 2/1(%)	4. Consumption	5. 4/1(%)
1970	306,085	22,157	7.2	222,323	72.6
1971	313,136	24,126	7.7	229,699	73.4
1972	334,591	26,997	8.1	240,349	71.8
1973	364,102	29,726	8.2	256,375	70.4
1974	394,575	33,611	8.5	276,120	70.0
1975	414,448	39,688	10.0	284,078	68.5
1976	416,127	42,471	10.2	285,565	63.9

SOURCE: JLP A-EH, 1980, p. 41.

Table 2.12
Government Consumption, 1970–76
(In Millions of Pesos at Current Prices)

Year	1. Disposition of Goods and Services	2. Federal Government Consumption	3. 2/1(%)
1970	461,409	32,575	7.1
1971	494,865	36,712	7.4
1972	562,497	43,687	7.8
1973	685,059	56,118	8.2
1974	910,745	77,624	8.5
1975	1,095,871	109,986	10.0
1976	1,353,926	149,963	11.1

SOURCE: JLP A-EH, 1980, p. 40.

Even though the handling of their own budgets seemed to give the decentralized agencies great autonomy, not all of them had their own resources. Furthermore, the great majority of them functioned only because of budget supports from the federal government, as was the case with 176 decentralized entities and 211 trust funds in 1976. These organizations represented 46 percent of the total parastatal agencies at the time. During the period 1971–76 the supports of the federal government to the organizations and enterprises of the public sector represented the following percentages of the federal government deficit: 1971, 117 percent; 1972, 61 percent; 1973, 57 percent; 1974, 66 percent; 1975, 68 percent; and 1976, 47 percent.[24]

Thus, the autonomy of the enterprises was relative. The malleability of the agencies permitted the state to nurture them instead of increasing the number of ministries, which would have required discussion in Congress. Even though Congress is submissive, congressional discussion would have drawn public attention to the creation of a new department or the expansion of an old one. An enterprise, on the other hand, is created by presidential decree. Moreover, to expand a ministry implied increasing its radius of action and thereby increasing the power of a minister, which would aggravate internal power struggles. The sexennial system is very sensitive to changes in the internal balance of power, not least because the ministers are competing to become the next president.

The creation of autonomous decentralized agencies, firms, and organizations also allows the dispersal of political pressures and the isolation of their clientele. Distinct groups of citizens have their own trust funds or commissions through which they can apply pressure or negotiate. This situation could weaken the central power, but the central government retains control because budgetary allocations depend on it. The executive personnel of agencies can be controlled and the director can be disciplined if the central government retains power over the budget. Therefore, an expansion in the scope of the parastatal sector generally strengthens the power of the state.

The rapid growth of enterprises and trust funds can be explained in various other ways:

1. With Echeverría a younger generation came to power. Before 1970 the generational succession had been slow and regular, but with Echeverría a gap was created when the new group skipped a generation. That produced an excess of politicians—those who had arrived in good time and those whose generation had "cut in line."[25] In the face of this demographic explosion the state had to expand and give employment to all these politicians, because not to do so meant having to face individuals with frustrated political aspirations, a risky proposition.

2. The growth of the educational system produced an excess of professionals who did not always find a place in the private sector but usually did in the public sector. The moment they became employed by the state, however, they added a desire for power to their professional aspirations and began to look on their agencies almost as guilds. Because most of the new employment was in decentralized agencies, these organizations became almost like fiefdoms. For example, the architects' association, the College of Architects, controlled the Commission of the Central Conurbation, whose main objective is the urban planning of the central region of the country, including Mexico City and vicinity. Without questioning the professional competence of the architects, we can easily see that sociologists, economists, and others could do the same job, with the architects as consultants. In contrast, the architects seldom consulted social scientists.

3. The Mexican state is not known for its efficiency. If it had any intention of becoming more efficient in pursuing its objectives, it was necessary to sideline the most inefficient politicians. One way the leaders sought to do that was by trying to technocratize the bureaucracy, sending future bureaucrats to study outside the country (one possible reason for the creation of the National Council of Science and Technology, or CONACYT). Once the government became more technocratic, it could make decisions through a sophisticated process that could vertically control governmental chores, which had been largely computerized.

As another option, the government could consider the creation of decentralized agencies as a strategy akin to the "lateral arabesque" of Lawrence Peter,[26] that is, shunting aside incompetents so that they did

Table 2.13
Number of Parastatal Enterprises Registered in
the Department of National Resources, 1970–76

Type of Enterprise	1970	1971	1972	1973	1974	1975	1976
Decentralized organizations	45	54	61	63	65	117	176
Enterprises of majority state participation	39	148	176	229	282	323	403
Enterprises of minority state participation	—	27	24	28	36	41	55
Trust funds	—	48	167	383	387	325	211[a]
Total	84	277	428	703	770	806	845

SOURCE: Informe Anual, Secretaría del Patrimonio Nacional. Cited in Villarreal, *Las empresas públicas,* 217, and in Carrillo, *La reforma administrativa,* 217.
    [a] The decline was due to the purge of trust funds carried out by the Departments of Treasury and National Resources.

not get in the way of those who were really in charge. In this way the establishment of posts in the trust funds and decentralized organizations could leave the road open in the central government to those who were truly competent. The foregoing arguments do not pretend to be conclusive, but they suggest some reasons that could help explain the dynamic growth in the parastatal sector (Table 2.13).

4. Another explanation is worth exploring, since it is relevant to the aforementioned reasons with respect to the creation of clients. In this case we refer to the sectors of the population whose situation is explosive, because of the length of time that they have been exploited and deceived.

Bartra says that "the growing intervention by the state in the commercialization of certain agricultural products responds not only to the needs of economic rationalization but also to the urgency of reducing the growing discontent of the producers and their struggles against buyers and monopolists."[27] In this category he put Tabamex, Inmecafe, PROQUIVEMEX, and Fideicomiso de Productos Agrícolas Perecederos (the Fresh Produce Trust Fund). Without denying this assertion, I believe that we can assume it to be just one among several causes. Even though Inmecafe was the instrument of control of the coffee farmers in the mountains of Puebla and Oaxaca, it also covered coffee exports, one of the most important products of the period, and was the basis of the attempt to create a cartel similar to OPEC. PROQUIVEMEX was the result of a confrontation between the government and the transnational pharmaceutical enterprises (this case is discussed further in Chapter 5).

Finally, one should not forget that economic policy was a product of the times. That was also true of the trust funds, which were created to resolve specific problems, as can be noted by the fact that the 387 Fideicomisos existing in 1974 had been reduced to 211 by 1976.

INFLATION AND THE INTERNAL MARKET

One of the major problems facing the Mexican economy was the narrowness of the market. The pattern of wage distribution was polarized, with the highest strata able to engage in excessive consumption of legal imports as well as contraband, while the six or seven lowest strata had incomes that made it difficult for them to subsist and kept them at the very margins of the market. Only about 20 or 30 percent of the population made up the internal market; this group was about 12 to 18 million people, a market of considerable scale, but far short of the entire population. It basically comprised the salaried sector, which suffered inflation, a deterioration of income, and thus a decline in purchasing power because salaries were not keeping pace with prices. Another aspect of income distribution is the great geographical inequality between rural and urban areas. In addition, some regions of the country are more advanced than others.

When Mexico entered the 1960s, it did not have a truly national market, and so it was a fundamental concern of the state to create one. The government, therefore, tried to expand capitalism throughout the country. Since it was impossible for business to compete abroad and grow "to the outside" by expanding exports, its protection in the Mexican market was all the more important. Its products were not characterized by either high quality or competitive prices. Of course, the economic situation in the sixties led many countries to protect their internal markets.

The only way in which the state could increase the existing market was to return purchasing power to the salaried workers, but as we can see in Figure 2.1, this became practically impossible. Only from January 1974 forward did the relationship between minimum urban wages and the consumer price indexes begin to level off. But we must add that the paying of minimum wage was sometimes evaded and that inflation was not uniform throughout the country.

On the other hand, inflation in this period originated not in the price of goods but in high profits[28] and in the management of government spending. Inflation occurred despite the fact that the state tried to correct several of the distortions that had emerged during the previous 30 years.

One example of such distortions was the decapitalization of the rural areas. The guaranteed prices for the peasants' agricultural goods had not changed for many years. That was not a serious problem as long as

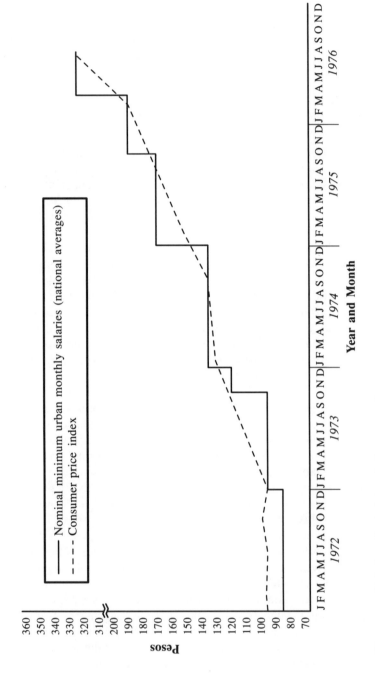

Figure 2.1. Relation of prices to salaries, 1972–76

Table 2.14
Guaranteed Prices of Selected Products, 1971–76
(Pesos per Ton)

Year	Corn	Bean	Wheat	Rice	Soya
1971	940	1,750	800	2,080	1,600
1972	940	1,750	800	2,121	1,800
1973	1,200	2,150	870	2,600	2,700
1974	1,500	6,000	1,300	4,250	3,300
1975	1,900	4,750	1,750	5,700	3,500
1976	2,340	5,000	1,750	5,700	3,500

SOURCE: JLP A-EH, 1979, pp. 476–77.

inflation was around 3.5 percent, but when it began to jump in 1971, the effects were significant. Moreover, various adverse agricultural cycles during the 1970s made the volume of production drop to the point that by 1974 Mexico had its first negative balance in commercial agriculture. By 1975 corn imports had reached $400 million,[29] almost one-fourth of Mexican corn production.[30]

These developments did little to motivate investments and work in rural areas, something the government was forced to correct through changes in guaranteed prices. The price of beans increased 23 percent in 1973 and 70 percent in 1974 but declined in 1975. Corn increased 28 percent in 1973 and 27 percent in 1974. In 1976 it increased 24 percent. The price of beans increased 23 percent in 1973, then soared 179 percent in 1974 before declining again in 1975 (see Table 2.14 and Appendix D).

Without discussing whether farmers deserved the price increases, we can say that the way it was done led to an increase in inflation. In 1971 agricultural product prices to the consumer dropped 2.7 percent but "throughout 1973 they increased no less than 30 percent, and in particular, foodstuffs increased more than 27 percent, slightly more than the general price index, which increased 21 percent."[31]

The government demonstrated that it was not capable of controlling prices. In March 1973, 95 percent of the 10,000 butcher shops in the Federal District closed in protest over the lack of price controls. The butchers blamed the cattlemen, who were interested in exporting to the United States, and the middlemen for the high prices.[32]

In addition, the government took contradictory measures that neutralized each other. For example, on September 24, 1976, a wage increase was agreed to; the following day CONASUPO announced an increase in the guaranteed prices, which was logical. In the face of the effects of devaluation, the state acted so that the salaried workers would not lose purchasing power and increased the subsidies to peasants so they would not be worse off. But the large landholders were the ones who could best take advantage of the guaranteed prices. And as its sense of justice impelled the Mexican government to require those who have the least to have a little less still, the Department of Industry and Commerce authorized a 10 percent increase in prices on September 25.[33]

Guaranteed prices have a great effect on the distribution of income; they benefited the wealthier "capitalist" peasants because they could plan their production and reduce costs by increasing their scale of output. The country could also improve the balance of payments by producing much of what it currently was importing.

With respect to the small producer, the regime became aware that the *coyotes*, or intermediaries, were the ones left with the profits. That is why it created organizations, or increased the ability of those already in existence, responsible for buying or distributing products (Tabamex, Inmecafe, CONASUPO). But to everyone's great "surprise," there appeared the eternal guest of Mexican politics: corruption.[34]

In this way income was not redistributed, the marginalized peasants were not benefited, and instead the rich were helped to get even richer and the state collaborated with them to push inflation even higher. This unrestrained inflation not only kept the market from expanding but also directly affected industrial salaries. If the production of cheap foodstuffs helped to keep the cost of labor down, with higher prices there was no remedy but to increase salaries. But industries passed on the costs to the consumer in order not to lessen their earnings, and the inflationary spiral burst out of control. Even here the state had to face rabid opposition from the bourgeoisie, who blamed the state for all its ills; yet while claiming innocence, it was filling its pockets with money.[35]

The problem was not that the industrial bourgeoisie had lower profits than before, but that the market continued to contract. In 1970 Mexican industry functioned at 50 percent of its installed capacity; it did not reach the scale that modernization had required from 1940 onward.[36] To increase the level of plant utilization would have meant increasing the prices of products to the point that they would have been difficult to sell. Such an outcome would have caused the closure of a great number of industries and would have meant economic crisis. For the generation of governing politicians and observers, the situation represented a real parallel with the crisis of 1929, for they understood the economic implications. If one adds the political instability that existed, the consequences were incalculable.

Forces concerned with the problem of prices and salaries had become even stronger. The bourgeoisie blocked price controls by all conceivable means—corruption (taking into consideration that with price controls the

Table 2.15
Real Salary in Mexico, 1972–1976
(1972 = 100)

Year	Minimum Urban Wage	Consumer Prices	Minimum Real Wage
1972	100.0	100.0	100.0
1973 (October)	118.8	121.0	97.5
1974 (October)	166.8	148.4	112.4
1975 (December)	166.8	171.1	97.5
1976 (August)	184.8	186.1	99.3

SOURCE: Tello, *La política económica*, 72, 144.

possibility of corruption increases), speculation and the black market, and even civil disobedience. While the representatives of the bourgeoisie were compromising with the state and making declarations of submission, the rank and file of that class sabotaged the accords.

In 1974 the state was forced to implement a program of price controls on five basic products (corn, beans, rice, cooking oil, and sugar) to combat the hoarding and speculation of foodstuffs.[37] But perhaps the most significant event was the accord of the "Mexican Basket," signed on August 3, 1974. Commerce, industry, producers, and public officials agreed to maintain prices on more than 300 products until December 31 of the same year, for five months of price stability. But Echeverría's finance minister later wrote that the basket accord was "stillborn. . . . The prices of many of the products were increased before the publishing of the list, protecting those merchants against the eventual price freeze."[38] Opposition to the state's proposals was continuous, as the bourgeoisie was more interested in demonstrating its strength at blocking programs and increasing its profits than in cooperating in economic recovery.

The National Fund for the Promotion and Guarantee of Consumption for Workers (Fondo Nacional de Fomento y Garantía al Consumo de los Trabajadores, or FONACOT) was created in May 1974 to grant credit to workers, establish stores and consumption centers, and promote savings.[39] FONACOT was intended to provide an impetus to industry and presumably to neutralize both the recessionary and inflationary tendencies the economy was experiencing. Also, being able to control the supply of many products, the state supposedly could curb inflation to a large extent. It seems that the state decided not to put a halt to inflation, however, because that meant having to confront the commercial bourgeoisie. Instead, it continued to make constant concessions to business interests.

The working class, at least the most numerous and organized portion, also stood firm, forcing the state to satisfy its wage demands. Yet as the years went by, the real minimum wage decreased (Table 2.15).

Even though the Labor Congress and the CTM were politically strong, they felt threatened by the independent unions. The only alternative left to the workers' leadership, which had collaborated with the state since the years of the Confederación Revolucionaria de Obreros Mexicanos, or CROM, was to assume pro-worker positions; that is, to manage the demands of the working class. Thus during the most difficult moments of inflation, in December 1973, the unions were able to press the federal Congress to create a commission for the defense of the popular economy, which would investigate the causes of shortages, monopolization, speculation, and the high price of products for popular consumption.[40] In April 1974 the Mixed Committee to Protect Wages was constituted to "defend the patrimony of the workers against damage or diminution and to struggle against inflation, speculation, and monopoly."[41] When the "Mexican Basket" failed in August 1974, the Labor Congress called a strike of all business throughout the country to recoup real wages.[42] All this activity demonstrated the radicalization of discourse among the labor leadership.

When in March 1973 the merchants rejected a government anti-inflationary program (see Appendix E), the union leaders took a hard line. In the 82d National Council of the CTM, Fidel Velázquez declared: "The CTM will no longer speak only of strictly following the law, but it may now have goals that go beyond the law. The confederation will not go beyond the Revolution, but will try to create within the Revolution a new proletariat that will be reintegrated into the Revolution." Angel Olivo, of the COR, said: "The worst enemy of the Mexican working class is the type of society that we suffer from." Mauro Gómez Peralta, president of the Labor Congress stated: "Private business is committing suicide; if it does not give in a bit, voluntarily, in the near future all that it has will be taken from it by force, just as has happened in many other places." And in Mérida, Yucatán, Fidel Velázquez said: "The sacking of stores by workers is valid when they are struggling against the abuses of merchants."[43]

As the bourgeois position became more rigid, the workers' position became more radical. The state found itself between two fires, and it tried to force one to back down while attempting to control the other until the difficulty passed. It ended up giving each side a little until the situation went out of control. One central element that provoked the internal inflation was external inflation; thus part of the inflation was imported.

The increases in the internal prices were 48 percent in 1971, 80 percent in 1972, 73 percent in 1973, 44 percent in 1974, and 12 percent in 1975,[44] roughly corresponding to the changes in international prices. In addition, the so-called dollar crisis of 1972[45] produced a scarcity of capital and resultant increases in interest rates that further expanded Mexico's debt. The Mexican economy was attacked by two sources of inflation, the internal and the external. Even if external inflation was abating, its lingering impact on Mexico was devastating when added to the country's internal inflation.

The system was kept in turmoil as the state defended capitalist accumulation at all costs, while it fought the bourgeoisie over increasing state intervention in the economy, promoted the demands of the exploited and oppressed sectors, and confronted signs of rebellion, discontent, and dissidence throughout the country.

CONSUMPTION

The state continued to search for policies that would give credence to its claims to revive the Mexican Revolution, and one of them was intervention in consumption. To increase the internal market by increasing consumption could be done by influencing purchasing power, a factor that could imbalance supply and provoke major inflation. Thus it was necessary to stimulate an increase in the use of installed capacity by an increase in demand, so the market would grow without suffering inflationary pressures in addition to those already mentioned.

Moreover, it was necessary to break the concentration in the market to stimulate economic dispersal throughout the country. Thus, the stimulants that the government offered to industrialists to tempt them to relocate their plants from the large cities were strengthened by the prospect of distributing these products regionally, which would add to their profits. Regionally based production could count on a certain market, lower shipping costs, and enhanced profits. The deconcentration of production presupposed the creation of a consumer market in those regions. Thus it implied a process that would contribute to slowing the unbridled growth of some cities. This measure would rein in the mounting costs of infrastructure and provision of services in such areas which had become ever more expensive and difficult because of their great magnitude.

The idea was correct from an economic point of view, but in Mexico the economy suffers from an almost chronic imbalance between supply

Table 2.16
Contribution to GNP, by Activity, 1970–77
(Rate of Annual Increase, Prices of 1970)

Economic Activity	1970	1971	1972	1973	1974	1975	1976	1977
1. Commerce	6.50	3.0	6.90	7.62	5.18	3.40	-1.0	2.0
2. Textiles (natural fibers)	11.59	6.50	8.83	9.63	0.69	5.39	3.1	5.9
3. Other textiles	0.0	-3.38	2.10	-6.86	18.42	-32.97	-3.9	26.6
4. Footwear/ Clothing	10.0	7.56	8.38	9.59	2.66	4.25	1.7	3.2
5. Soaps and detergents	6.91	0.0	13.73	5.68	8.60	10.02	7.0	11.8
6. Perfumes and cosmetics	15.43	3.38	10.05	8.85	4.49	3.61	2.1	4.7
7. Services (food and lodging)	7.07	8.95	6.90	6.11	4.21	3.60	5.6	4.6
8. Government	9.70	9.0	13.40	11.16	8.19	10.89	8.2	1.8
9. Manufacturing (misc.)	16.96	1.57	11.83	7.82	-9.55	-9.20	9.5	16.2
10. 2 + 3 + 4 + 9	38.55	12.25	31.14	20.18	12.22	-32.53	7.0	51.9
11. 5 + 6	22.34	3.38	23.78	14.53	13.09	13.63	9.1	7.1

SOURCE: JLP A-EH, 1979, pp. 29–30.

and demand, in which the latter exceeds the former. Thus the bourgeoisie seeks in state promotion and protection only the ability to speculate and increase immediate profits. For this reason, the effort to take production to the countryside contributed to the accumulation of capital without achieving the other desired economic effects. The production data do not indicate that the distribution programs increased consumption; rather, they suggest a tendency toward contraction of consumption (Table 2.16).

After the economic decline of 1971 all economic activities behaved erratically. Only a few industries managed to maintain themselves. Soaps and detergents continued to do well until their fall in 1976, which nevertheless reached a higher level than in 1970 (in reality, soap was always available in CONASUPO stores). Services also generally continued at a high level. Lodging and preparation of food fell after 1971 but were recuperating by 1976. This behavior can be explained in part by the free breakfasts provided by the government in the schools. Industrial activity (rows 2, 3, 4, and 9 of Table 2.16) fell in 1971, recovered markedly in 1972, declined strongly in 1975, and began to increase again in 1976. The previous data demonstrate that attempts to regulate production and therefore control the market were not successful, but not for lack of trying.

During Echeverría's term state stores were opened throughout the country, so that by 1975 CONASUPO supplied and operated 2,800 stores and supplied 2,200 others managed by other entities. Various government departments opened stores for their workers, following a traditional practice of the unions.

According to Grindle: "The consumers toward which CONASUPO aimed its activities were those with incomes less than 2,000 pesos monthly and producers who earned less than 12,000 pesos annually; both categories included 90 percent of the active economic consumers and 94 percent of all the peasants in the country."[46] The span of CONASUPO included the Distributive Company for Popular Products (Compañía Distribuidora de Subsistencias Populares, or CODISUPO), which operated 62 trailers with daily routes covering 300 worker barrios and serving an estimated population of more than 2 million persons. CODISUPO operated 405 stores (included in the 21,800 in the system) in poor barrios to ensure a minimum diet.[47]

While this system contributed to the increase in distribution and consumption, it also may have contributed to the slowing of inflation by reducing the price of foodstuffs, thus making it easier for the working class to obtain them. That is possibly what provoked the distortion in the economic plan. CONASUPO dedicated itself to fighting inflation by producing its own goods (milk, cornmeal, wheat flour, and bakery goods); in 1975 it bought a business that produced cooking oil. As Grindle says: "The control over this business was expected to bring about a significant increase in the influence of CONASUPO over consumer prices."[48]

Critics raged against Echeverría, and the popular classes resented the effects of his economic policies, which forced salaried workers to carry the load of inflation, and yet the CONASUPO budget continued to increase. The enterprise was gradually becoming a suitable instrument for putting the national economy back on its feet.

Once again corruption appeared, however, as suppliers often sent CONASUPO defective or low-quality merchandise.[49] So although these state-supported stores made the accumulation of capital easier, the associated corruption harmed the popular economy. Though the program bought cheaply, it also bought badly, thereby costing double.

Another problem was inefficiency. When the government created programs without sufficient study or planning, it was forced to improvise in its organization and implementation. With CONASUPO, for example, instead of developing the administrative system to carry out planning, it proceeded in reverse. First it launched the plans and works and then added the bureaucracy. The consequent proliferation of state agencies fragmented the power of the central government and developed new factors of regional power, often neutralizing the real objectives of the

Table 2.17
Salaries in CONASUPO, 1971–76
(In Millions of Pesos)

Year	Current Income	Rates of Increase (%)	Current Expenditures	Rate of Increase (%)	Wages and Salaries	Rate of Increase (%)
1971	3,071	7.5	3,737	9.3	68	74
1972	3,614	17.7	4,274	14.4	637	387
1973	5,202	43.9	7,031	64.5	103	-618
1974	9,207	77.0	14,861	111.4	139	35
1975	10,137	10.1	18,871	27.0	1,884	1,255
1976	13,632	34.5	16,895	-10.5	293	-643

SOURCE: JLP A-EH, 1980, p. 141.

enterprise. In this manner the goals that CONASUPO had to meet were diverted by the administrative disorder. Take, for example, the salaries of CONASUPO employees (Table 2.17), which did not seem to have any relation to the income or expenses of the CONASUPO stores. If the government stores were the only program, it would not be logical for salaries to have dropped in 1976, since the closing of stores began only in 1977. The 1972 jump in salaries in the budget is also unexplainable, as is the dramatic drop the following year. The same can be said with respect to 1975–76. However, one can also say that the information used to make decisions was as erratic as the decisions based on that information.

These results sabotaged the good intentions of planners, but another factor was the opposition of business to the economic regulation that the state intended to achieve through CONASUPO. For example, the proposal to provide medicines at CONASUPO stores was rejected by the Business Council after an intense propaganda campaign launched by the pharmaceutical industry. The idea of opening popular pharmacies was rejected, therefore, just as the plan to manufacture steroids in Mexico under state control had been.[50]

The state came to the realization that to initiate a program for creating stores under state control it would have to confront the commercial bourgeoisie, and as things were, possibly the rest of the business class as well. Nevertheless, according to data on contributions per sector to the gross national product, commerce did not behave in a different manner from the rest of the economy, although it did register increases while the other sectors registered decreases (see Appendix G). Only the activities of the government experienced a constant increase, climbing from 6.2 percent of GNP in 1970 to 9.6 percent in 1976. Here it is pertinent to clarify a point: if the activities of CONASUPO are included in the governmental sector, the data on the commercial sector give a more realistic picture.

But if CONASUPO's data are included in the commercial sector, the government sector loses some importance. The same point is pertinent to all economic activities in light of the increase in state intervention.

It seems apparent that the merchants did not lose. On the contrary, they took advantage of inflation, monopolies, speculation, and so on and then protested state intervention in areas that might lead to price controls.

From the point of view of the regime's strategy for economic development, hurting business would not fundamentally affect the model. But if business lost confidence, the result could be capital flight and sumptuary consumption, and as I mentioned, that is where speculation and other causes of the acceleration of inflation were located.

Commerce does not need to reinvest capital, and its capacity to create jobs is minimal. When it increases its level of concentration, it simply eliminates many small businesses, and therefore its multiplying effects in the economy can be somewhat limited. In any case industry is capable of creating commerce and not the opposite, because the merchant prefers to import merchandise rather than to produce it.

All these characteristics put commerce in a privileged position reinforced by the organizational weakness of the workers in that sector. The small and medium merchant is practically left out of labor conflicts, since the Federal Work Law stipulates a minimum of ten persons in a firm to form a union. In the large commercial sector the absence of labor organizations is so marked that it is difficult to hear about labor conflict within it. That puts the commercial bourgeoisie in a strong position relative to the state. It has great capacity for negotiation and maneuver in matters affecting it.

The opening of state stores was intended to accomplish two objectives: (1) Finally create a national market, since it had never been sufficiently lucrative for the bourgeoisie to do so, and (2) weaken the commercial sector to control prices, then support the increase of production and regulation of demand to avoid further inflation. The regulation of prices would make possible increased competition, and since state stores functioned without the profit motive, the system would force private business to reduce its profit margin. Speculation would be attacked by controlling basic merchandise through a good distribution system.

The state was not interested in profits or in collecting taxes from the stores under its control, because both factors would have made merchandise more expensive. State stores were intended to be an impetus to industry to increase its output, which would increase taxes, create jobs, and so forth. Also, if the state controlled distribution, it would be easier for it to minimize tax evasion, and if the system functioned properly, it would succeed in raising the popular standard of living.

To explain why this scenario was not achieved, I have two hypotheses.

First, inflation was not curbed because a national market was never achieved and hence there was little increase in effective demand. On the one hand, basic products were commercialized, but on the other hand, inflation contracted the market and there was little increase in production. Besides, part of the inflation was imported, and hence domestic actions could have little effect on that. To slow inflation, the state would have had to confront the bourgeoisie far more decisively than it did. That would have been difficult, however, since conflicts among the workers and between workers and the government meant the state could not count on much political support. Furthermore, middle class backing of the PRI had slipped after 1968.

Second, through CONASUPO the state intended to break the isolation of some of the local economies and thereby contribute to the creation of a national market, one requirement for halting inflation. If this objective had been achieved, the director of CONASUPO would have gained great power, but internal political pressures prevented such a result.[51] Add to this the inefficiency and corruption in the enterprise in particular and in the political system in general, and we see why CONASUPO had less impact than might have been expected.

All these measures should have forced the bourgeoisie to pay the minimum wage, which it steadfastly avoided. But Echeverría's policies clashed with so many opposition groups that the efforts of his government to restructure the social and economic system were dissipated. The bourgeoisie attempted to create the impression that the government was directed by a heretic who tried to get the bourgeoisie to pay taxes, fair salaries, and so on. The inquisitional Mexican bourgeoisie felt that a bonfire had to be started to purify the political system.

Finally, the CONASUPO stores became an instrument of negotiation and control in the hands of the politicians. A politician could obtain a store for his area, circumventing any system of planning. Thus CONA-SUPO was converted into one more plum in the basket of promises of the Mexican Revolution, thwarting the purposes for which the stores were intended.

Turning once again to the economic policies of the regime, we see that the government did attempt to correct basic or structural errors. The state intended to recapitalize rural areas and decentralized enterprises, improve the standard of living of the masses, correct distortions in the distribution and production of merchandise, and facilitate production. In other words, the regime tried to restructure and modernize the godfathered capitalism.

The state was, however, incapable of controlling the existing contradictions or of preventing new ones. It became caught in a hurricane of demands and economic, social, and political pressures that eventually took it off course. The government tried to correct the deteriorated situation but was unable to do so. In the words of Whitehead: "Mexican economic policies were too restrictive in 1971 (accentuating the depressive effects of the downward movement of 1971, which in fact turned out to be very brief), too stimulative in 1972–74 (accentuating the overall tendency toward an unsustainable rhythm of reactivation), but not sufficiently restrictive when the 1975 United States recession proved to be unexpectedly deep and prolonged."[52] The moral of the story is perhaps that the state should understand that even the most benevolent godfathers let their godchildren get hurt from time to time.

CHAPTER 3

Management of Politics

The term *politics* has become a confusing concept, especially since Marxism formulated the concept of an economic infrastructure and a political superstructure. The problem is that decision making is the final aim of politics, and such decisions include both economic and noneconomic factors. Ultimately, all decisions, even those that appear only political, have economic repercussions and vice versa. On the other hand, all decisions taken at the state level are political, whatever their immediate effects. This does not imply that all state decisions directly affect the economy. Let us examine several examples of this assertion.

In May 1971 one hundred peasants from Michoacán received land in Yucatán and Quintana Roo.[1] This policy was an attempt to reduce political pressures, resolve demands, and fulfill peasant hopes, all through political measures, and additionally to begin populating the uninhabited zones of the country to make them productive. In other words, it was an attempt at economic management through political means.

In December 1973 PEMEX doubled the price of gasoline.[2] This action seemed to be an economic measure, and its impact was certainly economic, but in reality it had a strong political component, because it signaled the state's intent to revalue the goods and services of the parastatal sector. Therefore, this measure had both economic and political implications. Dealing with price controls or controlling enterprises with credit problems and indebtedness to the state were typical of the actions taken by the government during Echeverría's sexenio.[3]

70

Another example of the interrelatedness of politics and economics was the arrest of the Acapulco police chief and twenty-two detectives in 1971 following a rapid rise in crime.[4] Undoubtedly, this crackdown had economic motives, since Acapulco is the number-one tourist port of the republic; it was therefore important to show tourists that they were secure from criminal elements, especially because at the time, the U.S. was consistently mentioning the crimes being committed by Mexican police. Politically, this measure allowed the government to show that it was fighting corruption. In like manner the following year the chief of police of the Federal District dismissed two commanders and arrested twelve motorcycle officers.[5]

The battle against corruption was one more sign that the government was in a struggle against the "emissaries of the past," as Echeverría called them. This effort culminated in the proposal for a "democratic opening," which Abel Quezada renamed the "demographic tightening" (*"apretura demográfica*," as opposed to *"apertura democrática"*).

From the beginning, this opening was typical of the Echeverría administration. It was initiated with the conviction that repression was not the only way of controlling and directing change, and as the liberal alternative it was presented to the public as a stark choice: Echeverría or fascism.[6] To unify the country, it was necessary to create the illusion of "a common enemy" to "all Mexicans"; to put Echeverría at the head of the fight for unity, to the left of Díaz Ordaz; and to initiate the policy of rumormongering, which would wreak havoc in the years to come. Ironically, this pattern of rumormongering that was begun by the regime itself ended with the most dramatic of rumors—that Echeverría would be overthrown in a coup d'etat.[7]

RURAL POLICY

An area of focus of all Mexican regimes since the end of the 1910 Revolution had been agrarian reform—not only continuing to sustain Zapata's banner (the peasant expression within the armed movement of 1910), but also, from 1917 to 1970, encouraging peasants to put their hopes (and patience) into the possibility of receiving land. The importance of agrarian policy stemmed from that hope, permitting the regime to manipulate peasant support, and maintain control and political tranquility. It allowed the government in turn to preserve the "revolutionary" halo that has characterized the postrevolutionary Mexican state.

By 1970, however, agrarian reform was exhausted and the physical realities of continuing it were null. One observer wrote:

In conformity with the standing legislation in 1969, it was estimated that there were around 13 million hectares susceptible to being partitioned. These were, however, lands that were fundamentally not arable, and on which fewer than 150,000 landless peasants could be accommodated. . . . It has been calculated that the possible number of people that could benefit from this land, if private property was reduced to 50 hectares of irrigable land or its equivalent, would be only 200,000 peasants. Supposing a more drastic reduction to 25 hectares of irrigable land, there would be land for some 330,000 peasants.[8]

The law finally reduced the size of property susceptible of being partitioned to 20 hectares of irrigable land in 1971, a figure not very far from estimates, which favored 7 percent (in the case of the 20 hectares) of the economically active population in the rural areas. Yet even this reduction was able to benefit only a small portion of the rural population, which grew at an annual rate of 3.5 percent.

The real situation was even worse.

Up to 1979 more than 8,550 solicitations for land had been pending, for 510,000 presumed applicants, at an average of 44 hectares per person, 22 million hectares would be required; 10,700 requests for extensions submitted by 749,000 heads of families would require 25,446,000 hectares; 10,340 solicitations for new population centers represented 872,000 solicitors and required no fewer than 62,852,000 hectares, for 2,131,000 peasants. Added to that were 560 proceedings seeking restitution of communal goods which supported 112,000 communal members with 3,248,000 hectares, and 2,287 applications for confirmation of lands controlled by 655,000 communal peasants, adding up to 13,248,000 hectares."[9]

These numbers represent a total of 127 million hectares required to support 2,898,000 peasants. The fact that the data begin nine years after the period I am analyzing does not detract from their validity. Even if, to be cautious, we reduce it by half to 62.3 million hectares for 1.4 million peasants, it still represents a major burden that could not be satisfied. If, on the other hand, we take into consideration that the Department of Agrarian Reform quantifies the agrarian frontier at 95,000,000 hectares, of which it still needs to parcel out some 10 million, we see that the necessary hectares simply do not exist.

Thus not many options remained for the governing regime. The first consisted in parceling out land at a faster rate than usual[10] to achieve more militant support from the peasants. The second option was to pursue an economic development model that could change agrarian policy. That implied two basic steps: (a) to transform the terms of the discourse on the peasant question in a symbolic sense and (b) to attempt to change the political rules of the game and to press the next president to accept and continue the new approach, because, if not, rural pressures would worsen.

Both measures carried an incalculable potential for conflict because it would now have to be suggested to the peasants that "the ideals of the revolution" were changing. This kind of answer would be fuel for the political groups that wait expectantly for the change of power every six years, hoping to go forward with their own projects and ideas. The second alternative was to distribute land so slowly as to defer peasant expectations for several more years, thereby gaining time while another type of solution to the peasant problem was planned.

The government opted for the first solution. Echeverría received 1,994 presidential declarations not yet executed which would have benefited 186,072 peasants and protected 3,812,715 hectares. Of these, 1,312 related to *ejido* actions, 203 to new *ejido* population centers, and 277 to communal lands, not to mention extensions, parcels, or restitutions (see Appendix H).[11]

Echeverría published 2,208 presidential resolutions and executed 2,202, covering an area of 13,328,852 hectares and benefiting 206,452 peasants.[12] Of these resolutions, 1,578 were actions related to *ejidos*, 263 more than the number published, distributing 7,304,984 hectares (3 million more than distributed by the 1,315 published resolutions). These distributions benefited 112,309 peasants, 15,224 more than contained in the published resolutions.

In arithmetical terms it is clear that Echeverría left a great deal of land undistributed. Nonetheless, he did attack the problem with far greater fervor than had previous governments, although not enough to satisfy the pent-up demands of the peasants. One important aspect of the land problem was that most presidents would declare more resolutions than they would execute, thus leaving unfulfilled demands for their successors. For example, Abelardo Rodríguez published 985 more resolutions than were executed during his term, and Lázaro Cárdenas published 590 resolutions that did not get carried out during his term. This tremendous backlog could not be resolved by the succeeding four presidents, even though they actually executed more resolutions than they proclaimed. Díaz Ordaz produced a new backlog, and Echeverría tried to reverse the tendency and just about came out even, executing almost exactly the number published (see Appendix H).

The value of the distributed land to the economy declined steadily, since the agricultural quality of each new distribution tended to be worse than the last. During Echeverría's term the government adhered to the letter of the law, maintaining the minimum area per beneficiary of 20 hectares of irrigated land or its equivalent in summer pasture land. The

Table 3.1
Land Distributed per Inhabitant, 1935–80

Year	Hectares		Beneficiaries		Hectares/ Beneficiary
	Total	Monthly Average	Total	Monthly Average	
1935–40	17,906,429	248,700	811,157	1,277	22.08
1941–46	5,944,449	82,562	157,836	2,192	37.66
1947–52	4,844,123	67,279	97,391	1,352	49.76
1953–58	4,936,668	68,565	231,888	3,220	21.29
1959–64	11,361,370	157,797	304,498	4,229	37.31
1965–70	14,139,560	196,382	240,695	3,343	58.44
1971–76	13,328,852	185,123	206,452	2,725	67.93
1977–80	3,139,803	65,418	72,270	1,505	43.47

SOURCE: Wilkie, *La revolución mexicana*, Table VIII-4; Appendix H.
NOTE: There is a small difference between the two sources cited, which becomes greatest for 1965–76, because of an official revision of data after the publication of Wilkie's book.

government distributed almost solely pasture land, rather than irrigated land for growing crops. This practice allowed the average plot to reach 68 hectares per beneficiary, but the distributed land was of worse and worse quality (Table 3.1).

Nevertheless, land was distributed, and though politically this policy may have been a step toward fulfilling hopes, it did not provide economic satisfaction. What is important is that the land distribution gave the regime a popular base of support, while it took support away from subversive forces in the countryside and sought to improve peasant conditions politically and economically.

Agrarian reform was limited, however, and could not be maintained indefinitely. To bring the program to an end, there would have to be measurable economic development in the countryside. Several objectives could be accomplished by an increase in production. Such an increase would:

(a) Raise the standard of living in the countryside, thereby reducing the poverty level[13] which had worried Mexican economists. This action would demonstrate that there could be a redistribution of income without threatening capital.

(b) Increase agricultural production in order to reduce inflationary pressures, which if allowed to keep rising would become a destabilizing factor for industry. The growth of inflation also forced the state to increase expenditures, without the same flexibility of increasing revenues. This rise in production would alleviate some of these inflexibilities. Increased production could also help satisfy the demands of the growing population, without further importation of foodstuffs, which increased the deficit in the balance of payments.

(c) Reduce peasant pressures, especially those derived from increased unemployment and pauperism, which resulted in further demands for land. The development of the countryside would permit peasants to earn wages or would at least bring them some of the economic benefits derived from this development. This improvement would lessen the conflicts that were hampering the actions of the peasant unions.

(d) Create a more successful national market, since with production there would be demand and economic integration.

(e) Disarm national and international criticism and demonstrate that the state takes care of its people and satisfies the needs of marginal or impoverished elements.

(f) Stop the migration from rural to urban centers, which had begun to turn the marginalized urban centers into zones of conflict. The increase in urban populations also exhausted the infrastructure and services provided by the state. From 1960 to 1970 the majority of the important cities in the country registered population increases of more than 3.5 percent (see Appendix I).

One of the measures immediately taken was restructuring credit for peasants, accomplished by unifying various branches of the National Bank for Rural Credit. At the same time, the government pressed the peasants to organize collectively, a step that later became a fundamental prerequisite for attaining credit. In addition, various governmental entities initiated programs to provide organization and the means for peasant action (Secretariat of Agriculture, Banrural [Rural Bank], Ministry of Agrarian Reform, and CONASUPO).

Another important aspect of this policy was the new way in which peasants were controlled. In essence, the old methods were reformed. The peasant unions had become bureaucracies and acted to support the political aspirations of their leaders, not necessarily the needs of the masses. Although the pyramid structure of the CNC[14] could be an effective method for learning about peasant needs, the truth is that it produced a system not for supporting peasant demands but for corrupting local, regional, and national leaders. The structure also supported political groups whose interests corresponded with those of union politicians and not necessarily with the political demands of the peasants themselves. Perhaps the most striking example was the CNC's acceptance of the government's position on land reform, since the CNC itself was under the sponsorship of the state.

There came a time when peasants staunchly resisted being used as the "masses" of support and began demanding what had been promised to them. They took a more active stand, taking over lands, offices of government, and offices of the CNC. Examining the serious conflicts, we find that in Ciudad Juárez, in May 1971, more than 2,000 peasants squatted on lands, and two people were killed; in Veracruz, in August 1972, a land invasion cost five lives. In June 1973 twenty-nine invasions in Colima, Guanajuato, Michoacán, San Luis Potosí, Tamaulipas, Tlaxcala, and Querétaro occurred in which the army dislodged the squatters. In March 1974 twenty-five hundred peasants invaded lands near Cuernavaca, Morelos, land that later became the Rubén Jaramillo colony. The army also intervened during the 1975 squattings in Colima, Sinaloa, Tamaulipas, Chihuahua, and Morelos. In September of the same year, 2,500 peasants in Veracruz asked a large landowner for land; he refused to comply and was murdered and his house burned down. In May 1976, in Chiapas, peasants killed three landowners, and the army killed fifty-eight peasants. Two months before, the peasants had hanged the chief of police in Poza Rica.

Without attempting to provide an exhaustive list, we can note a common pattern: (1) The number of invasions was large, involving thousands of armed peasants. (2) Peasants expressed their demands with a great deal of violence. (3) Military and police intervention used a high level of violence to put down peasant unrest.

We also need to take into consideration a fourth point. Peasants began leaving the traditional unions and forming independent organizations and unions. In San Luis Potosí, after 30 years of negotiations, the peasants invaded Los Otates and Crucitas, later named Land and Liberty Camp. In Cuernavaca peasants invaded lots that the sons of the governor were going to convert into a golf course and formed the Ruben Jaramillo colony. In Monterrey, Nuevo León, peasants invaded lands and formed the Land and Liberty Camp. They did the same in Ciudad Juárez, Chihuahua. In Sonora, Sinaloa, Colima, and Veracruz, groups formed independent peasant fronts.

After so many years of control and manipulation the masses had decided to reorganize and seek justice. They formed popular colonies and even fervently supported the guerrilla movements in such states as Guerrero, Oaxaca, and Puebla. The state responded by using all kinds of methods, including violence, to stop the unrest:

1. Increased land distribution: 1,000 peasants from Michoacán received lands in Yucatán and Quintana Roo. This action was intended to develop sparsely populated areas and to pacify the peasants.
2. The use of troops in the areas of most conflict. In July 1971

12,000 soldiers, almost 15 percent of the army, were sent to Guerrero. Troops put down the sugarcane strike in 1972.

3. Law reforms benefiting the peasants: for example, the granting of social security benefits to peasant workers.
4. The expropriation of lands for symbolic political purposes. In Chihuahua, for example, land belonging to two senators and the brother of a former governor was expropriated.
5. Increased repression through large-scale arrests and summary executions.
6. The launching of an economic development program to create jobs.
7. The restructuring of political control.

The last point is important because of its innovative aspects. In December 1975, in Villa de Ocampo, Coahuila, four peasant organizations laid the foundations for the creation of a new peasant union.

The CNC, CCI (Central Campesina Independiente), UGOCM (Unión General de Obreros y Campesinos de México), Jacinto López, and the Mexican Agrarian Council formed the Ocampo Pact and sent requests to the president.[15] With this measure the government intended to stop the divisions and rivalries among the peasant organizations and to form a powerful entity providing more representation for peasants.

The new concentration of peasant unions did not succeed in changing the balance of forces, however, which had always favored the CNC, and the Pact of Ocampo was put under its aegis. The problem with this arrangement was that after the death of Alfredo V. Bonfil, the leader of the CNC, a power struggle ensued which did not allow the CNC to take advantage of the new political situation. The new secretary-general, Celestino Salcedo Monteón, was not able to control the *bonfilista* group that supported the chief of the Department of Agrarian Affairs and Colonization, who later became the secretary of agrarian reform (Augusto Gómez Villanueva).

The Ocampo Pact was not able to create a binding unity and became just one more of the "letterheads" of the Mexican Revolution, while the organizational and representative void continued. The attempt to fill this void through political parties is discussed later.

POLICIES TOWARD WORKERS

The imbalance in the economy had direct effects on employment, causing a polarization in the working class. This class consisted partly of a protected sector that was employed in businesses under state control or in large businesses with strong unions to protect employment.

Some of these enterprises included clauses in their collective contracts that gave hiring preferences to family members of employees. At the other extreme were substantial groups of workers whose employment conditions were so precarious that often they did not even receive the minimum wage. In the middle were a large number of jobs in which workers had little possibility of counting on representation by a real union but were controlled by shadow unions.

The state intended to give all workers the same employment protection that it gave its own workers. It reformed the Federal Labor Law, attempting to end the practice of temporary contracts. The first effect of the law, however, was a decline in investment, since the capitalists thought that the prolonged contracts would provoke major labor problems, expensive settlements with labor, and lower profits.

The state took the worker problem seriously, but it did not become worried when some of the important unions in the parastatal and private sectors began organizing and declaring their independence from the CTM and the Workers Congress. On the contrary, the government encouraged the weakening of these organizations, hoping that they would feel the threat and thus would realign themselves closer to Echeverría's government. At least, that is my hypothetical explanation as to why Rafael Galván, leader of one of the unions in the electricity sector, SUTERM, received so much government support. Galván hoped to become Fidel Velázquez's replacement as leader of the CTM.

Nevertheless, the independent unions created various problems for the state and political society. First, they could not guarantee the control of the masses as the CTM had for so many years. I will not discuss the moral aspects of the CTM's methods; the reality is that the organization was able to maintain control. Second, there was no guarantee that if Fidel Velázquez left the scene the followers of the CTM would accept a replacement selected by the president. In other words, the loyalty of the labor leadership could not be ensured. Third, the independent unions, even though they had won major labor victories, could not guarantee the control of their followers. Some of the unions already had problems, such as the university unions. These newly formed groups did not have the experience that the official syndicates had acquired through time. And fourth, the fact that there was leftist influence within these groups made the government hesitant to let them operate freely, especially since it had such an anti-Communist phobia.

Amid all these problems the state followed an apparently ambiguous policy. It allowed independent unions to carry out demonstrations and rallies, making them believe that they had won that right. But it was the government itself that benefited from this escape valve, because it was thereby able to evaluate the magnitude of dissidence and discontent.

Such independent union movements demonstrated the cathartic character of rallies: common citizens often joined demonstrations to vent their anger at the government, the bureaucracy, and the political society, to scream obscenities against the president, and yet to be protected by the anonymity of the crowd and to be able to go home the minute the rally was over. In this way many citizens relieved their frustrations and the government was able to gauge the extent of popular support for the cause that led to the demonstration.

When they saw the thousands of protesters in the streets, the independent unions fooled themselves into thinking they were about to gain political power, but they did not take into consideration the numbers that would break ranks the moment the showdown began. This miscalculation made many unions think that they could do more than they were capable of, and in some cases, such as the incident involving SUTERM, in which the military took over its facilities to end its protests, the organization was destroyed.[16]

Moreover, the independent unions were struggling for their very existence,[17] and for legal registration, something that hindered them from concentrating their strength on the global concerns of the working class.

The state took part in some of the disputes between workers and labor, and Echeverría initiated the practice of tripartism for resolving differences. The state, the owners, and the workers sat at the same table, and it was the partisans of Fidel Velázquez and the CTM who represented the workers. Suárez sums up well the effect of this practice: "Tripartism offered the official '*charro*' leaders the opportunity to legitimize themselves as the leaders of the workers, and in doing so they adopted the theoretical positions of the class."[18]

Legitimizing governmental representation in the talks helped to legitimize the government itself. The state was thus given the opportunity to manipulate certain matters, such as the forty-hour week, wage increases, worker problems, and energy rate increases,[19] so as to heighten aspirations and dilute conflictive issues in some of the more problematic cases. In these situations all representatives were accepted as legitimate negotiators. For its part, the state was able to get the involved parties to accept its role as arbiter. This practice had such good results that it was expanded to the peasant sector during the same sexenio.

The Forty-Hour Week

Some of the fundamental conflicts were a result of concrete cases. For example, the best defense that Fidel Velázquez had against those inde-

Table 3.2
Strikes and Workers Affected, 1969–76

Year	No. of Strikes	No. of Workers	Workers/Strikers
1969	144	4,464	31
1970	206	14,329	70
1971	204	9,299	46
1972	207	2,684	13
1973	211	8,395	40
1974	742	17,863	24
1975	236	9,680	41
1976	547	23,684	43

SOURCE: International Labour Office, *Yearbook of Labour Statistics* (Geneva, 1979), 593.

pendent unions sheltered by the state was his support of working-class demands. After many failed attempts to get the 40-hour week, labor finally threatened to strike.[20] The state responded by conceding the 40-hour work week to banking employees, perhaps thinking that this compromise would appease those employees, who had been previously denied by law the right to unionize. Concessions continued, and by the end of 1972 all government workers had gained the 40-hour week.[21] In January 1973 it was also extended to UNAM workers, sidestepping Rector Pablo González Casanova,[22] the representative of the leftist coalition that supported Echeverría's democratic opening as the solution to the nation's problems. Government's concession of the 40-hour work week in the tertiary sector was an economically "free" move because university employees, for example, seldom worked on Saturdays, as did the banking industry. This measure was also seen as an attack against CTM leader Fidel Velázquez, who had personally fought for the same issue and failed to win it in negotiations. Velázquez countered this attack with great vigor.

Strikes

The principal countermeasure adopted by the CTM was the strike, the weapon by which it could best demonstrate its true strength. The number of strikes during the sexenio were on the surface quite uniform, around 200 per year, except in 1974 and 1976 (Table 3.2). The difference in these years was that in 1974 the strikes were against minor industries and in 1976 they were relatively proportional to those of 1971, 1973, and 1975. In 1970 strikes were against major industries and in 1972 against minor industries.

It is obvious, however, that such data do not perfectly represent reality. For example, the Volkswagen conflict of 1974 sidelined 12,000 workers[23] out of the total of 17,863 who struck in 742 registered walkouts (see Appendix J).

In 1973 the publication *Latin America*[24] reported that 200,000 workers had struck more than 1,000 industries, while the International Labor Organization reported only 211 conflicts affecting 8,395 workers, and the government reported a mere 57 strikes in one source (see Appendix J) and 11 in another (José López Portillo, *Tercer Informe de Gobierno, Anexo Estadístico Histórico*).

The truth is that these conflicts were the response of Fidel Velázquez. As mentioned before, his only recourse was to gather workers' demands and launch them into the political arena. The basic issues concerned wage increases to counter inflation. Velázquez succeeded relatively well in his objectives, killing two birds with one stone, first by showing himself to be the true controlling and mobilizing force of the working class and second by regaining his position as the great leader of the masses.

Velázquez threatened a strike in 1973 that forced the government and owners to meet his demands and declare an emergency wage increase. In his way Velázquez demonstrated the power of the 3.5 million workers that he represented.[25] In 1974 he threatened strikes on 180,000 enterprises (including some owned by the state), involving 4 million workers in all areas of the economy,[26] and succeeded in having workers' demands met. Again, in September 1976, he used the resources at his command to strike 15,000 firms to achieve a salary increase.[27]

Not only did Velázquez have solid victories, but he also managed to show that he was the legitimate representative of the organized working class and was knowledgeable and ready to negotiate on its behalf. The independent unions were generally unable to achieve such victories. Besides, they represented a smaller portion of the working class, most of whom worked in parastatal industries or in the tertiary sector, where their ability to apply pressure on management was substantially less.

By 1976, forces united under the Congress of Workers (CT) was pressing the government to outlaw independent unions. The government did so, with the aid of strikebreakers and police. If the independent unions had hoped to lessen the power of Fidel Velázquez, the results were exactly the opposite; their actions helped create a great worker czar who had more influence than ever in Mexican politics.

The state did, however, gain something out of all of this. It succeeded in protecting the market by using the worker movements to demonstrate the need for increasing expenditures to meet demands, and it won the support of those classes by demonstrating that it was sensitive to their needs.

The government also succeeded in experimenting with various forms of violence and found out how far society could be pushed in this manner. At the same time, the state showed great capacity for controlling conflict and demonstrated that it still had the ability to maintain law and order in the country. Besides, the more violent the labor conflict became, the more margin the state had to repress it.[28]

THE STATE, POLITICAL SOCIETY, AND
THE GUERRILLA MOVEMENTS

Political society encompasses all the levels of institutionalized representation that exist in society (see Schmidt, *La autonomía relativa del estado*, 1988). Mexico's recent past has demonstrated that many of the powers that defined and structured political society had deteriorated and worn out, consequently loosening their social control, especially over the dominated classes. Lacking effective relegitimizing instruments of representation, these classes were inclined toward options of extrainstitutional participation which were more dependent on violence.

Kenneth Johnson found ample evidence of popular alienation against local governments and of attacks against local functionaries.[29] A close reading of the Mexican and foreign press of that period supports Johnson's perception. The people's patience had reached its limit: in Mérida, Yucatán, for example, one hundred peasants kicked to death an agrarian functionary when he refused to pay them more.[30] Not only were there numerous and violent confrontations, but it seems that the bureaucrats' halo of omnipotence and invincibility was disintegrating. In reality, officials and major landowners could be kicked to death, shot, or chopped up with a machete.

The people started to attack city halls, and PRI offices, and in general lost all respect for authority. If the authorities wanted to react with violence similar to that used against the students in 1968, it now did not have a concentrated group on which to render a lesson. On the contrary, dissent was spread widely throughout the country, and the government had to search for new forms of control to reinstate a peaceful compact with the masses that would get them to love and adore the godfather government.

One attempt was the issuance of rulings of neighborhood committees of the Federal District, auxiliaries of the chief of the Department of the Federal District, which were supposed to be instruments of citizen collaboration.[31] It was a good beginning, directly supporting inhabitants' pleas for greater democratic participation in the country's largest city. This type of policy was a point in favor of the regime. In the final analysis, however, it was another means to exert control over civil society. Article 8 stipulated: "The delegates will communicate to the members of the neighborhood councils their designation by the chief of the department."

In this way democracy functioned by degrees. The bases would choose their representatives by blocks and neighborhoods, ostensibly to form the councils, but the members of each council were designated by the chief of the Central Department. Throughout 1979 I was able to attend some of the meetings of these councils, where blue folders were handed out to the speakers (who were designated for each session by the political delegate). When I asked about the contents of the folders, I was told that they were petitions that were going to be made to the chief of the Department of the Federal District.

This way the state thought it had achieved a new form of organization for civil society, in which all the political middlemen were eliminated so that control could be exercised by functionaries, who in most cases are designated by the president.

Such initiatives for independent organization extended to all sectors of society, raising doubts about the efficiency of the structure of political control. Associations of businesses were affected by the rise of the Business Coordinating Council (Consejo Coordinator Empresarial, or CEE). The worker unions were affected by the mobilization of independent organizations, and the forms of urban control by the rise of fronts such as the Comité de Defensa Popular in Chihuahua. Also, police control was challenged in a surge of guerrilla activity throughout the country.

The guerrilla movement of the seventies differed from that of the previous decade because it reflected antigovernment activities by a sector of the population that refused to use the normal channels in which to exert its demands. This movement did not believe in the existing channels, and it held a political vision calling for the destruction of the system as the only means to achieve the social change that had been postponed in Mexico.

Many of these individuals had participated in the student movement of 1968, which actually dates back to the attack made by a group of youths on the military base in Ciudad Madera, Chihuahua, in 1966. It continued through the Spartacist movement inspired by José Revueltas in 1967 and received political nourishment from the guerrilla movement encouraged by Professor Genaro Vázquez Rojas in Guerrero. He demonstrated that a guerrilla movement supported strongly and decidedly by the people, even if it does not take power or defeat a government, can at least provide some justice.

It is necessary to differentiate the two guerrilla movements that existed during Echeverría's term: urban and rural. Although combining forces might have increased their effect on the society at large, there is no evidence that their activities were coordinated, even though rumors existed about such unification. It might have been possible after the death of Lucio Cabañas and the subsequent escalation of antiguerrilla activity, when twelve existing groups decided to unite and form the Communist League of September 23. Nevertheless, the only official reports on the subject are police documents, which are of doubtful validity.

The Rural Guerrilla Movement

The most important rural guerrilla movement emerged from the repression suffered by the Civic Association of Guerrero, directed by Genaro Vázquez. Its demands from 1959 to 1968 included political freedom, scientific planning of the economy, retrieval of the mineral wealth from the hands of the North American imperialist firms, respect for labor unions, distribution of land possessed by large landowners and appropriation of timber riches, and the cultural development and literacy of the people.[32]

Some of these demands were not new and had been promoted by the Partido Popular Socialista (PPS) and other left-wing groups. However, the violence that the group suffered pushed its leader, when he escaped from jail, to the conclusion that Mexican institutional channels were not the means for promoting these demands.

Genaro Vázquez took to the hills and turned his group into the National Revolutionary Civic Association (ACNR), and in 1971 he declared that it would struggle for the "overthrow of the oligarchy of large capitalists, large landowners, and governing pro-imperialists. He hoped to establish a coalition government of workers, students, and progressive intellectuals; to achieve the political and economic independence of Mexico; and to install a new social order for the benefit of the working majority of the country."[33] He was killed during an overwhelming assault by 12,000 soldiers (15 percent of the army) in the state of Guerrero in February 1972.

The movement gained strength, however, when Lucio Cabañas became commander. The organization became known as the Party of the Poor and put the army on the run by kidnapping and ambushing the troops that were sent to pursue it. The army initiated a policy of terror to weaken the guerrilla's bases of support. In April 1973 it executed six peasants in Peloncillo, Guerrero, who were accused of sending food to Cabañas. This action started the general repression of the peasants, and the army put down marches and removed land squatters. The dense coastal region of Oaxaca, Guerrero, and Michoacán was penetrated by soldiers who put up roadblocks throughout the countryside. Rumors, not confirmed, mentioned that the army used napalm in the hills to isolate the guerrillas.

In December 1974 Senator Rubén Figueroa decided to go to the hills and "persuade" Cabañas to quit his guerrilla activities. By this means, Figueroa strengthened his campaign for governor of the state of Guerrero.[34] Soon afterward, the army killed Cabañas. Although many believed that the guerrilla movement had been exterminated, it was not. It is very important to recognize that the guerrilla movement was one of the excuses for repressing the peasant movements. Such was the case in the suppression of the leaders of the Rubén Jaramillo colony in Morelos, who were accused of being the leaders of the Party of the Poor. They were persecuted in hopes of weakening them and making them disappear from the political scene.

The Urban Guerrilla Movement

In March 1971 the Mexican government expelled five Soviet diplomats and accused them of having connections with the Movimiento de Acción Revolucionaria (MAR), a group apparently trained in North Korea and with established bases in various states in the republic. In August of the same year, the police kidnapped two UNAM researchers and provided protection to the embassies. In November the Mexican government proposed an arms control law, which was ratified in January 1972.

During the first year of Echeverría's government a great deal of urban guerrilla activity took place; it intensified after the student killings at San Cosme in Mexico City on Corpus Christi Day, June 10, 1971. Urban guerrilla groups began to flourish, and the big cities felt the effect, to the point that in March 1973 the American consul in Guadalajara was kidnapped and the government responded by releasing and sending thirty political prisoners to Cuba and publishing a guerrilla letter. In November the chief of police of Guadalajara resigned because he could not control the guerrillas.

The wave of kidnappings by guerrillas was so intense that even the president's father-in-law, José Guadalupe Zuno, was kidnapped; when Echeverría was asked if the kidnapping was legitimate, he answered: "Unfortunately, it happened, just like many others; lamentably, no kidnapping has been our fabrication, but have been aspects of a profound social and moral crisis of many countries, or have been provoked by a generalized repression."[35]

It could be said that the state knew that it was managing the provocations in a way that would lead to greater repression,[36] or even that it was the state that was causing the provocations, as could have been the case in the kidnapping of the president's father-in-law. It should be noted, however, that even common criminals were hiding behind the guerrilla disguise, as in the case of Comando Armado del Pueblo, which operated in the Federal District in 1971. But the state also took advantage of the opportunity to blame many things on the guerrilla movement, especially the Communist 23rd of September League, after it was formed in 1973 with the uniting of twelve groups.[37]

The most important guerrilla groups during this period were:

1. Movimento de Acción Revolucionario (MAR), trained in North Korea, which robbed banks, planted bombs, and operated in several states.

2. Asociación Nacional Cívica Revolucionaria, Guerrero peasants who kidnapped landholders, attacked the army, and rarely left their zone of operation. Their leader was Genaro Vázquez Rojas.

3. Fuerzas Armadas de la Revolución, active in Sonora and Tampico.

4. Frente de Liberación Nacional, which robbed banks, kidnapped, and started shootouts between unions and police; active in Monterrey.

5. Comando Armado del Pueblo, seven thieves disguised as guerrillas, active in the Federal District.

6. Central Revolucionaria de Acción Armada: It is believed that they kidnapped Julio Hirshfield Almada, director of airports. Little is known about them.

7. Liga de Comunistas Armados: No one had heard of it until a group of fifty members was arrested in Monterrey; thirty bank robberies are attributed to them.

8. Unión del Pueblo, Maoists. Apparently, they had connections with the guerrillas of Guatemala.

9. Fuerzas Armadas Revolucionarias: This group kidnapped the American consul in Guadalajara in 1973; nothing else is known of it.

10. Frente Urbano Zapatista, active in the Federal District.

11. Frente Revolucionario Estudiantil: Also supposed kidnappers of the American consul in Guadalajara in 1973; they were active in Jalisco, Sinaloa, and Nuevo León.

12. Frente Revolucionario de Acción Popular, also kidnappers of the American consul in Guadalajara and of José Guadalupe Zuno, Echeverría's father-in-law.

13. Liga Comunista 23 de Septiembre, began in 1973 but apparently joined other groups later on.

14. Comando de Guerrilla Salvador Allende, apparently part of the 23rd of September League.

15. Partido de Liberación del Pueblo Urbano, apparently joined the 23rd of September League in 1975.

16. Partido de los Pobres, derived from the ANCR of Genaro Vázquez, led by Lucio Cabañas.
17. Liga Lacandona, operated in Jalisco.
18. Comando Guerrillero Fidel Castro, operated in Guadalajara, Jalisco.[38]

This profusion of groups and commandos carried out a series of kidnappings, bombings, and robberies that gave the appearance that the government was losing control and could not guarantee the nation's peace. In 1972 there were 23 bombings, 2 in 1973, 28 in 1974, 13 in 1975, and 8 in 1976. In 1973 there were 17 kidnappings, and in 1974 there were 12; after that, such activity declined. In 1974 there were 15 shootouts and 11 the following year.

Thus the press had much to talk about until the government found and dismantled the guerrilla movement, which did not happen until near the end of the presidential term. Echeverría had to endure the abuse of a representative of the Monterrey bourgeoisie after a commando assassinated Eugenio Garza Sada, leader of the powerful Monterrey Group. Presidential candidate José López Portillo felt the threat when his sister was almost kidnapped.

The government's response when it came was very violent and was mixed with kidnappings and tortures, including 17 children in Monterrey and academics from El Colegio de México. In addition, innocent citizens were accused and extorted by the police for alleged guerrilla activity and many peasants in Guerrero were summarily executed. In 1972 the government abducted 30 people and tortured 10; in 1973, 24 and 22, respectively; in 1974, a year of great conflict, the figures were 65 and 20.[39]

This repression was the other face of the "democratic opening," the government's firm hand against the violent dissident movements whose energy was out of control, which shows the danger and limits of the opening. The guerrilla activity was the expression of a part of civil society that was not interested in listening to the revolutionary demagoguery of the PRI, whether of a "revolution from within" or of "institutionalized change." This element was not apathetic, but apparently the system's limits of tolerance did not include a certain type of militancy.

CO-OPTATION, TECHNOCRACY, AND NEW POLITICAL PARTIES

The criticism that some Mexican scholars made of the Mexican economic miracle and of the achievements of the Revolution seemed to enjoy some receptivity on the part of the government. The claim that a new revolution was being carried on from within the system was adopted at the same time that such critics were being employed by the government and given opportunities for coming into contact with "the people" ("*el pueblo*"). The idea was to turn them into "revolutionary detonators" without requiring them to undergo the pain of affiliating themselves with the PRI or forcing them into armed dissent.

In this way the state co-opted or recovered many young university people, who were converted into promoters of various state agencies, such as CONASUPO, Banrural, Inmecafe, IMPI, and others. These young people were given the opportunity of getting close to the peasants and of gaining employment, although many soon recognized that they had become just additional bureaucrats. Some saw that they were "promoting development" by being converted into consumers and that they contributed to the protection of the capitalist cycle without really changing conditions in the countryside, which had been their original goal.[40]

Some of the students who did not enter into the government directly did so indirectly by receiving scholarships to improve their preparation and then to return to the country. There they found the doors of employment open, not only in the government but also in the universities, which had received substantial aid and thus had experienced significant expansion. It is in this context that the National Council of Science and Technology (CONACYT) was created and the scholarship programs of the Bank of Mexico were strengthened, at the same time that intergovernmental agreements were improved. The logic was that these better-prepared young people would strengthen the technical capabilities that the country so lacked.[41]

In part, this strategy was the way in which the technocracy—understood as the elaboration and domination of technical solutions for economic, social, and political problems—was created. It attempted to order and organize information, introducing computers and giving the impression that the regime was behaving technically. That was not bad in itself, but it was fictitious. Although the basis was laid for more rational management of public expenditure and investment, it is certain that in the face of the great national problems, the overriding criterion was political, not economic (see the case of land conflict in Sonora, below, as an example).

It is suggested, therefore, that Echeverría chose the path of high economic costs to achieve political successes. The Mexican political-economic structure was simply not prepared to tolerate the preponderance of technical methods in order to achieve political solutions.

In any case the opening of the doors to the technocrats and the attempt to create a technocracy motivated youth to see the state as a real option, at least in terms of employment and for making a revolution from within.

That motivated them to continue studying, lengthening the student cycle and putting off their entry into the job market.

Groups that were considered progressive were invited to participate. They supported the democratic opening, because finally it permitted them to come closer to where decisions were made, that is, closer to power. It is in this context that Pablo González Casanova was named rector of UNAM and Carlos Fuentes functioned as a link between Echeverría and liberal U.S. intellectuals and was later appointed ambassador to France. Some members of the Movement for National Liberation assumed important positions, such as Enrique González Pedrero, who became a federal senator and director of television Channel 13; Francisco López Cámara, who became an official of CNOP; and Víctor Flores Olea, ambassador to the Soviet Union. Even some leaders of the student movement of 1968 entered the government.

That was not unusual. Generally, the student movements have served as vehicles for the political promotion of their leaders, and some students participate with their own advancement in view, just as many professionals use UNAM to impel themselves into national political positions.[42] In addition, the attraction to the regime of bitter critics of the Mexican "Revolution" such as Fuentes[43] or experts on Marx such as Flores Olea[44] gave a distinct vision to the government and in a sense returned to it the respectability that it had lost in 1968 or 1971. I believe that the point of agreement was that these intellectuals supported the view that the choice was "democratic opening or fascism."[45]

Echeverría's other step was to try to heal the wounds of the sixties, promoting a political amnesty that was based on an offer of conditional liberty for the political prisoners, which some took advantage of, and the dropping of charges for the rest. By April 1971 50 had accepted amnesty, by March 1972 33 more were freed, and that same year Echeverría met with some of them in Veracruz. In 1976 an initiative was launched to pardon 250 more prisoners. This policy served to put a smokescreen over the repressive policy that the government was developing in the social conflicts that it could not control.

All these measures served to reconcile the state with the middle class, which had protested so strongly in 1968. This is important, because the state had been nourished by this sector for a long time, and this class also nourished the guerrilla movement and the opposition movements, including the new labor unions of the service sector. It is obvious, therefore, why the state saw such urgency in relegitimating itself with the middle class and regaining its support.

As the discontents were reconciled and new opportunities were offered to the banished, it was necessary to manage the third aspect, to open the possibilities of participation for those who wanted to make Mexican pluralism a reality. The government indicated through the amnesty program that it was disposed to pardon those who attacked the system and thereby to demonstrate to the world that political imprisonment had ended. It also sought to create an image of Mexico as a mature country that could play the multiparty game.

The López Mateos reforms[46] that created the party deputies had to be maintained because some of the parties (e.g., Partido Auténtico de la Revolución Mexicana, or PARM) had difficulty achieving the minimum requirements for electing deputies. Therefore, it was necessary to find a formula that would truly bring "the people" into the electoral game in such a way that the PRI would be strengthened against an opposition that would lose election campaigns. In this way the people would vote for the system, and the winner, PRI, would be legitimate.

The impulse of the young people would achieve this objective, and therefore in 1973 a measure was enacted that gave the vote to 18-year-olds and reduced the minimum legal requirements for party deputies. At the same time, it was made much easier to organize opposition parties. The government thereby sought to demonstrate that the struggle of the youth and the opposition had been with Díaz Ordaz and not with the system. Thus Echeverría used both student leaders and former political prisoners to show that his vision of a political opening was widely accepted.

That was especially true of the Socialist Workers Party (PST),[47] which had split with the National Committee of Information Gathering and Organization (CNAO) and had dedicated itself to organizing peasants. The political positions of this group coincided with Echeverría's. One of CNAO's most strongly held tenets was that a progressive and leftist sector existed within the government and the PRI, a sector with which the party should forge an alliance.

The PST viscerally rejected the positions of the Mexican Communist Party (PCM), not from being in disagreement with its practices, but because some PST members had left the PCM and had had a serious confrontation with its leaders. PST's anti-Communism was an ideal justification for accepting the domination of the PRI. Thus the economic support of entities such as FIDEURBE, IMSS (Instituto Mexicano del Seguro Social), Inmecafe, or vehicles of IMPI permitted the PST to register significant growth and to manipulate the masses to convince them of its effectiveness.

In two significant meetings of coffee growers, organized in conjunction with Inmecafe, Echeverría called PST leaders "my young revolutionary friends." The PST was managed by the PRI as an instrument of control in areas where the peasant unions had failed, and it was always under the vigilant eye of the government.

The Mexican Workers Party (PMT) continued with the line laid down by the CNAO, whose fundamental programmatic points, as expressed in the first national plenary (November 23–25, 1973), were:

1. Respect for the workers' rights of strike, association, and protest.
2. There should be a real labor democracy that includes the rights of the workers both in the countryside and in the cities to choose and reject leaders, in order to eliminate *"charrismo."*
3. The problems of the countryside should be resolved by bringing an end both to *latifundios* and to untenable small plots.
4. The right of *amparo* (special legal protection) in agrarian affairs should be eliminated.
5. The banks should be nationalized.
6. Capitalist monopolies should be eliminated.
7. Corruption should be eliminated in public administration, in private business, and in workers' organizations.
8. There should be a right to education that permits the children of the working class to have access to all levels of instruction.
9. For the economic independence of Mexico and the support of the peoples that fight to free themselves from the oppression of the common enemy, "Imperialism."[48]

Note how similar these positions are to those of Echeverría.

The only members lost by the PMT, other than the PST, were some of the intellectuals who started the CNAO in 1971, such as Fuentes and Octavio Paz. The party remained under the leadership of Demetrio Vallejo and Heberto Castillo.[49]

According to Kenneth Johnson, Castillo was freed from prison under the promise that he would create another party in order to reinforce the facade of democracy in Mexico. Johnson wrote: "Another party will prevent the embarrassment of 1970 when the PAN threatened to withdraw its candidate (which did occur in 1976) and which would leave the PRI as virtually the only party in the election."[50]

Even if this were so, the truth is that the PMT managed to attract a good number of young people who were looking for a solid position from which to participate within the Mexican political opposition. Nevertheless, the personalistic control of the leadership, the lack of influence of the rank and file in the party, and the harshness of the political position of its directors contributed significantly to its weakness.[51]

Two other leftist groups emerged or organized during this time. The Communist party, for its part, could breathe anew and, if not exactly legalized, was allowed to operate openly. In 1975 it presented as its presidential candidate Valentín Campa, who would allow the party to carry on a strong propaganda campaign. In addition, the Trotskyite groups grew and decided to unite and create the Revolutionary Workers Party (PRT).

The right was also active. In February 1971 the sinarquists announced their intention of forming a party that would be legally constituted within 3 years.[52]

In this way two tendencies came together: on one side, the state permitted the emergence of parties in an attempt to neutralize the guerrilla movement by drawing discontent within new channels that controlled the masses. The fact that the parties of the left hurled themselves against the 23rd of September League demonstrated the degree to which they accepted and reinforced the position that political change should come about only through the use of bourgeois rights and law.

On the other side, the youth, tired of the PRI and its manipulation, found a way to express its discontent. The following opinion about the PRI is indicative of this sentiment:

> The party is a bureaucracy of specialists in the organization and the manipulation of the masses. Its influence extends horizontally across the entire country and vertically it extends to the *ejido*, the union, the municipality, and the cooperative. Throughout its permutations and changes of color (PNR, PRM, PRI), it has not changed its function. It is the organ of control of the masses; but by the same token, until a few years ago and for better or for worse, it was their organ of expression. The most immediate and sharp expression of the present crisis resides in the fact that the PRI, even though it continues to control the masses, has completely ceased to express their interests. In any case, the survival of the party reveals that it is an essential organ of the postrevolutionary Mexican state.[53]

Thus the failure of the guerrilla movement was helped along by the creation of parties, and the failure of the guerrillas in turn reinforced the parties. The state, by creating, supporting, consenting, and nourishing the opposition, felt that it was thereby legitimizing itself. Nonetheless, the elections of 1976 would destroy illusions, for abstentionism was higher than six years earlier.[54] But despite the discontent of the middle classes, they returned to the fold, once again disposed to play at democracy.

THE USE OF THE MASSES

It is clear that the Echeverría years brought a great mobilization of masses, balanced with a constant and systematic repression, widespread yet selective. Even if this fact contradicted in practice the rhetoric that inaugurated and sustained the "democratic opening," it really served to strengthen the president, because he made the greatest use of it and extracted the greatest advantage from it. In other words, the repression served to "tranquilize" the country and to demonstrate that the regime still was in control. The mobilization of the masses allowed the government to open the escape valve to a society tired of the obvious domination in which popular participation was so limited. It appeared to show that the government truly had a "democratic vocation," but in fact it allowed the government to evaluate the extent of internal dissent. And both measures—mobilization and repression—permitted the regime to resolve some conflicts among the states and to achieve a readjustment of power. I analyze some of these cases below.

The Students and the 10th of June

In the mind of the public in general and of the students in particular, Echeverría was the image of the repressive regime. Outside of the mobilization of the army to repress the masses,[55] there was not the slightest doubt that, as secretary of government, Echeverría had been in charge of internal security and thus had been responsible in some measure for the form and dimensions of the repression of 1968.

Echeverría came to the presidency with the stigma of an intransigent and repressive high official, but he sought to clean up his image by his actions as president. He intended to achieve it by means of managing a "Dialogue" and "Opening," contacts with those who had been outraged, sullied, and beaten: the students. He perhaps thought that if he could improve his image in their eyes, it would extend to the rest of society.[56]

The student movement did not end in October 1968; it simply entered into a phase of demoralization and demobilization brought on by the shock of the students in the face of the regime's extremely violent and unexpected response. The dissident student expressions were reoriented toward plans and programs of study, toward guerrilla activities, and toward such legal forms of political activity as political parties. In March 1971 the governor of Nuevo León promoted the approval of a new university constitution that was seen as contrary to the interests of the university community, to such an extent that it provoked a conflict that led to the removal of the rector of the university. (In Mexico the public universities are governed by a basic charter [*ley orgánica*] approved by the state legislature. In the case of UNAM the charter is approved by the federal Congress.) Both measures—the new charter and the removal of the rector—incited a movement of such magnitude that the state governor was also dismissed.

The significance of this movement was that, together with demands of a local nature, the students called for the discussion of national questions. In Nuevo León the students demanded:

1. Annulment of the organic law.
2. Solution to the economic problem of the universities.
3. Automatic passage from the Preparatory School to the Autonomous University of Nuevo León (achieved at UNAM in 1966).
4. Public dialogue.
5. End of the repression and expulsion of the *porristas* (government-dominated university officials).
6. Unconditional freedom for political prisoners throughout the country.[57]

Even after the governor had fallen on June 5, the university demands still had not been resolved. A demonstration was called in Mexico City for June 10. Its demands were:

1. Support for the democratic organic law, proposed by the Representative Commission of the University of Nuevo León.
2. For democracy in instruction, and against the bourgeoisie educational reform.
3. For union democracy and against *charrismo*.
4. For freedom for all political prisoners.[58]

These demands were not opposed by everyone in the regime. Even more, the governor who had approved the objectionable law had fallen, which could be interpreted as a political concession to the opposition. Political prisoners were being freed, educational reform had been enacted but not well accepted, and the state had struggled against the CTM and agreed to allow independent unions. In the face of these events it is difficult to understand what motivated the paramilitary group, the Falcons, which under the vigilant eyes of the police attacked the demonstrators and even pursued the wounded into hospitals to finish them off. I have three hypotheses to explain this response.

First, by means of the use of paramilitary power to repress mass movements—begun in 1968 with the Olympic Battalion—the state showed the new type of repression that it was willing to employ.

Second, the state decided to end with one blow and with one exemplary lesson the residues of the student rebellion of 1968. Its purposes were to put in motion the plans of educational reform and to eliminate the political resistance in the universities and thereby to bring them once again under control.

Third, the movement of 1971 served to clear the decks of certain officials: Alfonso Martínez Domínguez, politician of Nuevo León and regent of Mexico City (it may or may not have been a coincidence that the conflict began in his state); Rogelio Flores Curiel, chief of police of the Federal District; Julio Sánchez Vargas, attorney general of the republic; and Enrique Herrera, subdirector of communications of the Department of Communications and Transport. Echeverría held the first two responsible. He said: "The resignations were carried out as a result of the conflict. Whether they intended it or not, their actions had deleterious effects on a large sector of the government."[59]

Nevertheless, Flores Curiel returned to his seat in the Senate and later became governor of Nayarit, delivering perhaps the most bitter electoral defeat suffered by the PPS, whose secretary general accepted a seat in the Senate in return for acquiescing in his own defeat. After this event, the PPS split up and formed the Party of the Mexican People (PPM), led by politicians from Nayarit.

Julio Sánchez Vargas, inherited from the previous regime, was appointed director of SOMEX for the remainder of the presidential term. This was an important step, because during his leadership the enterprise nationalized many firms. Apparently, Enrique Herrera's resignation had little to do with the conflict. But the career of Alfonso Martínez Domínguez remained frozen, and he was unable to advance for several years until he became governor of Nuevo León.

According to Guerra Leal,[60] in 1969 Echeverría's only support for his presidential candidacy was from Martínez Domínguez, who had a brilliant political career at the same time that he managed an important political team. Thus, June 1971 acquired considerable importance in terms of political readjustment. Echeverría was able to eliminate a future political rival who by virtue of his political power could gain the presidency in 1976. It is possible that Echeverría wanted to exclude Martínez Domínguez from consideration because he had not supported "*continuismo*" by indicating that he would allow himself to be manipulated by Echeverría if he became the next president. In addition, by this action Echeverría was able to demonstrate that he was willing to negotiate with other interests. He thus eliminated one of the stars in order to bring under control interests that he still did not dominate. Finally, the scoffing at the regent of Mexico City was intended to cleanse himself of responsibility for the incident in the view of history, by saying that the attacking group was paramilitary and was not formally under the president.

Attacking the Nuevo León politician who had contacts with the Monterrey Group, Echeverría demonstrated to that group that political power had not yet passed to the industrialists, indicating to them the limits of the political-economic game. In this way Echeverría made use of the masses to balance and sustain his political moves.

On the other hand, the president followed a policy of drawing near to the students. Until June 10 he had at least ten related meetings with students or university officials, and four days later he received officials of the University of Sinaloa where he experienced another conflict in 1972.[61] On June 29, 1971, he received students from the University of Puebla to recognize their organization officially. At this university a conflict in 1973 brought about the fall of the governor;[62] in this case the Communist party had already surfaced and operated openly.[63] Thus some of the skirmishes that occurred in the city of Puebla, among them some assassinations of members of this party, can be seen through the lens of confrontation between parties and factions.

It is necessary to clarify another point. Outside Mexico City, university conflicts acquired major importance by virtue of the fact that a rector can become governor with great ease. The political weight of the university in a state is relatively great, so that some conflicts result in the dismissal of the governor by the president, perhaps because in such cases the university becomes a crucible of sociopolitical pressures.

Luis Encinas, former governor of Sonora, said: "The conflict that we had in Sonora in 1967, just before the conflict in the capital, also was important, as it was to a greater or lesser degree in Durango, Morelia, Mérida, Puebla, Villahermosa, etc."[64] It became clear that the turmoil in Sonora was provoked by the imposition of an undesirable PRI candidate and by the recognition of electoral fraud.

Echeverría did not relax in his desire for reconciliation after the repression of June 10, and in March 1975 he visited UNAM's central campus, where after Communist students yelled at him during his speech, he shouted back: "Listen to me, fascist youth, agents of the CIA. . . . That's the way the Mussolini and Hitler youth yelled people down."[65] As he was leaving, he was hit on the head by a stone thrown by the groups that had opposed his visit. Thus the triumphal entry into the heart of the university was converted into an attack on the sacrosanct person of the president, like the incident that had so annoyed Díaz Ordaz and the politicians in 1968. In 1975 the students proved something else, that the president is also vulnerable. But Echeverría demonstrated boldness in going to the campus of UNAM. The problem was that by 1975 his detractors were looking only for things to criticize; if not, they would have admitted that this was a bold deed.

It is clear that Echeverría had a strategy for regaining the support of the heterogeneous student sector,[66] a strategy that included an increase in the availability of middle, technical, and preparatory education; an increase in subsidies to the universities and other centers of instruction; and the opening of new opportunities for work.[67] But because of the political dynamic of the period, his name was never inscribed in gold in the pages of Mexico's history, which was perhaps his ultimate goal.

The Governors

Three cases involving governors seem to have been used by Echeverría for his political purposes. The first concerned the govérnor of Hidalgo, who in 1975 had opposed Echeverría in the choice of his successor as governor. The president used peasants to march in front of the state governmental palace, stone it, and insult Governor Otoniel Miranda, who finally fell from power.

In Guerrero in 1975 Governor Israel Nogueda was accused of fraud by a group of peasants who applied a new law that authorized the attorney general to investigate the "inexplicable enrichment" of officials. The fact was used that in Acapulco serious conflicts had arisen with *ejidatarios*; the governor was dismissed in order to placate them. According to Carlos Loret de Mola, Echeverría threw out Nogueda to pave the way for the candidacy of Rubén Figueroa for governor of Guerrero. Figueroa was czar of auto transport and a supposed associate of Echeverría.[68]

The third case, in Sonora, was much more important. It began in 1975 and reemerged and had its final solution under López Portillo. One of the outcomes of this conflict was the destruction of the political career of a very promising politician, who was so prominent that he was mentioned as a possible future president of Mexico.

Carlos Armando Biebrich began his political career as a student leader in Hermosillo, Sonora; rose very quickly; and thanks to the support of Governor Faustino Félix Serna, became a speaker in Echeverría's campaign. From there he became undersecretary of government, and after a hasty change in the constitution of the state of Sonora he became at age 33 the youngest governor in the country.

It appeared that Biebrich would be one of the most favored governors, since Sonora was a state whose agricultural exports were vital for Mexico. Its areas of large ranches characterized by capitalist exploitation of the land had been the unattainable desire of the agrarians, who were blocked by the great economic power of the large farmers. The young governor, a prime example of Echeverría's effort to draw young people into power, spoke the language of the president, talking of social and economic justice at the same time that he demonstrated his desire to resolve the problems of landownership.

Biebrich managed his government strongly, maintaining direct communication with the president, who visited the region relatively early in his term and frequently thereafter. But by 1974 the demand for cotton had fallen, and even though the government promised to buy part of the crop, the area under cultivation fell the following year.[69] (see Appendix K). Even though production began to fall in 1965, profits continued to increase. By 1975 only half the area was cultivated compared to the amount in 1974, with Sonora experiencing the greatest part of the reduction. This cultivation was considered socially desirable because of the great employment that it produced, occupying 15,000 peasants for four to six months.[70] Some of the workers were "swallows," or migrant workers who came to Sonora for the picking season, and others were residents of the area who had no land but were petitioners for land. As the area of cultivation was reduced, many of these workers lost their jobs.

The unemployed chose then to ask for land. Along with workers in Sinaloa who became unemployed as a result of a decline in the production of vegetables, they began a wave of land invasions to press the government to give them land. Beginning in October 1975, property in Sonora and Sinaloa was invaded by groups of 20 to 200 peasants. In Sonora the conflict was centered in the Yaqui Valley, where 45 percent of Mexican wheat was produced.[71]

But the conflict began to get very specific, dividing into two groups: the bourgeoisie of the north (Hermosillo), who supported the governor, and on the other side the bourgeoisie of the south (Yaqui Valley), who opposed Biebrich's government for its agrarian policies. On the night of October 19, approximately fifteen hundred peasants invaded two properties: San Isidro in the Yaqui Valley and San Ignacio de Rio Muerto in the Guaymas Valley. The army and the judicial police intervened on the 23rd and dislodged the invaders of San Isidro. At San Ignacio a flurry of bullets was unexpectedly loosed, killing seven peasants, including their leader, Juan de Dios Terán. According to the government, the peasants fired first, but in an interview in the area in December 1976, the peasants told me that they were suddenly fired on. This version seems more likely, because if the peasants had fired they would have killed at least one policeman or soldier, which did not happen. In fact, neither the police nor the army reported any wounded. (The head of the judicial police, a military man, disappeared after the massacre and, according to information from Jesús Blancornelas, later appeared in López Portillo's personal escort.)

With great speed the leaders of the peasant organizations met on October 24 and mounted a demonstration for the next day. Fifteen thousand peasants marched, demanding the removal of state government leaders. On October 26, after fruitless attempts to communicate with the president, Biebrich resigned and was replaced by Alejandro Carrillo Marcor, a senator. Carrillo Marcor had tried to coerce large farmers into giving land to peasants during the time of Cárdenas, an act that forced him to leave the state.[72]

There are several possible explanations for the fall of Biebrich. First, Loret de Mola[73] suggests that the young governor overshadowed Augusto

Gómez Villanueva, secretary of agrarian reform, prompting the latter to orchestrate his overthrow. In the meantime Gómez Villanueva had arranged matters so that Biebrich would fall in Echeverría's estimation. This seems likely, because the secretary managed to arrange for the survival of the Ocampo Pact, even though until then it had merely been a facade. As Gómez Villanueva had been one of the drafters of the pact, he would reap some of the benefits if it became a success. Also, Porfirio Muñoz Ledo, a young and ambitious politician who was undersecretary of the presidency, and Hugo Cervantes del Río, secretary of the presidency, were interested in destroying Biebrich's power in order to hurt his political mentor, Mario Moya Palencia, secretary of government.

Second, according to rumors, Biebrich belonged to Moya Palencia's political group and was beginning a brilliant political career. Moya had arranged that five governors would announce their support for him for president in Monterrey on September 22, 1975. The five governors were Biebrich of Sonora, Pedro Zorrilla Martínez of Nuevo León, Enrique Cárdenas González of Tamaulipas, Antonio Calzada Urquiza of Querétaro, and Luis Ducoing Gamba of Guanajuato.

Always in tune with rumors, Leopoldo González Sáenz, at the time mayor of Monterrey, did not want to take responsibility for such a meeting and communicated with the president (an act of discipline that earned him an undersecretaryship in the following presidential term). The presidential office ordered that the meeting not take place, and the only governor who came to Monterrey was Biebrich. That same day Moya Palencia accompanied Echeverría to a breakfast at the military social club in Mexico City, and Fidel Velázquez unveiled López Portillo as the next president.

Still, Biebrich's trip to Monterrey does not seem to be an adequate reason for his harsh punishment. The larger reason was probably that he led the campaign for Moya Palencia for president, and even after López Portillo was "unveiled" as the PRI candidate, Biebrich tried to persuade Moya to run as an independent candidate, thus rebelling against Echeverría.[74]

The fall of Biebrich can, therefore, be explained as an exemplary punishment by the president of an undisciplined governor. The president's team also intended to overthrow Zorrilla Martínez, using the urban land invasions as a pretext. But more politically astute than Biebrich, Zorrilla Martínez regained momentum and became stronger. The president's men imposed on Calzada Urquiza a successor who was not to the governor's liking. The other governors finished their terms in peace, and Moya Palencia, despite being the strong man of Mexico, did not succeed in becoming president.

Third, in an interview in Hermosillo I was told that Biebrich fell because he was a homosexual. Supposedly, Felix Serna, his protector, also was one and was allied with the group of Ernesto Uruchurtu, powerful former regent of the Federal District, who also allegedly was a homosexual.

The interesting thing about this rumor is that after the persecution of the governor, the only thing left was to try to disgrace him by attacking the most important symbolic value of the Mexican male, his *machismo*. In Mexico a man can be almost anything except a homosexual, so that the epithet hurled at Biebrich in this context was intended to make firewood out of the fallen tree. Mexican politicians do not publicly accept homosexuality as just another individual right.

Fourth, on the same level, Johnson mentions that when Biebrich gave the order to the army, the governor was under the influence of alcohol and cocaine. According to Johnson, "this seemed to be a matter of public knowledge in Sonora and was used to permanently discredit him."[75] Johnson also indicates that Biebrich was accused of corruption—of collecting money for public works projects that did not exist, using his brother to obtain the money, up to 4 million pesos. (Biebrich was accused of stealing silver bars, and he responded that the bars were used to make jewelry for Mrs. Echeverría. He was also accused of taking money from the Banco Agrícola y Ganadero, a charge that, according to Blancornelas, was true. Interview in Tijuana, March 6, 1989.) The charge of corruption served to allow the incoming governor to appear as a knight of honor while attending to his own business affairs. In this case Carrillo continued the punishment for indiscipline by persecuting Biebrich, which provoked strong political reactions in the state. This explanation seems even less likely than the previous one.

In this case it is obvious that the use of the masses to define a political conflict, including provoking a massacre, demonstrates the lengths to which Mexican politics can go in the struggle for power.

But the conflict did not end there. The land invasions continued, and the bourgeoisie counterattacked. A work stoppage occurred in December 1975. In August 1976 peasants kidnapped a pro-landowner union leader, and two hundred peasants stoned the offices of the newspaper *El Debate* to impede its publication. During the summer as many as thirty land invasions a day occurred.[76] By November 1976 the conflict had come to its climax. In Sinaloa, according to landowners, 200 properties were invaded. In Sonora armed peasants took 12 properties in the Yaqui Valley, where three thousand peasants demanded 2,422 pieces of property totaling about 150,000 hectares.[77]

Nevertheless, it was no longer the Ocampo Pact that controlled the land invasions. In Sinaloa the UGOCM, managed by Governor Alfonso Calderón, directed the invasions, but in Sonora it was the Independent

Peasant Front (FCI), led by a former militant of the CNC and a former militant of the Mexican Communist Party, who managed the armed invasions after the failure of legal efforts. This was a challenge to the established forms of domination over the masses, a challenge to the government and to the landowners, and it received an immediate response.

The army surrounded the invaded property but did not attack. Orders were issued for the arrest of the FCI leaders, but according to local accounts, they flew to Mexico City in the governor's plane. A great deal of aid for the land invaders was provided by *ejidatarios*, who often were relatives of the invaders. Solidarity began to develop in the student centers, and the conflict expanded. In Durango two thousand peasants invaded twenty properties.[78]

From another viewpoint, the largely untouchable area of concentrated landownership in the north tempted Echeverría to take the opportunity to finish off his sexenio with a grand act of "popular justice." Such an event would solidify his image as the president who achieved what even Cárdenas could not. Facing a ferocious opposition from business, which carried out a commercial strike that was somewhat unsuccessful because it did not include small and midsized entrepreneurs, and amid rumors of a coup d'etat, Echeverría decided on November 19 to expropriate about 100,000 hectares belonging to seventy-two families.

The acts of expropriation took place the following day, November 20, to pursue two objectives: (1) to present an accomplished fact to the *latifundistas*, who would vehemently oppose it, and (2) to achieve a rapid expropriation and to demonstrate that benefits went to those who cooperated with the regime. The government allowed land to be given to those represented by the Ocampo Pact, thus showing the peasants that organizational independence did not bring benefits or resolve demands. The regime destroyed the groups of petitioners by benefiting some individual members of some of the groups without dealing with any group as a whole. The other members of the group not only did not receive land but even lost their individual seniority. Property was given to peasants who had not petitioned, so that there would be problems of disagreement and confrontation among them. In this way the state stayed within the letter of the Ocampo Pact and yet eliminated dissidents.

Therefore, the great loser was the Independent Peasant Front, which, after carrying out the invasions, managed only to be excluded from the benefits.[79] The *latifundistas* did not lose, because they were paid for their land.

Once more Echeverría used the masses to achieve a great victory, but at a high economic cost. The expropriation was costly, the credit for the *ejidatarios* arrived late, and the National Agricultural Insurance Agency refused to insure the crops. The production of wheat fell by 15 percent just when the country was already importing a large amount of food-stuffs.[80]

The entire conflict had another political basis already hinted at earlier in this chapter. The bourgeoisie of central and northern Sonora had always retained political power, even though the bourgeoisie of southern Sonora, especially the Cajeme group, was more enterprising and dynamic. The northerners consider themselves aristocratic and are not inclined to cede their political domination, either in the local legislatures[81] or in the state government, which are generally linked to their interests. For example, Governor Carrillo Marcor came from two northern families with great landholdings. Apparently, the northern elite felt itself threatened by the rise of the southern group, which lacked only political power. The northerners apparently persuaded Echeverría to support them in demonstrating to the southerners in no uncertain terms that they would not be allowed to come to power.

The most important evidence for this view of power relations in Sonora was that about 30,000 irrigated hectares in the southern part of the state were affected by the land distribution program, whereas in the north (Hermosillo, Altar) nothing was touched. The alleged 300,000-hectare ranch of the Pesqueira family—if such a ranch exists—was not even mentioned. In any case the possibility of expropriation in the north was never even discussed. On the contrary, the concern was how to resolve the problem of salinity along the coast near Hermosillo, which resulted from the drilling of many wells for irrigation, allowing seawater to seep into cultivated lands.

In conclusion, the Echeverría government demonstrated a great ability to manage the masses and to take advantage of popular mobilization to achieve political successes. But many of the political gains for officials often were losses for social harmony. A success based on peasant support was a failure in terms of middle-class and business support, and in the final analysis the Mexican state depends far more on the bourgeoisie than on any other group.

PART III

Echeverría in Decline

Nobody respects anything or anybody, not the police or the president, or even his own heritage. I believe it is that way throughout the entire world.

—JORGE ACOSTA
SUBDIRECTOR, INSTITUTO NACIONAL DE
ANTROPOLOGÍA E HISTORIA, 1974

CHAPTER 4

Business Opposes the President

The actions taken by the regime during Echeverría's term to pacify dissent and calm the people had a strong effect on the factors that had provoked the discontent. The discontent stemmed quite simply from the maldistribution of wealth that forced the majority of Mexicans to pay, with growing misery, for the enrichment of a minority.

To stabilize the economy, it was necessary to modify the existing economic development model, but the modifications became a principal cause of the deterioration of relations between the president and the bourgeoisie. It also led to a questioning by the bourgeoisie of the president's influence and power.

Since Echeverría began his term in conditions of systemic deterioration, he needed to demonstrate that his was a government of national unity in which the entire country would go "upward and onward,"[1] enacting all the changes that were necessary.[2]

During his first month in office the president proposed three new laws in very sensitive areas: (a) Reforms in the tax laws on the production and consumption of beer and bottled alcoholic drinks. Beer, however, was one of the most important products of the Monterrey Group, a powerful set of businesses in that northern city. (b) Reforms to the General Law of Credit Institutions and Auxiliary Organizations and the Organic Law of the Bank of Mexico. This was a sensitive area for government intervention because banking was the only sector of the economy in which unionization was prohibited, and for that reason banks believed themselves to be untouchable. (Under López Portillo, bank workers were allowed to unionize. (c) Laws that reformed various other taxes. For example, a tax of 10 percent was imposed on luxury items. One observer noted that, "given the opulence and ostentation of the new upper and upper middle classes, this increase in taxes would not seriously affect their purchasing power, but would serve as an indication of the prophetic concern of the government for the poor."[3]

To understand the position of the Mexican bourgeoisie, it is necessary to recognize that this class was worried not about losing purchasing power, but about losing decision-making power. Regarding a particular policy proposal, the president of the Confederación Patronal de la República Mexicana (COPARMEX, a leading business association) declared: "On this occasion we were not invited to discuss the proposal." He added: "This could interrupt the dialogue between government and business."[4]

Thus, the godson indicated the kind of response he would give the godfather. CONCAMIN, CONCANACO, COPARMEX, and the Mexican Association of Insurance Institutions all demonstrated their opposition to further taxation by saying: "Government revenues should be based principally on an effective collection system that ensures the just and timely payment of taxes by the payer." These organizations were, of course, precisely the ones that evaded and corrupted the tax system, but they screamed when the new law eliminated 50 percent of the deduction for advertising expenses. They were not disposed to concede any profits, and so the government was left only with the option of increasing taxes on salaried workers. CANACINTRA added that the tax "was inflationary and would contribute to smuggling." But many who claimed to be bothered by a 10 percent tax could still afford a yacht, the latest model car, or a color television set on the black market. The American Chamber of Commerce rendered the ultimate comment: "It is the consumers who will pay." Green says that in return for the 10 percent luxury tax, certain items that could have been sources of funds for the government, including radios, clocks, and some appliances such as refrigerators, were exempted from the list of taxed items.[5]

Nevertheless, as strident as the voices of the bourgeoisie were, the president's was just as shrill. After hearing business's response to the proposal of the 10 percent tax, the president declared: "They should not think only of their own interests; they should reduce their unbridled love of money, animate their national spirit, and understand for once that the government is going to look out for the general interest instead of the interest of only one sector."[6]

When the president played host to the sugar industrialists and they complained of the suspension of the sugar subsidy, he told them: "Much of the money from the subsidy is not applied to the industry, but has been detoured and used to build private homes and large office buildings on the Paseo de la Reforma."[7]

Thus the clashes that began within two weeks of Echeverría's inauguration and that set the pattern for the rest of his term later intensified into both political rhetoric and actions. When the Agrarian Reform Law was announced which, among other things, reduced the area irrigated, COPARMEX protested because it was not consulted. Echeverría responded: "The organization was not consulted with respect to the Agrarian Code because COPARMEX is not involved with people with these problems, such as *ejidatarios*. Also, if the Constitution commanded me to send COPARMEX my policy proposals for its consideration, you would have them just as do the deputies and senators."[8]

My hypothesis is that from the beginning of the efforts to reform the tax system, the clashes and confrontations between government and business occurred because it appeared that profits would be directly affected. This conflict existed despite the fact that tax evasion was widespread and hence Mexican business could therefore expect to continue to do well.[9]

The government did not retreat, however, and in 1972 it planned another reform. This one also did not go as far as the president had hoped, because of "the powerful resistance of the financial, industrial, and commercial sectors."[10] According to Whitehead, "at the last minute the president met secretly with the leader of the business elite [no name given], and the result was that the reform was put aside. From then on, the relations between the president and the secretary of the treasury (who had proposed the reform) got worse until the latter was replaced. Likewise, relations worsened between the president and the private sector."[11]

Deteriorating relations between the president and business were apparently due to Echeverría's forceful responses, as the bourgeoisie was doing all in its power to attack his autonomy and ensure that his fiscal policies failed. It was salaried workers, however, who most strongly resented the increase in taxes. The economic reality was that taxes increased only 11.2 percent as a share of the gross national product between 1971 and 1976, yet this figure represented a significant decline in the standard of living for consumers who lived on salaries. The increase was attributable mainly to indirect taxes "that affected the general index of prices, causing the fiscal burden to fall disproportionately on the lower and middle classes. The taxes on income derived from capital were not significantly affected; for example, ownership of stocks was not taxed."[12]

In 1971, 1972, and 1974 new tax proposals were introduced that met strong resistance from entrepreneurs and intensified the friction between government and business. And so the old relationship did not change; on the contrary, protection for the bourgeoisie became more firmly entrenched. When Carlos Torres Manzo resigned as secretary of industry and commerce in 1974 to become governor of Michoacán, he was replaced by José Campillo Sáenz, former president of CONCAMIN. During José López Portillo's term, Campillo Sáenz became director of INFONAVIT, the organization that had brought Echeverría so many conflicts with business.

To stimulate exports the Mexican Institute of Foreign Trade (IMCE) was established and a program was initiated to give tax exemptions for export products (Certificados de Devolución de Impuestos para Exportaciones, or CEDIS). Industrial parks were created where government provided credit, tax breaks, and physical infrastructure. Under the Law of Technology, payments for patents and trademarks were canceled. Yet despite all these advantages, business continued to attack Echeverría and even called Campillo a traitor to the business community from which he had come. Perhaps that was because he proposed the Law of Control of Foreign Investment, which improved the maneuvering capacity of *local* capital.

In addition to the measures described above, the government strengthened SOMEX to save floundering firms. In the case of the Banco Internacional, for example, the government bought 51 percent of the stock to save the firm when fraud was discovered. Considering all that this government did for business, one must ask, as did Suárez, why entrepreneurs continued to harbor so much hatred for Echeverría.[13]

The Mexican bourgeoisie vehemently defended its territory, as when it accused CONASUPO and ISSSTE of providing "disloyal competition." It also practiced solidarity with other factions of its class against the government. For example, in Sonora it gutted the protectionist package that the government had imposed for the purpose of allowing Mexican business to make more money.

Business attacked the government on any pretext. In June 1974 commerce in Monterrey came to a standstill during a strike of gasoline station employees. Then the owners of transport, mostly buses, in Sonora announced their determination to stop service until the government authorized increases in fares. Afterward, 20,000 farmers went on strike in Sonora and Sinaloa in December 1975, demanding assurances that their property would not be expropriated. From Monterrey a campaign was launched against the new free textbooks, and Echeverría was attacked for not having decreed national mourning after the murder of Eugenio Garza Sada, the head of the Monterrey group. In fact, the bourgeoisie of Monterrey actually blamed the president indirectly for the death of the kidnapped businessman. And in Monterrey a secret meeting was held in which a coup d'etat was apparently discussed.[14]

Business found reasons to oppose nearly every measure that the government announced. In the area of price controls, for example, CANACO would say that the government should control the black market, the American Chamber of Commerce would ask for the freedom to import, and even when taxes were exempted and subsidies for the importation of certain products were granted, business would ask for more. Not only that, but entrepreneurs put more pressure on the government and reaped more benefits by conjuring up the apparition of inflation that they themselves were helping to cause.

For the Mexican bourgeoisie, none of the measures proposed by the government was seen as good, since in October 1971, through the president of COPARMEX, it had asked for the reprivatization of government firms that had operated at a loss. But business did not realize that such problems had been brought about by the fact that those firms operated by buying at high prices and selling at low prices. That is, many firms had operated inefficiently by not keeping their costs down or by being unresponsive to the market. But they usually blamed the government for their troubles, and whatever aspect of economic policy the Mexican bourgeoisie did not like—even if the policy had been in place for three or four presidential terms—was blamed on Echeverría and his "Communism."

This attitude was carried to the point of fierce anti-communist libels, such as the collection of articles by Gustavo de Anda[15] and the fact that scholars, editorialists and many ordinary citizens came to regard Echeverría as a leftist.[16]

The serious breach that had been created between the government and the dominant class was stronger than ever. Many people interpreted events as evidence that Echeverría was trying to emulate and even surpass Lázaro Cárdenas in his "leftism." In response, the bourgeoisie repeated some of its practices from the Cárdenas period, 1934–40.[17] The president tried to remain neutral between the warring forces or at least to placate both sides. That approach can be seen as a reason for the fall of Horacio Flores de la Peña, secretary of natural resources, recognized as an "open leftist,"[18] who was proposing that Mexico join OPEC. He was replaced by Francisco Javier Alejo, who was often mentioned as a student leader of 1968. Thus, one explanation for the change was that Echeverría removed Flores in order to please the right and to demonstrate the limits of his leftism, even though neither the ideological balance of his cabinet nor his policy positions were fundamentally changed, because Flores was replaced with another apparent leftist. Another possible explanation was that the United

States put pressure on Mexico not to join OPEC and that the pressure isolated Flores.[19]

At the same time as Flores' resignation the Law of American Trade, which criticized OPEC, was introduced. After Alejo became secretary, he denied that Mexico had any intention of joining the OPEC cartel. Thus, Echeverría emerged triumphant from this controversy on several counts. He was able to show his willingness to negotiate with the United States, to manage with greater freedom his rumored candidacy for the leadership of the United Nations, and to free himself somewhat from the pressures of the domestic bourgeoisie.

Echeverría was generally cautious in responding to the attacks on him. When he was asked why he did not reply to Margain Zozaya at the funeral of Garza Sada, he said: "I did not understand what that old man said."[20] But there were exceptions. In 1976 he said publicly to Páez, the director of Alfa: "Instead of congratulating me for having helped you sell your patent, go tell your bosses they should be patriotic." To Páez's amazement, the president continued: "Tell them not to send their money abroad. This is a serious message." And he said to two assistants: "Tell him that he should go right now with that message."[21]

Echeverría concentrated his attacks against the bourgeoisie on the Monterrey Group. In October 1976 he said in Monterrey: "To the rich and the powerful of Monterrey who call themselves Christians and beat their breasts but who refuse to help their fellow man, even though you create industries, you lack a sense of social responsibility and you have become profound reactionaries and enemies of the people."[22] In response, in addition to their public actions, entrepreneurs renewed their pressure on the government, spread rumors, and engaged in the old tactic of capital flight.

THE RUMORS

Echeverría's term of office began with a rumor of the imminence of fascism which, along with a rumor of devaluation, remained the two most persistent rumors of the period. The two rumors appear to have had different origins, since the one about fascism could be manipulated by the government and the one about devaluation could be used by those who stood to profit from the speculation that followed.

Such rumors quickly demonstrated that they had political value, and many people saw them as useful weapons. Here is a list of some of the more common rumors during the Echeverría years, illustrating the turbulence of this period.

Doctors were going through the schools giving vaccinations to
pupils to sterilize them (1974). Because of the resulting fear, more
than 100,000 children were not vaccinated against polio.

A strangler of women was at large. (1972)

There was rationing of basic foodstuffs, provoking panic buying.
(1972)

There was a scarcity of gasoline, at a time of a price increase. (1973)

A widespread program of nationalization of urban and rural property
was being prepared through the law of human settlements which
was "sovietizing, anti-Christian, and confiscatory." (1976)

There would be a freezing of bank accounts. (From 1972 forward)

The following rumors were all heard in 1976:

Banks would be nationalized.

Echeverría was a Communist.

Echeverría was one of the richest men in the world.

Augusto Gómez Villanueva, the secretary of agrarian reform and
closely associated with Echeverría, changed 400 million pesos into
dollars a few days before the devaluation of 1976.

Mrs. Echeverría suffered a murder attempt.

Luis Echeverría, his wife, and their children were all murdered. (This
rumor had various versions: sometimes one or another survived
but was gravely injured.

A coup d'etat was being organized, sometimes from the left and
sometimes from the right.

Cuenca Díaz, secretary of defense, was a prisoner in Military Camp
No. 1.

Echeverría would lead a coup d'etat and install a dictatorship.

At the end of the term, in 1976, rumors seemed to gain control of the
popular imagination.[23] In November 1976 I was standing in a very long
line at a bank in Guaymas, Sinaloa, and began to chat with a middle-aged
woman behind me. She said that she was going to withdraw all her money
from the bank. I asked her why, and she said that she did not know, but
was just going to do it.

The government decided to confront the rumors, and on November
10, 1976, a deputy from Coahuila (who became governor in 1981)
proposed an anticalumny law. On November 18 the Chamber of Deputies
announced that it would investigate the origin of the rumor campaign.
Initial indications implicated private business. The leader of the CTM in
Monterrey—an eternal legislator—accused Marcelo Sada, head of
COPARMEX, of sabotage and treason.

Echeverría later recognized that "the oligarchy now understands two things: the political value of a campaign of rumors as a mechanism in the service of a policy of public intimidation, and the value of domestic and foreign economic priorities during an economic crisis. . . . The campaign . . . in my case was intent on the destabilization of the regime."[24]

In March 1977, early in López Portillo's term, Jorge Sánchez Mejorada, a business leader, declared: "If we were previously spreading rumors about a coup d'etat and a freezing of bank accounts, now we should paint a positive picture, since conditions have improved so much."[25]

This evidence strongly implies that Echeverría was correct in accusing the bourgeoisie of spreading antigovernment rumors. Of course, rumors occur in all political systems at all times, but the question is, Why were the rumors so effective against Echeverría? The following are possible answers:

(a) People did not have confidence in the media, because of the history of media corruption. Major decisions of society and government were made in secret, and the Mexican media had little tradition of probing that secrecy. Politicians used that secrecy to benefit themselves politically, and so the rumors became believable.

(b) People did not understand what was happening during these years, and thus the more bizarre the rumor, when reinforced by repetition, the more credible it became.

(c) The rumors demonstrated the peculiar social cohesion that exists in Mexico.[26] People tend to believe their relatives and friends and what they hear in the café, the bar, or at the shoe-shine stand more than they believe the mass media, which merely repeats the government's version of events.

The political weight of the rumors was clearly demonstrated when they began to interfere with the effectiveness of the government. To say that a strangler was on the loose was to make it appear that the government was incapable of ensuring the safety of its citizens. To mention that children were being sterilized created a lack of confidence in the actions of the government and suggested sinister motives. This type of rumor seeks to terrorize the population, creating suspicion and resentment with regard to everything that emanates from the government.

Moreover, a public accustomed to such fantasies as the claim that the people choose their governors, that they live in a system of equal opportunity, that Indians can be president, and so on, are inclined to believe lies anyway and therefore are prone to pay attention to rumors, no matter how outrageous. In addition, rumors are useful to some people because they can profit from them. For example, rumors can powerfully affect the stock market or the value of the currency, and speculators can profit from rumors that they themselves help to originate and to spread.

THE JOKES

It is common to hear jokes about Mexican presidents, but in the case of Echeverría the jokes were aimed at impairing his authority and ridiculing him, and they were an effective reinforcement for the rumors (see Appendix L). Linking the two areas, a rumor circulated that anyone who told jokes about Echeverría would be thrown in jail.

The majority of the jokes attacked Echeverría's intelligence and manliness. A common joke claimed that his wife ordered him around, including a rumor that on one occasion someone was appointed general director of an organization because he had choreographed a play for the folkloric group Las Palomas de San Jerónimo, sponsored by doña María Esther Zuno de Echeverría.

Echeverría's detractors began to use sonnets and even religious "prayers" to round out the attack. The following anonymous list of examples was circulated widely throughout Mexico City. First we give the Spanish version and then a translation.

Oración al Piadoso Señor Echeverría
　　¡Salve, señor Echeverría! Dueño absoluto de dos millones de kilómetros cuadrados de tierra, pasto immaculado de cincuenta millones de animales bípedos, que humildemente bajan la cerviz para adorarte.
　　¡Salve, soberano de tantos males, a ti bondadoso señor, te debemos el encarecimiento del azúcar y el alza inmoderada de los precios y los artículos indispensables para nuestra existencia. Gracias a ti ha bajado el número de estudiantes, de campesinos, de profesores y de agentes de seguros, pues gracias a tu inmenso respeto por la vida humana los has trasladado a la vida eterna!
　　¡No tenemos señor con qué pagarte! El pueblo te idolatra entrañablemente, gran benefactor, eres incansable para darnos tanta miseria y, aún no conforme, viajas a tres continentes, visitas muchas ciudades, te gastas muchos millones de pesos en pasajes y regalos, haces el ridículo y sigues, divino y piadoso señor, elevando impuestos, llenándonos de privaciones y careciéndonos de empleos, en lugar de proporcionarnos trabajo con las obras que tu espurio Gobierno entrega a la CIA. Contratista!
　　¡Oh Sapientísimo señor Echeverría! ¡Aborto de la naturaleza! En ti confía el pueblo, el "nutrido pueblo." La cosa tendrá que cambiar cuando despierte; mientras tanto te suplicamos te dignes seguir llenándonos con tu infinita misericordia, como hasta hoy, Amen . . . digo!

(Haz las copias que creas convenientes de esta hoja y repártelas entre tus parientes y amigos).

Prayer to Our Merciful Lord Echeverría

Hail, Lord Echeverría! Absolute ruler of two million square kilometers of the Earth, immaculate grazing land of fifty million biped animals, who humbly bow their heads to adore You!

Hail, sovereign of so many evils; it is to You, good Lord, that we owe the scarcity of sugar and the uncontrolled rise in the price of the necessities of life. Thanks to you the number of students, peasants, professors, and insurance agents have been reduced, since thanks to Your immense respect for human life, You have granted them life eternal!

Oh, Lord, we have no way to repay You! The people idolize You from the bottom of their hearts; great benefactor, You are tireless in giving us so much misery, and, not satisfied with that, You travel to three continents, visit many cities, spend many millions of pesos on fares and gifts, play the fool, and go on, divine and merciful Lord, raising taxes, bestowing privations, taking away our jobs instead of offering us work on the projects that Your spurious government contracts with the foreign CIA!

Oh, most wise Lord Echeverría! Miscarriage of Nature! The people trust You, the abundant, "nourished" people. Things will have to change when they awaken; meanwhile, we beg You to continue providing us with Your infinite mercy, as You have to this day. Amen . . . I say to you!*

(Make as many copies of this sheet as you see fit and spread them around among your friends and relatives.)

CREDO
(Según San Político)

Creo en el PRI Todopoderoso, creador de candidatos en la tierra, de Echeverría su único hijo. . . . Señor nuestro que fue elegido por obra y gracia del espíritu cuento; nació de la Secretaría de Gobernación y apareció bajo el poder de Díaz Ordaz; fue maquilado, retratado y amplificado; demostró ser el BUENO y, al tercer día resucitó entre los "tapados." Subió a los Pinos y está sentado a la derecha del PRI Todopoderoso, desde ahí ha de combatir y exterminar a los benefactores del pueblo.

Creemos en su espíritu santo . . . en la Santa Constitución la

---

* The literal meaning of *"Amen, digo"* is "Amen, I say," but it also implies *"A mendigo,"* or "Hail, son of a bitch."

amplificación de los empleos, el perdón de los impuestos, la reducción
de los precios y la vida tranquila del mundo futuro. Amén . . . digo!

CREDO
(By Saint Politician)
I believe in the PRI almighty, creator of candidates on Earth, of Echeverría, Its only Son . . . Our Lord, who was elected by and thanks to the Phony Spirit;* He was born of the Secretaría de Gobernación and appeared under the power of Díaz Ordaz; He was made up, photographed, and amplified; He showed us he was GOOD, and on the third day, he arose from among the veiled candidates. He ascended into Los Pinos, and is seated at the right hand of almighty PRI. From there he carries on the fight to exterminate those who would benefit the people.

We believe in His Holy Spirit . . . in the Holy Constitution, the rise of employment, the forgiveness of taxes, the reduction of prices, and the peaceful life of the world of the future. Amen, I say to you!

ADIÓS CHIVARRIAS
(Soneto)
Tu palabra cumplida, hijo de puta,
demagogo, fanático y farsante.
Que nos jodiste, no hay quien lo discuta;
el caos fue siempre arriba y adelante.

Y te vas muy feliz. ¡Que poca madre!
Y la pendeja Esther muy satisfecha
con su pinche labor, que fue un desmadre
dejan a la Nación casi deshecha.

Que nos robaron tú la compañera
todo el mundo será siempre testigo,
aquí, allá, en Cancún y dondequiera.

Te has de quedar sin perro que te ladre,
con todo el corazón yo te lo digo.
Adios, pinche pelón, ¡chinga tu Madre!
El Pueblo

---

* In the original prayer it is *espíritu santo,* meaning "holy spirit," but here it is changed to *espíritu cuento,* which means "fairy spirit" or could be read as *es pupo cuento,* "a big lie."

GOODBYE CHIVARRIAS
(Sonnet)
You did what you promised, son of a bitch;
You're a fanatic, demagogue, con man.
No one denies you screwed us up.
With you, chaos was always onward and upward.[*]

You're leaving quite happy, you bastard!
And self-satisfied Esther,[†] smug asshole,
with her shitty works, a complete foul-up.
You're leaving the country nearly destroyed;

You and your "comrade"[‡] have robbed us.
The whole world is our witness to that,
here, in Can Cun,[§] and all over.

All hate the sight of you; you'll be alone.
From the bottom of my heart I bid you
good-bye, you hairless asshole, fuck you!
The People

In this way jokes, sonnets, poems, grumblings, and rumors created a climate of instability and lack of confidence that put the government's back against the wall. Any action that the government tried to introduce was met with a rapid, biting, and destructive response. In a country where politicians seek office to benefit themselves financially, where business selfishly takes advantage of government policies to enrich itself, the ones who do not have these opportunities lie in wait for any information that, even if it does not benefit them, at least will not hurt them. And so the people were inclined to put the worst possible interpretation on anything that they heard. For that reason, by the way, rumors of devaluation led very rapidly to a large-scale conversion of pesos into dollars. (See in Appendix L a pamphlet that accused Echeverría of being in the pay of Rockefeller and the CIA; the party responsible for the pamphlet was also accused of being paid by Rockefeller.)

---

[*] *Arriba y Adelante*, "Onward and Upward," was the slogan of Echeverría's presidential campaign.

[†] Echeverría's wife.

[‡] Echeverría called his wife *la compañera* ("the comrade"), using the leftist language of equality between men and women.

[§] To this day, as with Alemán and Acapulco during the 1940s, people think that Echeverría built Cancún as his personal business.

Political humor also allows citizens to get even with a government that seems very distant and that has betrayed them. Some examples:

Since Díaz Ordaz ended his term resented, insulted, and reviled, it was said that he selected Echeverría as the next president in order to take revenge on the country.

(*Lo que sucedió con Echeverría fue una venganza de Díaz Ordaz, porque cómo éste terminó su sexenio vituperado, insultado y ofendido, para vengarse de México dejó a Echeverría.*)

It was said that after the devaluation, what was needed was not a new type of exchange (currency), but an exchange of types (i.e., leaders). (*Después de la devaluación, no era necesario un nuevo tipo de cambio, sino un cambio de tipo.* [This example involves a play on the word "*tipo*," which means both "type" and "guy."]

By means of jokes, the individual citizen could, in a sense, become equal with the president, by mocking him, scoffing at him, and hurling vituperatives at him. Yet the individual could protect himself through anonymity, avoiding persecution by a justice system that was often more concerned with protecting the image of the powerful than with safeguarding the individual and society. Thus by means of political humor, the individual could jab at the powerful even though the powerful usually had the last laugh.

CAPITAL FLIGHT AND DOLLARIZATION

Another of the tactics used by the bourgeoisie in its confrontation with the government was monetary pressure. Thus a distinctive mark of the period was speculation and capital flight. All the government's attempts to use fiscal policy to keep the economy steady were frustrated by the actions of the rich, who distorted the government's corrective measures aimed at reining in inflation and reducing the public debt and the fiscal deficit.[27]

Over time the economy was virtually converted to the dollar. The government authorized banks in 1973 to take deposits in dollars on fixed-term certificates of deposit in order to attract dollars from abroad. Undoubtedly, the intention was good, because attracting funds from abroad could slow the rise of the debt, but it did not work out that way. Liabilities in foreign currency increased considerably, and nonmonetary instruments went from $357 million to $588 million from 1972 to 1973.[28] That is, the economy became saturated with dollars, but the reserves of the Bank of Mexico did not increase at the same pace (see Table 4.1 and Appendix M).

Table 4.1
Monetary Liabilities of the Mexican Banking System, 1971–76

Year	National Currency (Millions of Pesos)	Annual Increase (%)	Millions of Dollars	Annual Increase (%)
1971	53,060.4	n.d.	3,209.0	n.d.
1972	64,327.6	21.2	3,409.7	6.2
1973	79,874.7	24.2	4,871.4	42.9
1974	97,473.7	22.0	6,403.0	31.4
1975	118,267.0	21.3	8,593.8	34.2
1976	154,800.2	30.9	13,648.7	58.8

SOURCE: Secretaría de Programación y Presupuesto, *Boletín Mensual de Información Económica*, México, D.F., August 1978, p. 140.

The second goal of the government was to slow capital flight, but this effort proved even less successful, and capital flight continued to increase (Table 4.2).[29] As the sexenio neared its end and the rumors about a possible devaluation grew, the economy continued to experience a conversion of pesos to dollars, but this money did not come from investors.

The government was forced to go further into debt to satisfy the demand for dollars. From August to November 1976, while checking accounts in pesos went from 63 to 65 billion pesos, an increase of only 2 percent, checking accounts in dollars went from $378 million to $445 million, an increase of 17 percent.[30]

The twin developments of capital flight and dollarization devastated the market, which was left without adequate money in circulation. The government was forced to print more paper money and go further into debt without having gained any social or economic benefit. The regime was left with no alternative but to devalue the peso and allow it to float, because this was the best way to stop speculation, even though it increased the profits and the negotiating power of the banks.

This argument is not meant to imply that indebtedness was the only reason for the devaluation. The government should have devalued the peso in 1973 when the dollar fell. To follow the traditional yet erroneous monetary policy of defending the peso with as much ferocity as defending the virginity of a fair maiden forced the government to pay a very high price for maintaining the parity of the peso.[31] Nevertheless, despite the tardiness of the decision, it was necessary.

Taken at the end of the sexenio, the devaluation allowed the new government to inherit a healthier monetary policy. If the devaluation was interpreted as a sign of the weakness of the government, at least it was the weakness of the government that was on its way out rather than the one that was coming in.

Table 4.2
Capital Flight to the U.S., 1971–76
(Millions of Dollars)

Year	Banking Liabilities		Nonbanking Liabilities	
	Short Term	Long Term	Short Term	Long Term
1971	709	31	22	1
1972	831	28	27	1
1973	1,296	44	46	3
1974	1,770	6	60	3
1975	2,078	10	82	3
1976				
January–March	5,951	—	92	6
April–June	6,413	18	72	6
July–September	6,759	55	74	7
October–December	8,173	60	—	—
Total 1976	27,296	133	238	19

SOURCE: Angeles, *Crisis y coyuntura*, 107.

The Mexican bourgeoisie interpreted the devaluation as an attack on it and immediately counterattacked. It continued capital flight, raised prices on basic goods from 30 percent to 60 percent, and demanded that the rate of exchange be fixed in view of the fact that the peso was now floating. In addition, the bourgeoisie pressed the government not to place heavy taxes on profits from speculation.

Mexican businessmen were overly provincial and unconcerned that the world economy was reeling, or perhaps they did not understand that Mexico was linked to the American economic cycle. The fact is that they needed to find someone to blame for the monetary difficulties and the economic recession, and the target of their attacks was Echeverría, the "villain" of the sexenio.

THE BUSINESS COORDINATING COUNCIL

During the Echeverría years a movement toward greater organizational independence emerged when the business associations joined in a peak agency called the Business Coordinating Council, or Consejo Coordinador Empresarial (CEE). This organization was able to present a united front for all the business factions and could thereby end the fragmentation in the representation of business. It was another challenge to the state, which had preferred that business organize itself into different associations to defend specific interests. With the new organization the most powerful interests were capable of dictating to various member organizations in order to promote their goals of limiting state autonomy.

The debut of this organization was even more problematical for the government because it presented its platform at the very time that the regime's basic economic plan was being launched. This timing made the business proposal look like a direct challenge to the government by the private sector. In addition, the council was created at a particularly tense moment in the relations between the state and the bourgeoisie, and was thus seen by the government as a provocative move and as another source of friction and conflict. Its confrontational image was minimized only by the fact that it emerged near the end of Echeverría's term.

In addition to all these internal pressures and conflicts, Echeverría was involved in strong confrontations abroad. We now turn to his foreign policy.

CHAPTER 5

Echeverría as Anti-Imperialist

Echeverría endeavored to match his foreign policy to his domestic policy; that is, if internally the participatory bases were to be expanded toward the left, then externally the leftist tendencies also had to be encouraged. All this had to be done while demonstrating that the government was capable of leading the initiatives for national recovery which reaffirmed Mexican "sovereignty" and "national dignity." Invariably, this program was manifested in anti-American positions, even though Mexico was in the American orbit and its economy was intimately related to the American economic cycle.

THIRD WORLDISM

It is a mistake to think that Mexican foreign policy was directed only at achieving for Echeverría the secretary generalship of the United Nations. To believe this is to underestimate both the foreign policy of the country and the international political reality.

From the formation of OPEC in the early 1960s, and with increasing emphasis after 1970–73, when the oil-exporting countries took control of the price and profits of oil (Iraq nationalized oil companies in 1972), "third worldism" (*tercermundismo*) began to make a greater claim on global wealth and technological benefits.[1] The new left assumed a more "liberationist" position, denouncing both Soviet and American expansionism. World domination by those two countries began to weaken with the emergence of China as a world power (a country considered to be part of the Third World) and the growing strength of Japan and West Germany as economic and industrial powers. Also, in the 1970s the world monetary system collapsed, inflation soared, and the exploited countries were exploited even more as the world economic powers unloaded on them the negative consequences of capitalist development.

Hypothetically, one can suggest that some of the political movements that overthrow democratic governments or ancient monarchies are a result of the difficulty that the latter systems have in imposing the social sacrifices that are necessary during the capitalist concentration phase of economic modernization. The transfer of these economic distortions by the industrial powers onto the shoulders of the so-called peripheral, underdeveloped, dependent, Third World, or exploited countries (for me, all synonymous) forces the afflicted countries to reassert their role in the world system in whatever ways are possible for them. The most notable option in this regard was the emergence in the United Nations of a Third World bloc, which made it obvious that political alliances had changed. However, the raising of Third World political consciousness only partly liberated the new countries from economic burdens and imbalances. In Mexico this imbalance was indicated by the analysis in Part II of this book.

As noted above, for Echeverría to protest the consequences that Mexico was suffering, it was necessary to pursue a discussion at the national level and for internal consumption about emancipation and justice through external foreign policy issues. As Gereffi argues,[2] Echeverría intended to expand Mexico's autonomy and negotiating strength with the international centers of power, but his error was in not understanding that this would require some transformation of Mexico's so-called status of dependency. Here it is necessary to make a basic clarification. It is incorrect to see actions of the state as if they were "fights to the death" or as if the motto of every political action were "conquer or die." Such is the case in the analysis of Rosario Green, who believes that it was always a fight to the death between the state and the bourgeoisie. Thus, when the state makes concessions to the business class, she concludes that it is really demonstrating its weakness,[3] when in fact the dominant class and its representatives engage in conscious give and take, in a constant redefinition of the balance of power. Thus a state's relatively little autonomy on one issue does not imply an overall weakness, because on another occasion it might have greater power. In short, the fact that a state or particular government sometimes makes a concession is no indication that it is weak. A similar "all or nothing" analogy is used by

Gereffi, who concludes that a redefinition in the terms of trade will lead to a break with the dominant powers. Both authors' conclusions are symptomatic of analyses that do not consider that capitalism is a complex international system bound to have local implications.

Echeverría succeeded in coalescing a feeling that had been developing since 1963 with the declaration approved by the Group of 77 at the end of UNCTAD I, which was reaffirmed in the Letter of Algiers in 1967 and in the economic declaration of the nonaligned states in 1973. It was called the Letters of the Rights and Duties of the States, or the "Echeverría Letter," and was one of the most deeply felt Third World measures.

According to Whitehead,[4] Mexico's great achievement in 1974 was to persuade the United Nations General Assembly to approve, by a vote of 120 in favor, 6 against, and 10 abstentions,[5] an instrument that formalized "much of what had been discussed in a less organized form for several years."[6] The letter enumerated various fundamental principles of international economic relations, among which were the following: sovereignty, equality among nations, nonaggression and nonintervention, peaceful coexistence, equal rights and free determination of peoples, peaceful settlement of disputes, respect for human rights and fundamental liberties, international cooperation, and others. The articles that follow illustrate these principles:

Article 1: Each State has the sovereign and inalienable right to choose its own economic, political, social, and cultural system.

Article 2: Each State has and freely exercises a full and permanent sovereignty, including possession, use, and disposition of all its wealth, natural resources, and economic activities. . . . [In consequence,] each State has the right to regulate and to exercise authority over foreign investments, including the right to nationalize, expropriate, and transfer foreign property or goods.

Article 4: There should be no discrimination in trade based on differences in political, economic, or social systems.

Article 5: States have a right to associate in producer organizations of primary materials [i.e., cartels].

Article 6: States have a responsibility to contribute to the development of international merchandise trade, especially through long-term multilateral agreements about basic products.

Article 7: The responsibility to cooperate in the economic, social, scientific, cultural, and technological spheres to promote economic and social progress throughout the world, especially in the developing countries.

Article 10: The rights to participate fully and effectively in the international decision-making process for the solution of world economic, financial, and monetary problems.

Article 13: Use of science and technology to accelerate economic and social development. . . . The cooperation to strengthen scientific and technological infrastructure.

Article 14: Cooperation for expanding and liberating commerce, especially in taking steps for ensuring additional benefits for the international trade of the developing countries.

Article 15: To link the achievement of complete and general disarmament under effective international control to the allocation of the resources freed thereby to economic and social development. Also, attention should be paid to the question of the resources of the oceans outside of national jurisdictions. The resources of the oceans are defined as the "common inheritance of humanity."

The physical environment was also considered in the letter as a common responsibility of the nations. The letter did not mention certain important subjects—population, energy, and food—and gave little indication of concrete suggestions for the long-run problems of human survival and of global relations. But it constituted a quasi-legal framework for orienting the policies of all the members of the United Nations toward specific objectives, and it was an instrument that could help to channel cooperative international efforts toward a new set of objectives.[7] As Suárez wrote, "The Letter contains a set of current aspirations of the underdeveloped countries for their liberation . . . and presents a list of existing possibilities for the development of the countries of the Third World."[8]

If Echeverría wanted to test the unity of the Third World behind his rumored candidacy for the secretary generalship of the United Nations, the reaction to the letter was a good opportunity. He could also look at previous votes, however, especially those that dealt with anti-Israeli positions, to test whether a bloc of support existed that could be easily mobilized for an anti-American initiative or some other unifying issue. Whatever the case, it is certain that the letter gave Echeverría an irrefutable Third World presence that strongly reflected the sentiment of most of the countries traditionally considered oppressed.

At the same time, Third World nations wished to combat the manipulation of mass information by agencies of the so-called First World.[9] The message seemed to be directed mainly at the United States, since Mexico strongly resented American newspaper campaigns that often had devastating results inside Mexico. Since 1975, newspaper articles had speculated about a possible monetary devaluation in Mexico. In addition, a press campaign in the U.S. about crime in northern Mexico implied that such conditions were endemic throughout the republic, just at the time of the tourist boycott.[10] This action is important because of the tremendously strong ties between the two countries, reflected in the great importance of Mexico in the U.S. press (see Appendix N).

In this case the demand for freedom of information appeared to be a well-intentioned but ill-timed and poorly managed initiative that provoked a spate of denunciations by the imperialist powers about "ideological and information control."[11] It appeared that the government was trying to control the Mexican television monopoly created by the merger of Televicentro (Channels 2, 4, and 5) and Mexican Independent Television (Channel 8) to form Televisa, requiring it to broadcast government material for at least the minimum amount of time specified by law. The rumor began to circulate that Echeverría was trying to grab control of all of Mexican television. Since the government already controlled two channels (the government's Channel 13 and the National Politechnic Institute's Channel 11), the rumormongers believed that they had scored a bulls-eye. As a result, the proposal for freedom of information was distorted, and the wildfire of antigovernment rumor spread even faster.

All this rumormongering was supplemented by the fact that the Bank of Cinematography, headed by Echeverría's brother—former leader of the actors' union—had displaced private movie producers.[12] Thus Mexico went to the international film festivals with the film "Actas de Marusia," directed by the leftist Chilean producer Miguel Lithin and funded by the Mexican government.

Such rumors ignored the fact that the films of Costa Gavras were not allowed into Mexico because of government censorship. Many wanted to see Echeverría as the villain in all this, extending his tentacles even into the area of communications. It was also rumored that he had grabbed control of the newspaper chain *El Sol de México*.[13] Thus the public perception grew that Echeverría wanted to enhance his position in international agencies such as the UN purely to foster his selfish interests. But this view was obviously the result of pure speculation rather than of analysis.

The government's position regarding the 200-mile coastal limit was also a question of bad timing. In reality, Mexico had never been a leader in the movement for an extension of coastal rights and was not in this case. Mexico had fishing agreements with the United States that would be affected by the adoption of such a resolution, and the U.S. had always rejected the proposal to extend the coastal limit. An attempt to extend the limit would inevitably bring Mexico into conflict with the U.S. as Mexico tried to enforce the law against American boats that entered into Mexico's expanded territorial waters.

American opposition, therefore, meant that the decision to extend the limit had to be unilateral and that the countries that favored it would have to impose their new sovereignty against the countries that did not accept it—and these were generally the economically most powerful countries. In addition, expansion of territorial waters also implied greater control of the ocean floor, which would diminish the ability of the economic powers to look for minerals and energy in those areas.[14] Although the international situation seemed favorable for most of the countries that supported the extension of coastal limits, for a country like Mexico, which had to confront the U.S., and Japan, the external and internal political conditions were not favorable for such a policy. It was an unfortunate situation for Echeverría, because the policy precisely fit his Third World strategy and corresponded exactly with the content and spirit of the Echeverría Letter.

THE ANTI-ZIONIST VOTE

The issue of the anti-Zionist vote was perhaps one of the most disconcerting of the Echeverría years. On the one side, Echeverría had maintained the traditionally cordial relations with Israel established previous by Mexican governments. This policy included the willingness to refrain from interference in affairs that were particularly sensitive to Israel. On a personal level it was even rumored in Mexico that Echeverría's children had spent a short time on some Israeli kibbutzim.

Nevertheless, on his trip to the Middle East, after making the usual declarations in Israel, Echeverría embraced Yasser Arafat, compared him to Benito Juárez, and later facilitated the opening of a PLO office in Mexico. Continuing in this vein, at the conference of the International Year of Women, which took place in Mexico City, the Mexican delegation voted with an Arab-Communist bloc for a resolution condemning Zionism. The effect of the action was intensified by the fact that the delegation was led by the attorney general and included the participation of the president's wife. During that same year the Mexican representative at the General Assembly of the United Nations took a similar position. At this point the Jewish community of the United States imposed a tourist boycott on Mexico, which forced Echeverría to stumble badly in his actions and declarations.

It is difficult logically to explain Echeverría's policy in this area. It is arguable that the anti-Israeli position was a consistent part of an overall Third World strategy. If this is so, it suggests that Mexico attached considerable significance to such forums as the Conference for Women. The Mexican delegation at this conference, however, although formally led by an individual appointed by the president, consisted only of temporary representatives and one could argue that the anti-Zionist position taken there could not necessarily be attributed to the president. Mexico's permanent representative to the United Nations, on the other hand, did strongly reaffirm the position instead of repudiating it.

To see the policy as an attempt to gain Arab support seems untenable for two reasons. First, the Arab world, even after it had achieved the oil boycott in 1973, was not very united with regard to the Palestinian problem. Therefore, it would seem that Mexico had little to gain from the Arabs in taking such a strong position on that question. Second, Mexico already had sufficient petroleum reserves to enter OPEC but had declined to do so. The Mexican government did not consider it desirable to join a movement that could not guarantee any advantages for the Mexican national interest while it would certainly antagonize the United States. The Arab members of OPEC were so displeased with Mexico's unwillingness to join that the anti-Zionist vote would have done little to change their attitude. Therefore, the position does not seem to have been an attempt to placate the Arabs.

Third, the anti-Zionist vote makes even less sense if one considers that Mexico had for years taken refuge behind the Estrada Doctrine of nonintervention in international affairs that did not concern it (especially if they were risky). Mexico's position of nonintervention is so well known in the world that the country is usually allowed to remain aloof from entangling international matters and hence avoids making enemies unnecessarily. If Echeverría had particularly wanted to take a position on the matter, however, he could simply have ratified previous UN resolutions, which were sufficiently ambiguous to allow countries to get along with both sides without getting too caught up in the specifics of the matter.

Neither Echeverría nor his advisers predicted the magnitude of the international response to Mexico's position. They did not dream that the U.S. Jewish community would react in such a rapid and forceful way, especially after years of experience with Mexico's politically inactive Jewish community.

The effect of the tourist boycott was augmented by the fact that the government had suspended the procedure for quick divorces in 1971, eliminating the foreign exchange that was generated as a result of the many Americans who took advantage of the old law.[15] In addition, the Condor Plan with the U.S. cut off to a great extent the export of marijuana, which also reduced the foreign currency coming into Mexico. Tourism also declined as a result of the tax on restaurants and airline flights, the U.S. recession, and the increase in the price of gasoline. The rate of increase of tourism declined from 12 percent in 1973 to 5.6 percent in 1974.[16] All these factors together had a devastating effect on the amount of foreign currency entering the country, especially in conjunction with the capital flight that began to increase after 1974.

Table 5.1
Exports, 1970–76
(Millions of Dollars)

Year	Exports[a]	Exports[b]
1970	1,429	2,933.1
1971	1,511	3,167.1
1972	1,882	3,800.6
1973	2,419	4,828.4
1974	3,443	6,342.5
1975	3,461	6,303.6
1976	4,010	6,971.7

SOURCE: Nafinsa, *Statistics on the Mexican Economy*, México, D.F., 1977.
[a] Goods only.
[b] Goods, silver production, tourism, border transactions, international tariffs, *maquiladoras*, and others.

Mexico's revenue from foreign exchange fell dramatically in 1974–75 in all areas, including tourism and merchandise export (see Tables 5.1 and 5.2). Even in 1976, any increase was canceled out by inflation and exacerbated by the deficit in the trade balance and in the balance of payments. Thus the foreign debt reached unexpected proportions.[17]

Therefore, the boycott by Jewish tourists was destined to hit Mexico where it hurt most. This issue also demonstrated that the Mexican government made decisions in a vacuum and was often blind to the consequences of its actions.

While the wave of tourist cancellations hit Mexico, former president Miguel Alemán met with Jewish travel representatives in New York and Chicago and declared: "The Mexican government acted unilaterally, the people are not in agreement, and what happened at the United Nations does not reflect the feeling of the average Mexican, nor does it cause any prejudice against Jewish visitors."[18]

Nevertheless, Jewish organizations in the United States canceled all tourist activities in Mexico. For example, the Jewish-American Congress and B'nai B'rith suspended their planned trips to Mexico for 1976. The greater problem, however, was that the boycott was expanded to include 80 percent of all U.S. tourism in Mexico.[19] This decline was also a result of the fact that the Mexican government had become identified with the Third World movement in general.

In an effort to offset these developments Echeverría met with American and Canadian Jewish leaders and told them that Emilio Rabasa, Mexico's secretary of foreign relations, was at the United Nations to make sure that future votes by Mexico would not be misunderstood. For his part,

Table 5.2
Tourism, 1971–76

Year	No. of Tourists	Spending (Millions of Dollars)	Average Spending (Dollars)	Average Stay (Days)
1971	2,590,000	461.0	183.72	11.9
1972	2,915,000	562.6	193.04	10.5
1973	3,226,000	724.2	224.47	11.0
1974	3,362,000	842.0	250.44	10.9
1975	3,218,000	800.1	248.65	10.6
1976	3,107,000	835.6	268.94	11.3

SOURCE: Secretaría de Programación y Presupuesto, *Boletín Mensual de Información Económica*, México, D.F., August 1978, p. 112.

Rabasa also went to Israel; placed a wreath on the tomb of Theodore Herzl, the founder of modern Zionism; and declared that Zionism was not racism.[20]

By the end of 1975, 120,000 tourist cancellations from the United States had been reported, amounting to perhaps $50 million in foreign exchange losses.[21] Rabasa resigned after the press denounced him for going to Israel to "ask forgiveness." Thus, the government, by castigating one of its instruments rather than correcting the mistake itself, was trying to distract public attention and create the impression that a serious political mistake could be corrected.[22]

In July 1976, after Mexico condemned Israel for the rescue of the passengers of an Israeli aircraft that had been hijacked and taken to Uganda, U.S. Jews proposed reinstating the tourist embargo and extending it to trade. In September, apparently in an effort to end the boycott, the initiation of Israeli airline flights to Mexico was announced.[23] At about the same time, Echeverría met with Jewish leaders during a visit to San Antonio to explain that Mexico was not anti-Semitic.[24] Echeverría seemed to believe that he could behave with as much ambiguity in international politics as he could in domestic politics.

Apparently, he believed he could play with a speech without giving it multiple interpretations. In this particular case, Echeverría achieved a certain agreement with the PLO, since on his visit to the Middle East he was photographed embracing Arafat. He then made a declaration with respect to "the recognition of the national rights of the Palestinians, the return of the territories illegally occupied by Israel, and the fulfillment of the resolutions of the United Nations." Echeverría announced that Arafat was similar to Benito Juárez and said that only Israel needed to make amends.[25] The following year the PLO opened its office in Mexico City and the anti-Zionist vote occurred. These actions implied a tilting to the left and were interpreted as an intent on the part of the government to demonstrate an opening to the left, as had been done inside the country. The affair had few domestic results because of the low political participation of the Jewish or Arab communities within Mexico (the Middle East conflict had few repercussions in Mexico), and therefore it was impossible for the opposition parties to use these incidents for political advantage.

Nevertheless, the issue had potential domestic political use. By means of its pro-PLO policy, the government could try to isolate the guerrilla movement, which, without the international support of such groups as the PLO, would find itself limited and isolated.[26] But even if the policy made good sense domestically, it had other implications in the international context. The United States did not look kindly on the anti-Israeli policy because of the way in which the U.S. perceived the Arab oil embargo of 1973, as well as its interpretation of the ideological attacks on Israel, its most important ally in the Middle East.

In this way Mexico collided with forces it did not take into account. These actions cost it a great deal because they occurred under disadvantageous conditions that magnified their effect. One could compare it to a person who has a sore foot that someone stomps on. Under healthy conditions, he might not protest the blow, but since he is already hurt, he lets out a howl. To the Mexican government, it seemed that critics were stomping on both feet when they were already hurting badly.

BARBASCO

One of the industries in Mexico most controlled by foreign capital is the chemical-pharmaceutical industry. From the beginning of the Echeverría period at least 15 of the largest 500 firms in Mexico were pharmaceutical firms, with a capital of 640 million pesos, of which 600 million, or 94 percent, belonged to 14 of them. These fourteen were branches of foreign firms, ten American and four European.[27] To control these firms would be a great achievement, and Echeverría therefore moved in that direction. He looked particularly for the weak point of the industry, which he found in barbasco, the basic material from which steroid hormones are extracted and from which the active ingredient in birth control pills is derived.

Steroids are so important to the Mexican economy that "they constitute over 60 percent of all Mexican pharmaceutical exports and 15 percent of all chemical exports. They occupy tenth place on the list of Mexican export articles of industrial origin, and with regard to the value of exports in the chemical industry they occupy second place, after phosphoric acid.[28]

The prospect of the earnings generated by barbasco was tempting, but the transnational firms would not allow Mexico to integrate all the knowledge for the final production of the product. Thus, even when PROQUIVEMEX, a state firm, was established to process barbasco, it had to allow the transnationals to manufacture the finished product. Mexico, therefore, found its hands tied because it could not compete with its resources and its own primary materials. In addition, the European companies that traditionally had extracted steroids from animals (mainly the ox) were becoming increasingly inclined toward synthetic production to reduce costs. That development collided directly with the plans of the Mexican government to control the industry.

Another basic problem was that the lands where barbasco grew were being reduced because of clearing and agricultural use. By 1974, 80 percent of the 7.6 million hectares that had been used for barbasco had been converted to other uses, while the yield per plant declined, from 6 percent to 4 percent of diosgenina (the chemical component used to produce the steroids).

At the beginning of 1975 PROQUIVEMEX began to control all the transactions relative to the picking, processing, and sale of barbasco. The announced objectives of the program were to improve the welfare of the peasants and to protect the natural resources of Mexico.

PROQUIVEMEX was a mixed firm of 80 percent state capital and 20 percent transnational capital. It followed a propeasant policy in which it tried to distribute part of the profits to the pickers. This policy was inspired in part by student protests about the exploitation suffered by the pickers. It intended to increase the resources of the peasants to the level of the *ejido* in order to reduce the power of rural intermediaries and local bosses (*caciques*) and to develop new rural industries using nonbarbasco vegetable resources. To industrialize the production of primary products is a dream that Mexicans want to realize in many areas.

The pharmaceutical firms opposed the policy, however, and stopped buying barbasco to press the government to reject the plan. They were prepared to withstand the assault, since they had accumulated one year's stock of the product, and they also hoped that the change of administration in 1976 would give them an opportunity to negotiate the matter. It should be noted that the government had rejected a plan to create popular pharmacies to control the distribution of medicines and to weaken the power of the foreign firms.

In 1976 the government found itself in the position of having to buy barbasco from the peasants and warehouse it, even though the state lacked the resources to subsidize such a policy. Thus Echeverría announced as a major goal of the government the sale of barbasco to Japan. That same year the production of henequen dropped, costing the government 2 million pesos a day in subsidies to the henequen growers. The production of rubber fell, as well as cotton, leading to the problems in Sonora already discussed. And even though the barbasco pickers were not organized on the basis of this activity, to stop buying their product could have provoked serious political conflicts.

The government made use of the peasants, and through PRO-QUIVEMEX it organized two massive demonstrations calling for the nationalization of the foreign chemical firms. At the same time, the government left **PROQUIVEMEX** out of the negotiations, and its officials became radicalized and began to transform the conflict into a broader political question.

They began to demand payment of the right to exploit the wild areas, such as hills (*derecho de monte*) for the term of 25 years, totaling 470 million pesos, and accused the Europeans of evading taxes of 1 billion pesos a year by overbilling. The private sector continued to oppose the government, charging it with intervening in business and of trying to give its policy an anti-imperialist appearance.

Finally, after losing a great deal of support and enduring more conflict, the government negotiated and accepted what the firms had offered from the beginning. This action caused friction and provided more basis for the antigovernment rumor campaigns and social disturbances of 1976.

THE LAWS OF TECHNOLOGY AND FOREIGN INVESTMENT

In 1971 spokesmen of diverse sectors joined their voices to those of some politicians and respected economists on the issue of the great quantity of money that was leaving the country in the form of profits and exemptions in the hands of foreign investors. Very quickly, the discussion was carried to the level of questioning whether Mexico's sovereignty was being threatened by the current rules of the game of foreign investment. The result was that at the end of 1972 the president introduced a pair of laws to promote national investment and to regulate foreign investment. It caused a great stir, as once again the government was attacked for intervening in the economy.

Nevertheless, the government and domestic and foreign investors were all interested in the creation of a legal framework to organize the fragmented body of laws that existed in the area of foreign investment. That would make it possible to readjust the responsibilities of the different participants[29] and permit the government to control investment more fully, as well as limit somewhat the percentage of participation in certain industries and economic activities. In itself, the foreign investment law changed only certain percentages, although it made the usual declarations of independence from foreign control.

The point at which the new legal framework perhaps most affected U.S. interests was perhaps in the Law of the Transfer of Technology, which lent support to the negotiation of technology at lower prices and to the stimulation of technological development in Mexico. It could also lead to greater freedom of trade and less payment of royalties.

But this law did not alter the agreements of exclusivity that accompanied the sale of "know-how," the competition for which had wreaked havoc among Mexican industrialists and had made them oppose such agreements. On the other hand, the paranoia of the Mexican bourgeoisie caused it to be so concerned about persuading people that this law was an unwarranted intrusion of government into business that the point was missed that both this law and the foreign investment law could play an important political and symbolic role.

Although these laws were considered complementary and were negotiated in one package, they were portrayed by business as a Third World and anti-U.S. maneuver. The U.S. response began to intensify, putting both the Mexican government and the economy in a difficult situation, while the Mexican bourgeoisie hoped that the neighbors to the north would resolve the problems caused by their own myopia and paranoia.

THE U.S. RESPONSE

The desire for Mexican independence and the new Third World policy came quickly into conflict with the American reality: there would be no concessions for Mexico. In the first place, the U.S. put the emphasis on illegal immigrants and began to return large numbers of Mexican workers. According to American sources, in 1975 the U.S. deported 700,000 Mexicans;[30] this figure was 100,000 higher than in 1974, according to Bartra.[31] From 1971 to 1975 the U.S. deported 2.8 million Mexicans.[32]

To slow the flow of Mexicans to the United States, or to deport them in mass, eliminates a great source of revenue[33] for Mexico, and thus the country is highly sensitive to this issue. To suspend this source of foreign currency strongly contracts the Mexican market and intensifies the misery in the country.

In 1971 Nixon imposed a 10 percent emergency excise tax on imports.[34] In 1974 U.S. exports of LP gas to Mexico were stopped and then rationed, affecting Northern and Southern Baja California, Sonora, Chihuahua, Coahuila, Nuevo León, Sinaloa, Durango, and Zacatecas, states that depended 100 percent on this source, and Jalisco, San Luis Potosí, and

Tamaulipas, which were dependent on this source for 50 percent of their gas. In July 1974 the U.S. government restricted the export of scrap iron to Mexico. Since 20 percent of Mexican steel production depended on this input, it gravely affected Mexican production just when the government was managing large construction projects such as INFONAVIT and FOVISSTE.[35]

That same year, 1974, the purchases of Mexican meat by the United States collapsed, just when Mexico needed to export more than ever as a result of a widespread drought. To cap off the year, the U.S. approved the Trade Law of 1974, which eliminated preferential treatment of a series of items exported by Mexico, such as textiles, electronic products, steel, glass, shoes, and more. Also, to protect U.S. commercial interests, the U.S. revised the antidumping statute even though there had been no charge that Mexico had engaged in such activity. Finally, the U.S. excluded all OPEC members from the generalized system of tariff preferences.[36]

In 1976, seventy-six U.S. congressmen sent a letter to President Gerald Ford advising him about a pro-Communist trend in Mexico. The letter made the following points:

1. The Mexican government had given amnesty to hundreds of Soviet agents, who had directed the bloody events of 1968.[37]
2. At least 1,000 non-Mexican Communists and radical journalists were in key government positions.[38]
3. The Mexican government had established political, economic, and cultural relations with all Communist countries in the world.[39]
4. As a diversion or provocation, Echeverría's government perpetrated waves of terrorist attacks that were not the fault of self-proclaimed leftists.
5. Recent changes in the constitution of Mexico undermined the legal basis of private property.[40]
6. Recent introduction of textbooks for obligatory use in schools.[41]
7. Persistent use of Communist rhetoric, anti-Communist demagoguery, and calls by high government officials for a domestic class struggle.
8. Political inaction with regard to thousands of land invasions throughout Mexico, usually by armed bands under non-Mexican leadership.
9. Open declaration that the collectivization of the countryside is a governmental goal, combined with strong government pressure on the rural population to unite collectively.[42]

The U.S. congressmen asked that serious attention be given to Mexico and ended the letter by saying: "We already understand the lesson of Cuba, and we do not want to see 65 million enslaved Mexicans nor a cactus curtain along the Rio Grande."[43]

According to the American Chamber of Commerce, the letter was in support of the political candidacy of Jimmy Carter.[44] It is clear, however, that the 76 congressmen were the spokesmen of the Mexican interests that for six years had blocked Echeverría's attempts to correct somewhat the deteriorated development model in Mexico. These interests canceled any initiatives that might have carried Mexico to a wealthier economic stage and with greater socioeconomic harmony. The letter to Ford was a good example of the distorted and deformed complaints that were raised like battleflags by the interests that opposed Echeverría. Some of the critics even tried to make it appear that the only way out of the problem was a coup d'état.

CHAPTER 6

End of the Sexenio: Coup d'État?

The constant use of rumor and innuendo unsettled and confused many citizens as well as some politicians and foreign observers. The double meanings were so confusing that even when the source was assumed to be internal, many times the implication was otherwise. Furthermore, messages occasionally evoked two responses: the left, to whom the message might be aimed, usually supported it, while the right would interpret the message in its own way and discuss it energetically. The stream of rumors in Echeverría's regime finally short-circuited communications in general and resulted in two versions of a rumored coup d'état found throughout the length and breadth of Mexico. They took the following forms.

The leftist version was that the right, led by the Monterrey Group, would carry out a coup in the South American style. That is, that the Mexican bourgeoisie was inclined to abandon democracy in order to let the military run the country. Echeverría reinforced this version when he denounced the meeting that took place in Chipinque, Monterrey, where in effect the coup possibility was mentioned and where money was collected for a press campaign against Echeverría, of which the president was aware.

The bourgeois version was that Echeverría would carry out a "self-coup" to remain in power and would install a *"maximato"* (dictatorship), supposedly supported by the army.

For its part, the army constantly made the traditional declarations about its neutrality and constitutionality. In addition, Echeverría had followed a very intelligent policy with the armed forces, one that ensured that they would stay within constitutional limits. During the period under study there were 1,519 army retirements, which apparently included 486 generals.[1] These retirements gave rise to a series of promotions (see Appendix O) that allowed younger officers to rise in the ranks. These young officers, therefore, had reason to be grateful to Echeverría. On the other hand, the army had also changed. It was now better educated and numerous officers were used by Echeverría in his administration.

This promotion process was inevitable, for the old military leadership that had emerged during the Revolution or during the Second World War no longer existed. By virtue of the fact that there had been no internal wars, but only repressive campaigns such as Tlatelolco, Guerrero, Plan Condor, and so on, the basis for promotion was through study and theoretical development, rather than success on the battlefield. The attraction for the soldiers was good employment, good salaries, privileges, and civil power.

Approximately 90 percent of army officers are products of the military schools. During the period 1935–76, 64 percent of military officials had university or military school education (considered to be at the university level); 53 percent of political-military officials had this level of education. By comparison, 82 percent of civil political leaders had a university education.[2]

This status allowed the military to participate at another level, no longer as a pressure group, but as part of the apparatus of decision making. Even though soldiers never left the PRI—they remained in the Leandro Valle Association and thus did not abandon their political status—now as part of the bureaucratic machinery they acquired greater importance.

Of course, the foregoing does not mean that the old soldiers did not enrich themselves. Echeverría also gave them the benefits of bureaucracy: stores, homes, improved pensions, and increased salaries. In addition, according to Alan Riding, they received lucrative customs appointments in the northern provinces.[3] Thus, soldiers were less interested than any other group in changing a system that favored them openly and allowed them to enjoy great benefits.

Moreover, the system demonstrated great agility and flexibility for resolving conflicts. By 1976 it had overcome the deterioration of the 1970s, and even if symbolically the system had deteriorated more, the state had made good use of its repressive capacities for tranquilizing dissidents within it.

Mexican authoritarianism consisted of the institutionalization of a limited pluralism, in which only certain types of associations were permitted: namely, those that were not hostile to the governing group.[4]

Such a political system showed itself to be useful for the continuation of Mexican capitalism, since it was not necessary to take radical measures in order to maintain the system.

In addition, the political system knew how to use rewards to maintain control. This aspect was important, since it is not sufficient for the system merely to co-opt; it must also reward, motivate, and provide incentives. For example, some of the senators who supported the president in October 1968 with a favorable declaration in the Senate had the following positions in the 1970–76 sexenio:

> Manuel Bernardo Aguirre, president of the Grand Commission of the Senate, became secretary of agriculture and livestock and later governor of Chihuahua.
>
> Gonzalo Bautista O'Farril became governor of Puebla, although he was subsequently ejected by students.
>
> Carlos Loret de Mola became governor of Yucatán.
>
> Hermenegildo Cuenca Díaz became secretary of national defense and later candidate for governor of Baja California. Although he died before the elections, his candidacy was a result of the direct intervention of Echeverría.[5]
>
> Rafael Murillo Vidal became governor of Veracruz.
>
> Manuel Sánchez Vite became president of PRI and governor of Hidalgo.
>
> Eulalio Gutiérrez Treviño became governor of Coahuila.

Thus, the system demonstrated that the investment in party discipline could produce considerable returns.

Another example is edifying. Of the four officials who resigned after the events of June 10, 1971, three returned to relatively high posts. General Flores Curiel, director of police and transit of the Federal District, returned to the Senate and later was named governor of Nayarit. Julio Sánchez Vargas, attorney general, was named director of SOMEX.[6] Alfonso Martínez Domínguez, chief of the Department of the Federal District, six years later reappeared as governor of Nuevo León.

The fourth politician was Enrique Herrera, subdirector of communications, who resigned. I have no information about his political future nor evidence that he resigned because of the student conflict. Possibly, his resignation only coincided with the events of June 1971.

The Mexican political system has a seasonality of sexennial change that functions as a refresher for the politicians and provides opportunities for aspiring young politicians through the retirement of older officials—as in painless dentistry, there are extractions and adaptations to change. The Mexican politician prepares himself for leaving as if it were a psychoprophylactic childbirth in which political power is delivered. But he knows that the system of rewards (power, money, prestige) is well worth the pain.

Echeverría's term came to its conclusion, but not without turbulence. The president himself provoked an unusual succession by naming six candidates for public discussion. This action spurred enormous political activity, giving Echeverría considerable capacity for maneuver on the eve of his departure. A shade of democracy was added to the system and contributed to discarding the coup d'etat as a political option. Echeverría did it to demonstrate that at least there was real political activity on the part of the PRI, since opposition parties were so weak as to be unable to put forth a single candidate. In 1976 not even the PAN was able to do so.

And so there were commentaries like this one of Marquis Childs: "The one-party system (neither revolutionary nor independent, according to the cynics), under the domination of the Partido Revolucionario Independiente [sic] of López Portillo, guarantees his election."[7] It is interesting that Childs inadvertently replaced Institucional with Independiente. An election with only one candidate, however, would rip the mask off of Mexican "democracy." For that reason, even though no one understood this style of political campaign, it was better to have six candidates, all from the PRI. By means of this preelectoral race López Portillo was able to eliminate the secretaries who were his competitors so that they would not hinder him.[8] Thus, Porfirio Muñoz Ledo, secretary of labor, became president of PRI; Augusto Gómez Villanueva, secretary of agrarian reform, became secretary general of PRI; Jesús Reyes Heroles, president of PRI, became director of the Mexican Institute of Social Security; Gálvez Betancourt, director of IMSS, became secretary of labor; Enrique Olivares Santana, leader of the Senate, went to Agrarian Reform; Mario Ramón Beteta, undersecretary of finance, became secretary of the treasury; and Hugo Cervantes del Río, secretary of the presidency, became president of the PRI in the Federal District.

Some were of the opinion that putting Muñoz Ledo and Gómez Villanueva (according to rumors, Echeverría's favorites) into the PRI was intended to impose on the candidate a new cabinet, but apparently the presidential campaign was managed by López Portillo and these two politicians were neutralized.

In any case the 1976 presidential campaign seemed to put the final touch on a presidential term characterized by conflict. López Portillo traveled to Monterrey, where he demonstrated before the press that there was an understanding between him and the Alfa business group. The result was seen at the beginning of 1977, when the secretary of the treasury announced that businessmen had signed ten agreements with the public sector in important industries. According to Loaeza, "The truce began, and the groups involved in the conflict seemed disposed to reconciliation and unity."[9]

That was not entirely true. The bourgeoisie was in fact negotiating with a new group in power and establishing new rules of the game. Sánchez Mejorada declared: "If we were rumormongers in talking about a coup d'etat and a freezing of bank accounts [under the previous government], then now we should talk about all the positive things that are likely to happen in the near future."[10]

With this thinly veiled threat about what business had done and what it could do, the only thing lacking was to say that Echeverría was an emissary of the past, and that while López Portillo lasted, there would be an understanding, but after that no one could predict what might happen. The bourgeoisie tried to make Echeverría an irrelevant "lame duck" right from beginning of his successor's presidential campaign in the fall of 1975. But the hand of the president was felt until November 1976 in Sonora and would be felt afterward as president-for-life of the Center for Economic and Social Studies of the Third World, as ambassador plenipotentiary, and most of all, as powerful expresident of Mexico.

CHAPTER 7

Conclusion

It is difficult to conclude the analysis of a presidential term in a few pages, as it is also difficult to conclude a book and to say that here are my conclusions and they must suffice. Nevertheless, in these last pages I want to summarize the outstanding aspects of Echeverría's term. But first I want to make a small digression.

I believe that it is a mistake to characterize distinct periods of history by the name of one chief executive after another, such as Cardenismo, Alemanismo, or Echeverrismo. Throughout this work I have tried to demonstrate that it is incorrect to attribute the events that occur in a country solely to the will of the president. I do not deny that the presidency concentrates great power and perhaps a great capacity for decision making, which can vary by historical period. But to go from there to the proposition that the president has an almost omnipotent power of decision and execution involves too large a leap. To call the period 1970–76 the age of Echeverría is simply a verbal convention.

That is not to deny, however, that there have been presidential periods in Mexico that have produced radical transformations in the economy and in politics. Indeed, some individual presidents have left profound impressions on the system, whether because of the importance of the period or because of the influence that their political associates had on subsequent events. This is true, for example, of Plutarco Elías Calles, with the creation of the Central Bank and the official revolutionary party; of Cárdenas, with his expropriation of oil and railroads; and of Alemán, with his irrigation projects and protection of business. In addition, both Cárdenas and Alemán continued to play important roles in the political life of Mexico long after their presidential terms, and their political "teams" (*grupos*) continued to be active for decades. Cárdenas's son, Cuauhtémoc, was a presidential candidate in 1988, and Alemán's son was appointed an ambassador in 1989. Echeverría's daughter was a high official in the government of Mexico City in 1989.

In the case of Echeverría it is difficult to assess his personal importance and the impact of his presidency on national life because insufficient time has passed to be able to judge the long-term importance of the president and his men. But as a first approximation we can say several things. First, Echeverría changed the rules of the game for the selection of the PRI presidential candidate. After him, all the candidates were of bureaucratic origin, rather than having come up through electoral office. Second, he showed the dominant class that nothing could be taken for granted as far as government-business relations were concerned. Third, he showed the dominated classes (workers, peasants) that the state still had powerful instruments for control and repression. Control was demonstrated by the promotion of dissidence in the electrical workers' conflict, and repression was illustrated by the paramilitary Falcons and the student repression of 1971.

Even though it is difficult to evaluate a historical period after such a short interval, I believe that the following remarks are valid conclusions.

First of all, Echeverría was confronted by rapidly deteriorating conditions at the beginning of his presidency. The regime experienced symbolic deterioration, too, in which the population ceased to feel unified around the PRI government, had stopped believing in the goodness of the Mexican Revolution, and found it difficult to participate politically because the "revolutionary family" had closed the doors to such participation.

Echeverría was unable to gauge the strength of the popular unrest from his position as secretary of government in 1968. After an extensive political-electoral campaign in 1970 he pursued the pacification of the country to reduce the likelihood of outright rebellion. But if the political calming of the country was the major goal during his presidency, some of the steps that he took toward that end can be seen as mistaken.

The first mistake was in trying to correct everything in one stroke, without creating the necessary political preconditions. In such matters the political risks and unintended consequences were seldom evaluated correctly.

I do not doubt that Echeverría acted from good faith and good intentions. But even if we recognize his great ability to pursue such a large objective as the pacification of the country, there is not sufficient evidence to persuade us that the errors committed in the pursuit of that objective were justified. Most notable among these errors was the high economic cost incurred in the effort to achieve social and political peace and the priority given to repressive measures, including the modernization of the army and its incorporation into civil power.

This policy of repression is all the more difficult to understand since the Mexican political system enjoys enough flexibility to permit its leaders to guide it at crucial times in the direction of co-optation instead of repression. I am convinced that in those six years there were sufficient conditions for coming to terms with civil society peacefully and leaving the repressive option, if necessary at all, for truly extreme situations.

The irony is that with the use of repression the state's control of the masses only deteriorated. With regard to labor the Congreso del Trabajo had been in existence only four years when it fell under the control of the CTM, without coming up with solutions for the challenge presented by independent unions. Echeverría allowed the two labor groups to confront each other in the electrical strike in order to weaken them both, the easier to keep them under government control. The conflict was eventually settled by military occupation of the firms and arbitration by the government. Among the peasants independent organizations also began to emerge that engaged in violent forms of action such as land invasions. In short, guerrilla activity made it very clear that Mexico was at the point of a generalized explosion in the countryside. In response, the government distributed more land to peasants and mobilized the army to repress dissent that could not otherwise be controlled. At one point 15 percent of the entire army was in Guerrero to annihilate the guerrillas.

In other words, Echeverría's responses were similar in the two areas. In the labor area he permitted union strife to weaken both labor groups to bring them under greater governmental control. In the countryside he accelerated land distribution to give at least the impression of a response, but used repression where co-optation did not appear sufficient.

Completing the social picture, the middle classes, which traditionally had sustained the system, rebelled by calling for greater political participation. That is why the events of 1968 so threatened the system. One sector of the population considered co-opted by the system—the one called "popular" by the PRI—broke out of and overflowed the channels of control. New political parties were formed in the aftermath of the events of 1968, indicating that the middle classes would no longer be as politically docile.

Considering how closely the middle classes had been integrated in the political system up to this time, however, the government responded with unaccustomed energy in its repression of the student demonstrations with the great massacre of October 2, 1968. This event had its epilogue in the police and paramilitary repression of June 10, 1971, whose function was to end with one quick stroke the vestiges of student activism. Echeverría incidentally used the student affair as a justification to discharge various officials and to pave the way for a government that recognized few limits on its power. In reality, Echeverría employed the entire student movement as a pretext for constructing a more authoritarian regime characterized by the practices of kidnapping, disappearing, and killing civilians who seemed to offer any resistance to the regime. These tactics, of course, alienated the large middle class, which had been a major support of the regime up to this time.

The situation of systemic deterioration involved a series of internal contradictions that impeded the realization of presidential goals. With the advantage of hindsight it can be seen that the president was very eager to achieve political triumphs without considering either the economic costs or the probability that immediate political victories might create serious political problems in the future.

An example is the case of land redistribution in Sonora in November 1976. In Echeverría's effort to recover the regime's image as champion of agrarianism, his government tolerated land invasions and then gave a great deal of land to the peasants. The land distribution not only resulted in a severe reduction in the production of wheat, but also demonstrated to the peasants that going outside the channels of regime participation could bear fruit. At the same time, the land redistribution left an important segment of the agricultural bourgeoisie angry at the government—and all this merely to recover the regime's agrarian image.

In the realm of the purely political the new electoral policy offered the vote to eighteen-year-olds and facilitated the emergence of new political parties. Although these developments may have been laudable in general, they created a problem for the Mexican type of democracy because of the attendant decline in the percentage of the vote going to the PRI. This change created future pressures either to allow the opposition to win elections or to force the regime to continue to steal elections through electoral fraud. The regime apparently chose the latter course.

Without denying that the government sacrificed economic considerations in favor of political ones, we can say that it is valid to engage in such a policy when the economy is strong and when the government has the support of the people. That, however, was certainly not true in this case, as the country was beginning to suffer serious economic difficulties. In addition, the regime faced an economically mature but politically myopic bourgeoisie that made such a change of policy direction an arduous task. Each time government actions made it appear that the state was trying to salvage Mexican capitalism and establish the basis for future expansion—including correcting an egotistical godson who wanted to satisfy only his immediate desires at the expense of his longer-term gains—his awareness of his own strength led the godson to undermine the authority of the godfather.

The situation was aggravated by the lack of evaluation of consequences, a constant in political decision making during his term. The anti-Zionist vote in foreign policy is an example of a policy decision that was made without any anticipation of possible results. In domestic policy Echeverría's opening of the doors of government to youth displaced a whole generation of politicians who lost their turn to exercise power, while it is doubtful that the regime gained from the students as much sympathy as it expected. Take the example of Francisco Javier Alejo, who replaced Flores de la Peña in the Department of National Resources. The government put forward the version that Javier Alejo had been a student leader in 1968, a claim that was unanimously denied by the militants of that movement. Instead, it was rumored that he was appointed because he was a relative of the president's wife.

This practice of not considering the effects of policies distorted the results relative to the original goals. Another example is population policy, as described by an American observer:

> Echeverría had had more difficulties than most Mexican presidents in consolidating his power with the Partido Revolucionario Institucional (PRI). The economic problems required that he take some major policy initiative to give the impression that something was being done and that he was in control. A dramatic, highly publicized population policy change offered just such a possibility. . . . It was no accident that Echeverría responded to the criticism of his economic policies with a policy to reduce population growth rates. Such a program could give the appearance of . . . "explaining" the recession as a consequence of too-rapid population growth rather than as a consequence of Echeverría's economic policies.[1]

This brings us to a most sensitive point: How do we judge a presidential term, policy, or system—by its intentions or by its actual accomplishments? In Echeverría's case his goals were laudable enough and can be summarized as nationalism, anti-imperialism, and revitalization of the system. It seems clear that he attempted to act according to these goals and ideological principles. Unfortunately, his achievements were extended confrontation, destabilization of the economy, repressive pacification of the country, and alienation of the regime's allies in all sectors of society.

Echeverría's positions challenged strong economic, ideological, and political interests, and thus his policies faced vigorous opposition from all sorts of groups, including some previously allied to the government. The bourgeoisie, for example, sped up the rate of capital flight and tied the country even more to the purposes of foreign capitalists, especially those from the U.S. Each measure advanced by Echeverría in an effort to limit foreign influence in the country was attacked by the bourgeoisie as being too interventionist. As a result, the regime was unable to restructure Mexican capitalism on a just and revitalized basis. The only outcome was that the bourgeoisie made more money than ever, without being required to reinvest it in the country. In fact, business sent its money as far as possible from the needs of the nation; in 1976 alone $27 billion fled the country, while the external debt reached almost $20 billion. A friend of mine in the government once jokingly said to me, "If this money hadn't fled the country, we could own Central America by now." It is clear that the dominant class and the government had totally different objectives.

Many people have commented that compared to the presidents that succeeded him, especially López Portillo, Echeverría was not so bad. A joke was told about how Echeverría came to the presidency: One day Díaz Ordaz was complaining about how much he was being criticized and attacked at the end of his term, and he reached the conclusion that the Mexican people had been unfair to him. So he decided to take revenge on Mexico by selecting Echeverría as the next president. Of course, the same could be said of Echeverría—that in order to make himself look good he took revenge on the country and selected López Portillo as his successor. Was this also true in the case of de la Madrid and Salinas?

Was Mexico simply going through a period of bad presidents? Or does the level of Mexican development point to the systemic inefficiency of an extremely powerful presidency? Perhaps the country is attempting a high level of economic and social modernization with an outmoded political structure.

Perhaps all of these ideas are part of the answer, although I would like to venture an additional hypothesis. Until Gustavo Díaz Ordaz, all Mexican presidents had experience as popular leaders, whether as revolutionary *caudillos* or elected officials, which gave them a certain sensitivity and taught them how the national political game works. Since Echeverría, however, presidents have risen in politics by ascending the bureaucratic ladder and through understanding the intrigues of palace rivalries that surround the exercise of power. They are accustomed to the backroom bureaucratic struggle, characterized by the presence of the professional automaton described by Lawrence Peter, where anything is justified in the name of discipline and conformity and where promotion is achieved by favoritism and not by political ability. They are far less accustomed to the actual realities of campaigning and governing and hence to the necessity of dealing with the many disparate and competing groups in Mexican political society, as opposed to the competing groups within the government itself.

Thus in 1970 began a new style of politics. The new type of electoral campaign may be an excellent spectacle of media and political cinematography, but it cannot substitute for the traditional presidential campaign or for the candidate's lack of previous electoral experience. Thus, the president, who is accustomed to receiving obedience, falls into all types of excesses, even those derived from whim, which ultimately place his personal imprint on the government. But perhaps he leaves no lasting results, because in the labyrinth of the bureaucracy the old-style boss is left behind and abandoned. Perhaps the era of the caudillo or political boss in the style of Miguel Alemán, Lázaro Cárdenas, or Gonzalo N. Santos of San Luis Potosí has passed.

In any case Echeverría appears to be a "political transition" between the two types of presidents: the politician and the bureaucrat. Although he emerged from the bureaucratic ranks, he refused to develop a regime totally confined to the office and he traveled all around Mexico and the world. Even though to an extent he sought the perpetuation of his power as a *cacique* beyond his term of office, as had previous expresidents, his conception of bureaucratic discipline was adequate to restrain him from going very far in that direction. Thus his term of office was a transitional one because it appeared to be a step toward a new type of presidency and a new form of government.

POSTSCRIPT, 1990

In 1987 I delivered a copy of this book to Luis Echeverría. As I left, he said to me: "Look, if you are going to write about the deterioration of presidentialism, you must write about my successor."

I have encountered many people who were of the opinion that in the light of the presidents that followed, Echeverría could almost be seen as a national hero. One friend of mine said to me in a sarcastic tone: "Recent Mexican presidents demonstrate very well the saying of George Bernard Shaw: 'There is nothing so bad that it couldn't be worse.'"

In reality, from Echeverría on, Mexican presidents have ceased to govern and instead have merely administered the government. This new role is the result of a change in the standards of politics and in the conceptual content of such standards. In the first place, the men who became president since 1970 have not had the experience of governing, whether as senators, deputies, or governors. Rather, up to and including the 1988 election, Mexican presidents have ascended by means of the bureaucratic ladder, where ability consisted of obeying, rather than setting policy and giving orders.

For the "political" presidents before 1970, politics was the art of guiding society within a framework of social peace, even if they used repression to achieve this objective. This "art" consisted, among other things, of negotiation, conciliation, co-optation, demagoguery, repression, and manipulation. Efficiency consisted of showing that the system maintained social peace, even if the economic and social costs were very high. Part of the process was to administer exemplary "lessons" to the working class movement, including putting dissident labor leaders in jail for decades, as was the case of the railroad union leaders Demetrio Vallejo and Valentín Campa, jailed in 1958 and released only at the beginning of the 1970s.

For the "bureaucratic" presidents who came to power beginning in 1970, efficiency is a problem of accounting. The national and international accounts (balance of payments, commercial balance, external debt) must be acceptable. Some of these presidents, such as Miguel de la Madrid, have had very interesting confrontations with the International Monetary Fund (IMF) in which they demonstrated their efficiency in achieving a surplus in the "primary budget" (excluding debt service). For this achievement, according to de la Madrid, Mexico deserves good treatment by the IMF and the foreign banks, so that the country can continue paying the foreign debt. Unfortunately, debt service (both internal and external) does affect the budget, whether primary or secondary. The government's main concern is to demonstrate that the accounts are efficient, independent of whether the economic and social situation continues along a catastrophic course (once again, Bernard Shaw?). Purchasing power is in decline, the economy is stagnant, but Mexico pays its debts. Both the (primary) budget and the commercial balance[1] have moved toward a surplus, partly because of good administration, but the government has no money to spend and the economy has ceased to import—but the balance sheet looks good. Thus the "bureaucratic" presidents (some call them "technocrats")[2] appear to be efficient.

Nevertheless, we must ask what happened. A transferral of power occurred from the politicians to the bureaucrats, or as I prefer to call them, "the financiers."

THE POWER NETWORK

Mexico appears to be governed by various groups of politicians related to each other in a network of power. Within this network is a series of groups and subgroups whose composition varies in terms of membership, location, activity, family relations, and so on.[3]

Part of the power network that Luis Echeverría brought to the presidency resided in two military men: General Rodolfo Sánchez Taboada, who had been president of PRI and with whom Echeverría was a close collaborator, and José Guadalupe Zuno, former governor of Jalisco and Echeverría's father-in-law. Sánchez Taboada, a native of Puebla, had strong interests in that state, which had been dominated by the Avila Camacho family. This connection suggests that Echeverría enjoyed the support of that group. For example, Díaz Ordaz was from Puebla and appointed Echeverría secretary of government. In addition, Manuel Avila Camacho had close relations with Cárdenas. Thus the network appears relatively clear. General Zuno was governor of Jalisco and had close relations with the revolutionary generals (Obregón, Calles, Cárdenas, Avila Camacho), which he could use to promote his son-in-law.

The transition from Echeverría to López Portillo seems to indicate two things. First, Echeverría decided to punish the supporters of Moya Palencia for having demonstrated a lack of discipline in attempting a *madruguete* ("early morning coup"), declaring their support for Moya before the president indicated his choice as the next president.[4] Second, Echeverría decided to name his good friend, companion of adolescent adventures, member of the same generation, and neighbor, who was also an "expert" in planning since his time in the Department of National Patrimony at the end of the 1950s and the beginning of the 1960s.[5] López Portillo received intensive training during the 1970–76 presidential term, moving from undersecretary of the presidency, where he controlled public investment, to director of the Federal Electricity Commission, one of the largest parastatal enterprises, and from there to secretary of the treasury, one of the most important posts in the government.

There is no doubt that López Portillo was a good bureaucrat who had expertise in the management of the financial and economic problems facing Mexico in 1976 in the form of monetary instability, increased indebtedness, high inflation, a slowdown in economic growth, and so forth.

The transition from López Portillo to de la Madrid appears as the natural transmission of power to one more member of the financial group. Miguel de la Madrid developed mainly in the ranks of the financial sector of the Mexican government. He began his financial-bureaucratic career in the Bank of Mexico, where in 1960 he was appointed adviser to the director. In 1965 he became assistant director general of credit in the Department of the Treasury; in 1970 he became assistant director of finance of PEMEX, but in 1972 he returned to the treasury as director general of credit. In 1975 he became undersecretary of credit in the same department with López Portillo as secretary. He remained in the treasury until 1979 and then moved to the secretaryship of planning and budgeting. Since he was loyal to the regime institutions as well as to the "political fraternity" of which he was a member, when he became president he appointed former members of the finance group to most of the highest positions in his cabinet. This policy was so notable that one could almost say that the cabinet was monopolized by former bankers of the Bank of Mexico or its subsidiary agencies.

This particular group of the network consolidated its political control with the nomination of Carlos Salinas de Gortari for the presidency. He also rose through the ranks of the Department of the Treasury, under the protection of Miguel de la Madrid. Salinas was assistant to de la Madrid in one position or another for more than twenty years. He was also helped by his father, Raul Salinas, who during a long career in the financial sector was secretary of commerce in the administration of López Mateos and a federal senator during the term of de la Madrid, in addition to being one of the major influences within CONASUPO.

The power network guaranteed that the presidency was retained in the hands of those members of the PRI who maintained close relations over the years, whether through official connections or blood relations. This is another way of describing the "revolutionary family" perceived by Frank Brandenburg.[6]

It is significant that in the election of 1988, when the government slightly opened the process of preselection of candidates for the presidency, of the six candidates[7] who were presented, two (Bartlett and del Mazo) were sons of former governors and two (del Mazo and Salinas) were sons of former secretaries of federal departments.

It is also significant that of the two contenders who received the most votes in the 1988 presidential election,[8] one was the son of a former president (Cuauhtémoc Cárdenas) and the other was the son of a former secretary of a federal department (Carlos Salinas). Even in opposition the power network seeks to maintain its monopoly.

DOMINATION AND DISEQUILIBRIUM

The transition from "politicians" to "bureaucrats" or "financiers" occurred with little conflict, perhaps because Mexico had not yet recovered from the trauma of 1968. Recently, the worsening of the economic crisis gave people reason to believe that if the "experts" took control, surely they would be able to set straight a critical situation that had become virtually permanent since the great industrial economic boom of the 1940s. Nonetheless, the crisis gradually became a catastrophe, including unexpected measures such as the nationalization of the banks, which resulted in the socialization of the debt that the private banks had contracted in the international money markets.

Not only did the external debt continue to grow rapidly, but the standard of living of the majority of the population consistently deteriorated. The transition from one "expert" president (López Portillo) to another (de la Madrid) failed to resolve problems and moreover created the impression of having a president who did not dare to take the reins of government. This widespread feeling manifested itself amply in the days after the earthquake of 1985 and took shape in the form of humor that attacked the president. The following are some representative jokes heard during de la Madrid's presidency:

Emilio Gamboa Patrón (de la Madrid's private secretary) did not seek the 1988 presidential nomination of the PRI because reelection is not permitted in Mexico.

Do you know who are the precandidates of the PRI for the presidency in 1988?
Manuel Bartlett, Alfredo del Mazo, and Miguel de la Madrid, because the latter still doesn't know that he is president.

A man comes to Los Pinos, the presidential house, knocks on the door, and says to the guard: "Say, I want to apply for the job of president."
"What!" responds the guard.
"Yes, I want to apply for the job of president."
"Are you crazy?" asks the guard.
"Why, is that a requirement for the job?" asks the man.

The external debt continued to grow, the purchasing power of the population continued to decline, and capital flight slowed only when the economic crisis cut profits so drastically that the number of dollars available for flight was severely constricted. In addition, the Mexican oil industry demonstrated once again how catastrophic it is for a country to become a monoculture with only one major export. The abyss between the rich and the poor continued to widen.

Nonetheless, contrary to what people in Mexico expected, violence did not break out. The population showed its repudiation of the government by refusing to vote, as almost 67 percent abstained from voting in 1988. The new "expert" president, who as secretary of planning and budgeting had designed the economic policies that brought Mexico to ruin, reinforced the police forces and consolidated the civil power of the military. The few outbreaks of civil discontent were met with the firm hand of a government that was seeking the approval of the United States, putting off the problem of political legitimacy because the government thought that with money—which the president believed could come only from the United States—the regime could recover the popularity that the PRI had once enjoyed.

Salinas de Gortari is collecting heads, just as all civilizations have collected the remains of the dead enemy to nourish their victories.[9] Thus the new president had numerous notorious miscreants arrested, especially leaders of government-related labor unions, who were accused of spectacular wrongdoing. Apparently, the new president believed that this type of "warfare" would provide the nutrients for legitimacy and consensus. But also apparently, the population quickly understood that the conquered "heads" were the result of a private war and the prize of a settling of accounts with those who had failed to support the nomination or election of the new president. The president no doubt hoped to achieve two things with the bold strokes—to settle accounts with political enemies and to persuade the population in general that he was both strong and different from previous presidents.

THE CONTINUED DETERIORATION OF PRESIDENTIALISM

The most interesting paradox regarding the domination of the financial group is that its consolidation of power was gained at the price of the destruction of the Mexican political system's fundamental structure of political equilibrium. In the first place, the cabinet was traditionally used by the president to provide a balance of political, regional, and other forces, such as the political families of Cárdenas, Alemán, and so on. The "financiers" broke this equilibrium by monopolizing the ministries and expelling other groups from the political battle. This practice left such groups with no option but to leave the PRI and to fight against it. At least this is the case with the "Democratic Current" within the PRI in 1988, which had as its antecedent the effort to launch Moya Palencia as an independent candidate in 1976.[10]

The "politicians" found themselves without political space within which to fight for power because all of the space was being monopolized by the "bureaucrats." Where the cabinet had previously provided a space, or a forum, for struggling "institutionally" for power, with the coming of the bureaucrats the cabinet has become an instrument for paying off debts of loyalty and a medium of obedience where dissent is not allowed.[11]

The cabinets of the "bureaucrats" have been more or less consolidated, but they have weakened the PRI regime in general. The president is bureaucratically strong but politically weak.

As far as the state governments are concerned, it appears that here is where the rupture of the political equilibrium is most advanced. On the one hand, regional interests that have been involved in great defeats for the PRI have been pushed aside; for example, the governors of Michoacán and Baja California were retired by Salinas and placed in the federal bureaucracy. On the other hand, the PRI has maintained its position of monopoly and has not recognized the victories that the opposition claimed to have won, most notably in Chihuahua in 1986. The governments of the states, perhaps more than ever, are selected by the central government, and the society reacts more forcefully than ever against this concentration of power. The president has a greater power of selecting candidates, but he confronts greater rejection of those choices by society.

The result is that presidentialism has continually deteriorated. Although on the one hand the president has concentrated greater bureaucratic and political power in the PRI, paradoxically he has lost power with respect to Mexican society and the world at large. The Mexican government no longer has a sufficient base of social support to confront the international banks or the IMF, even if it wanted to, which is not true in any case. The regime is therefore unable to negotiate favorable conditions for the debt because of this weakened domestic position.

As time passes and the crisis worsens, the government finds it increasingly difficult to apply its economic policies. Therefore, instead of convincing people, it imposes its will in an authoritarian way.

The president of the republic can deal with a firm hand with the striking unions and can declare the strikes illegal, as in the case of the transport workers of Route 100 in the Federal District in May 1989. This action can strengthen the government's policy of keeping salaries frozen for six years, but at the same time it strains the so-called Social Pact and jeopardizes the Mexican corporatism that has so strongly sustained the PRI regime, until at least the end of the 1970s (see figure 8.1).

I believe that the Mexican political scene one sees in 1990 is defined by the limits of authoritarianism. There seem to be only two ways out of the impasse: democracy or totalitarianism.

Facing the economic crisis, the PRI can choose to give political benefits instead of economic benefits. This policy would allow it to negotiate in the international arena under the rules of the game of austerity. But an increase in political benefits will bring Mexico a democratic system that will question the strategy of austerity and will interrupt the strategy of requiring wage earners to bear the cost of economic stabilization. This is the democratic scenario, in which the country will see itself ruined economically but will have political democracy.

The totalitarian scenario suggests that the PRI will continue to confront with a firm hand all the appearances of discontent, grounded in the fact that the United States continues to perceive the PRI as the only party that can guarantee stability. This choice implies that the PRI cannot concede electoral defeats or perhaps will concede only minor defeats in order to hide behind them and to maintain a policy of repression toward dissident movements.

This scenario implies two possibilities with regard to the army. It may continue to play its role of repressive arm of the regime, even while its specific power gradually increases. Or it may displace the civil officials that it believes are no longer able to control the situation in the country.

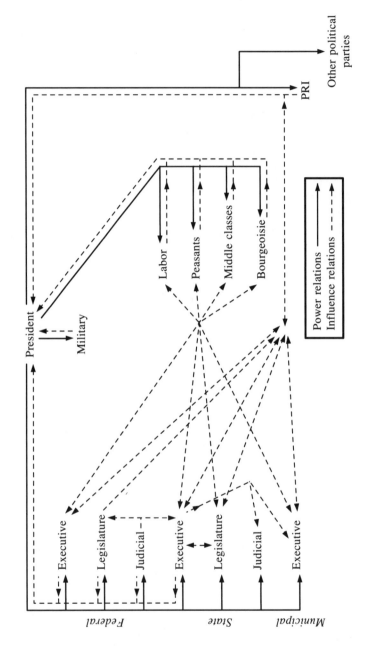

Figure 8.1. Mexican corporatism until the 1970s

A FINAL LOOK AT PRESIDENTIALISM

The strength of Mexican presidentialism is based on the fact that the presidency is at the summit of a pyramid of power that articulates all sectors of society.[12] Sectors are joined in a corporatist-representative structure that uses rewards and punishments of various sorts to maintain itself, as well as social peace. Traditionally, the president could intervene in the selection of deputies, senators, governors, local deputies, local and federal judges, mayors, and even university rectors. The president had the power to distribute favors and rewards, and thus the system of loyalties was oriented toward him.

In the old scheme of Mexican corporatism the president greatly influenced the National Executive Committee of the PRI, along with the various sectors of the party. The president was also the major authority in the selection of governors, and those governors in turn had great influence in the state legislatures. In addition, the president directly controlled local councils and judicial officials. His power extended even to the business organizations that were not formally included in the PRI structure, as well as to other political parties. Some political parties were mere satellites of the regime.

Now, by contrast, the unions have begun to lose the capacity to control their members, and the peasant federations can no longer direct the struggle for land because the government has declared that no more land is available for distribution.[13] The labor organizations can no longer offer political positions to their leaders because these positions have been severely restricted by the PRI's electoral defeats, such as when the PRI lost the Federal District in the 1988 election. The business organizations understand that the government must change its relationship with them to achieve a solution to the crisis. For example, the government must modify tax policy and actually begin to collect most of the taxes that business is currently evading. Political parties that have functioned as puppets of the PRI, such as PPS and PARM, now believe that they can have a better future if they are more independent. The opposition has begun to win positions in local councils, and in 1989 an opposition candidate even won a governorship for the first time in the history of this regime (PAN, in Baja California).

Thus the president's possibilities for continuing to guarantee the distribution of benefits to various groups have diminished greatly in recent years. Therefore, the basis of presidentialism continues to erode and hence presidentialism itself continues to deteriorate.

Appendixes

Appendix A.
National Index of Consumer Prices
(1968 = 100)

Year	Index
1970	108.7
1971	114.6
1972	120.3
1973	134.8
1974	166.8
1975	191.8
1976	222.1

SOURCE: JLP AE-H, 1979.

Appendix B.
Actual Expenditures of the Mexican Federal Government, 1971–76 (in Percent)

Year	Total[a]	Energy	Commu-nications	Social Develop-ment	Industrial Develop-ment	Agriculture & Fisheries	Admin-istration & Defense	Tourism
1971	100	2.7	13.2	23.1	13.2	10.1	37.4	0.4
1972	100	6.5	13.6	22.4	11.5	13.2	32.1	0.6
1973	100	5.4	14.1	21.2	9.7	13.5	35.6	0.5
1974	100	3.6	10.9	22.3	13.3	13.7	35.7	0.5
1975	100	7.2	8.8	21.9	11.1	17.3	33.2	0.5
1976	100	4.5	9.8	25.4	8.2	12.4	39.2	0.7

Actual Expenditures of Parastatal Sector, 1971–76

Year	Total[a]	Energy	Commu-nications	Social Develop-ment	Industrial Develop-ment	Agriculture & Fisheries	Admin-istration & Defense	Tourism
1971	100	56.5	10.9	25.9	—	6.6	0.0	0.1
1972	100	54.0	10.6	28.6	—	6.5	0.0	0.3
1973	100	48.8	9.0	22.6	8.3	8.1	3.1	0.1
1974	100	45.9	8.1	24.0	8.4	10.1	3.3	0.1
1975	100	46.9	8.9	20.7	9.8	11.0	2.7	0.1
1976	100	48.0	7.9	21.6	9.5	10.1	2.6	0.1

SOURCE: JLP AE-H, 1979, pp. 85–98.
[a] Totals may not coincide because of rounding.

Appendix C.1.
Acquisitions by the Public Sector, by Principal Purchasing Entity, 1975

Entity	Value (millions of pesos)	% Total	% Accumulation
Total	108,082	100.0	100.0
Sum of Selected Entities	100,166	92.67	92.67
Petróleos Mexicanos	16,510	15.28	15.28
CONASUPO	12,180	11.27	26.55
Comision federal de Electricidad	11,095	10.27	36.84
Siderúrgica Lázaro Cárdenas Las Truchas	10,023	9.27	46.09
Distribuidora CONASUPO, S.A. de C.V.	5,000	4.63	50.76
Altos Hornos de México, S.A. de C.V.	3,917	3.62	50.72
Instituto Mexicano del Seguro Social	3,899	3.61	57.95
Banco Nacional de Credito Ejidal, S.A.	3,614	3.34	61.29
Guanos y Fertilizantes de México, S.A.	3,475	3.22	64.51
Diesel Nacional, S.A.	3,278	3.03	67.54
Teléfonos de México, S.A.	2,583	2.39	69.93
Cia. de Luz y Fuerza del Centro, S.A.	2,286	2.12	72.05
Ferrocarriles Nacionales de México	2,185	2.02	74.07
Industrias CONASUPO, S.A. de C.V.	1,977	1.83	75.90
Departamento del Distrito Federal	1,636	1.51	77.41
Productora e Importadora de Papel, S.A.	1,484	1.37	78.78
Vehículos Automotores de México, S.A. de C.V.	1,197	1.11	79.89
Tabacos Mexicanos, S.A. de C.V.	1,191	1.11	81.00
I.S.S.S.T.E.	1,172	1.08	82.08
Sistema de Transporte Colectivo	1,131	1.05	83.13
CORDEMEX, S.A. de C.V.	839	0.78	83.91
Aeronaves de México, S.A.	737	0.68	84.59
Productos Pequeros, Mexicanos, S.A. de C.V.	686	0.63	85.22
Operadora Nacional de Ingenios, S.A.	629	0.58	85.80
Motores Perkins, S.A.	611	0.57	86.37
Banco de México, S.A.	604	0.56	86.93
Ferrocarril del Pacífico, S.A. de C.V.	596	0.55	87.48
Secretaría de la Defensa Nacional	596	0.55	88.03
Secretaría de Comunicaciones y Transportes	596	0.55	88.57
Nacional de Combustibles de Aviación, S.A.	573	0.53	89.10
Alimentos Balanceados de México, S.A. de C.V.	546	0.51	89.61
Constructora Nacional de Carros de Ferrocarril	533	0.49	90.10
Industrial de Abastos	533	0.49	90.59
Secretaría de Recursos Hidráulicos	512	0.47	91.06

Appendix C.1., *continued.*

Secretaría de Obras Públicas	446	0.41	91.47
Maíz Industrializado CONASUPO, S.A. de C.V.	445	0.41	91.88
Secretaría de Agricultura y Ganaderia	437	0.40	92.28
Mexicana de Autobuses, S.A. de C.V.	425	0.39	92.67
Other Entities	7,916	7.32	99.99

SOURCE: *Revista Expansión*, September 1, 1979, p. 9.

Appendix C.2.
Acquisitions by the Public Sector, by Industry, 1975

Industry	Value (millions of pesos)	% of Total
Total	108,082	100.00
Live animals	445	0.41
Vegetable products	16,367	25.14
Fresh, manufactured, and semi-manufactured foodstuffs, including beverages	4,651	4.30
Minerals	1,283	1.19
Fuels, lubricants and their by-products	6,746	6.24
Chemical products and substances	12,572	11.63
Rubber	1,156	1.07
Hides, pelts, and leather products (except footwear)	34	0.03
Footwear	136	0.13
Wood and wood products (except furniture)	868	0.80
Cellulose, paper, and cardboard products	2,914	2.70
Forms, books, and publications	458	0.42
Textiles and textile products	2,065	1.91
Non-metallic mineral products	1,136	1.05
Glass and glass products	260	0.24
Common metals and their products	8,822	8.16
Machinery and equipment (except electric)	23,185	21.45
Electrical machinery and equipment	5,033	4.66
Electrical materials and products	3,802	3.52
Electronic and communications equipment, goods, and materials	2,732	2.53
Equipment for transportation and service vehicles	3,082	2.85
Medical, surgical, dental, and ophthamological equipment, and instruments	1,591	1.47

Appendix C.2., *continued.*

Industry	Value (millions of pesos)	% of Total
Misc. equipment	1,169	1.08
Repairs, parts, and accessories for equipment and machinery	6,052	5.60
Personal property	997	0.92
Misc. goods otherwise not classified	526	0.49

SOURCE: *Revista Expansión*, September 10, 1976, pp. 10–13.

Appendix D.
Guaranteed Average Prices of National Agricultural Products per Metric Ton, 1970–76 (in Pesos)

Product	1970	1971	1972	1973	1974	1975	1976
Rice (white)	2,780	2,080	2,121	2,600	4,250	5,700	5,700
Rice (palay)	1,100	1,100	1,100	1,100	3,000	3,000	3,300[a]
Barley	0	950	950	1,200	1,200	1,450	1,740
Barley (for malt)	0	1,100	1,100	1,350	1,350	1,600	1,920
Bean	1,750	1,750	1,750	2,150	6,000	4,750	5,000
Bean (popular)	0	0	0	2,000	0	4,500	4,750
Bean (semi-preferred)	0	0	0	2,150	0	0	0
Bean (preferred)	0	0	0	2,300	0	5,000	5,250
Corn	940	940	940	1,200	1,500	1,900	2,340
Sorghum	625	625	725	750	1,000	1,600	1,760
Wheat	800	800	800	870	1,300	1,750	1,750
Sesame seed	2,500	2,500	3,000	3,000	5,000	6,000	6,600
Cotton seed	900	900	900	900	2,200	2,200	2,650
Safflower	1,500	1,500	1,500	1,600	3,000	3,500	3,300[b]
Soya	1,300	1,600	1,800	2,700	3,300	3,500	3,500
Sunflower seed	0	1,800	1,800	2,700	2,700	2,700	2,700
Coconut	8,475	3,725	3,725	3,725	3,725	5,500	6,050
Soya oil	0	0	0	0	0	0	9,401
Coconut oil	0	0	0	0	0	0	0
Soya paste	0	0	0	0	3,530	0	0
Powdered milk	0	0	0	0	23,012	28,948	30,650

SOURCE: JLP AE-H, 1980, pp. 574–75.
[a] Fixed price for sinaloa: 2750 pesos.
[b] Fixed price for irrigated zones: 3,200 pesos.

Appendix E.
Government Anti-Inflationary Program of 1973

1. The government will seek to adjust the pace of total spending in the public sector by reviewing its sectoral distribution and limiting its financing strictly to noninflationary activities.

2. Public sector consumption will be made more efficient through greater planning, more opportune payment schedules, and the rationalization of the purchases of supplies.

3. Care will be taken to allow the money supply to grow in proportion to the growth in real economic activity.

4. Productive activities, especially agriculture, will be financed more fully, and luxury consumption, speculative operations, and excessive accumulation of inventories will be discouraged.

5. Greater employment of industrial and agricultural capacity to increase the supply of foodstuffs, primary goods, and consumer goods.

6. Stimulation of private investment in areas where supplies have been low.

7. Greater monitoring and control of prices, especially between wholesalers and retailers.

8. Consumer education for more rational purchases.

9. Strict monitoring of the relation between price increases and cost increases.

10. Encouragement of the development of rural, urban, and union consumer cooperatives.

11. Promotion of centers of supply and consumption by industrial associations.

12. Rationalization of the export of foodstuffs, primary products, and other articles whose production exceeds internal demand.

13. If necessary, CONASUPO will continue to import grains and other products.

14. Facilitation of the import of products that are scarce in the domestic market.

15. Reduction of import controls and tariffs that adversely affect prices.

16. Encouragement of adequate relations among salary increases, price increases, and increases in productivity, with greater use of the system of tripartite commissions.

SOURCE: Carlos Tello, *La política económica en México* (México, D.F.: Ed. Siglo XXI, 1979), 65–66.

Appendix F.
Index of Imports from the United States, 1970–76
(1953 = 100)

Year	Index
1970	131
1971	135
1972	139
1973	162
1974	206
1975	230
1976	239

SOURCE: J. Wilkie and P. Reich, eds., *Statistical Abstract of Latin America*, vol. 20 (Los Angeles: UCLA) Latin American Center Publications, 1980), Table 2525.

Appendix G.
Distribution of GNP by Activity in Current Prices, 1970–76
(In Percent)

Year	GNP	Agriculture, Livestock & Fish	Industry[a]	Construction	Commerce	Services	Govern- ment
1970	100	11.3	16.6	5.1	29.6	23.8	6.2
1971	100	10.7	16.4	4.8	29.6	24.9	6.5
1972	100	10.3	16.7	5.3	28.9	25.3	6.9
1973	100	11.0	16.5	5.9	29.2	24.7	7.4
1974	100	10.4	16.7	6.1	29.9	23.2	7.6
1975	100	10.1	16.3	6.4	29.2	24.1	8.6
1976	100	9.7	16.8	6.4	27.9	25.3	9.6

SOURCE: JLP A-EH, 1980.
[a] Includes textiles and leather goods, wood, chemicals, minerals, and metal products.

Appendix H.
Published and Executed Presidential Resolutions, by Presidential Period (1915–June 1980)

Period	Published Resolutions			Executed Resolutions		
	No.	Area (hectares)	No. of Beneficiaries	No.	Area (hectares)	No. of Beneficiaries
VENUSTIANO CARRANZA, 1915–20	326	381,926	77,203	188	167,935	46,398
Ejidal actions	326	381,926	77,203	188	167,935	46,398
Endowments	—	—	—	—	—	—
Extensions	—	—	—	—	—	—
Restitutions	—	—	—	—	—	—
New centers of population	—	—	—	—	—	—
Communal plots	—	—	—	—	—	—
ALVARO OBREGÓN, 1921–24	748	1,730,686	164,128	628	1,133,813	134,798
Ejidal actions	739	1,715,582	161,788	623	1,123,944	133,686
Endowments	—	—	—	—	—	—
Extensions	—	—	—	—	—	—
Restitutions	—	—	—	—	—	—
New centers of population	9	15,104	2,340	5	9,869	1,112
Communal plots	—	—	—	—	—	—
PLUTARCO ELÍAS CALLES, 1925–28	1,622	3,186,294	302,539	1,573	2,972,876	297,428
Ejidal actions	1,620	3,173,149	301,587	1,569	2,972,445	296,685
Endowments	—	—	—	—	—	—
Extensions	—	—	—	—	—	—
Restitutions	—	—	—	—	—	—
New centers of population	1	196	607	4	431	743

Appendix H, *continued*.

Period	Published Resolutions			Executed Resolutions		
	No.	Area (hectares)	No. of Beneficiaries	No.	Area (hectares)	No. of Beneficiaries
Communal plots	1	12,949	345	—	—	—
EMILIO PORTES GIL, 1929–30	1,350	2,438,511	187,269	1,156	1,707,757	171,577
Ejidal Actions	1,343	2,433,223	186,684	1,150	1,703,360	171,005
Endowments	—	—	—	—	—	—
Extensions	—	—	—	—	—	—
Restitutions	—	—	—	—	—	—
New centers of population	4	2,981	519	4	2,988	519
Communal plots	3	2,307	66	2	1,409	53
PASCUAL ORTIZ RUBIO, 1931–32	540	1,225,752	57,994	582	944,538	64,573
Ejidal actions	538	909,617	56,724	580	942,994	64,450
Endowments	—	—	—	—	—	—
Extensions	—	—	—	—	—	—
Restitutions	—	—	—	—	—	—
New centers of population	1	646	110	1	646	110
Communal plots	1	315,489	1,160	1	898	13
ABELARDO L. RODRÍGUEZ, 1933–35	1,581	2,060,228	158,393	596	790,694	68,556
Ejidal actions	1,576	2,047,196	158,139	595	786,622	68,433
Endowments	—	—	—	—	—	—
Extensions	—	—	—	—	—	—
Restitutions	—	—	—	—	—	—
New centers of population	1	4,072	123	1	4,072	123

Communal plots	—	—	—	131	8,960	4
LÁZARO CÁRDENAS, 1935–40	811,157	17,906,430	10,744	764,888	20,145,910	11,334
Ejidal actions	808,271	17,864,779	10,721	760,407	20,074,706	11,309
Endowments	—	—	—	—	—	—
Extensions	—	—	—	—	—	—
Restitutions	—	—	—	—	—	—
New Centers of Population	2,106	25,695	16	2,802	32,339	15
Communal Plots	780	15,956	7	1,679	38,865	10
MANUEL AVILA CAMACHO, 1941–46	157,836	5,944,450	3,486	122,941	5,970,398	3,074
Ejidal actions	149,925	5,488,497	3,361	111,121	5,289,382	2,899
Endowments	—	—	—	—	—	—
Extensions	—	—	—	—	—	—
Restitutions	—	—	—	—	—	—
New Centers of Population	918	15,562	7	986	17,540	8
Communal Plots	6,993	440,391	118	10,834	663,476	167
MIGUEL ALEMÁN VALDÉZ, 1947–52	97,391	4,844,123	2,385	108,625	5,439,528	2,245
Ejidal Actions	84,442	4,016,270	2,251	87,686	4,167,252	2,066
Endowments	—	—	—	—	—	—
Extensions	—	—	—	—	—	—
Restitutions	—	—	—	—	—	—
New Centers of Population	724	11,857	14	3,368	43,226	22
Communal Plots	12,225	815,996	120	17,571	1,229,050	157
ADOLFO RUIZ CORTINES, 1953–58	231,888	4,936,665	1,864	226,292	5,771,721	1,745
Ejidal Actions	205,222	3,198,780	1,652	191,151	3,469,958	1,501
Endowments	—	—	—	—	—	—

Period	Published Resolutions			Executed Resolutions		
	No.	Area (hectares)	No. of Beneficiaries	No.	Area (hectares)	No. of Beneficiaries
Extensions	—	—	—	—	—	—
Restitutions	—	—	—	—	—	—
New Centers of Population	40	93,890	4,584	27	64,244	3,336
Communal Plots	204	2,207,873	30,593	185	1,673,641	23,330
ADOLFO LÓPEZ MATEOS, 1959–64						
Ejidal Actions	2,375	9,308,149	289,356	2,887	11,361,270	304,498
Endowments	1,984	5,274,836	210,804	2,588	8,235,638	252,786
Extensions	—	—	—	—	—	—
Restitutions	—	—	—	—	—	—
New Centers of Population	303	2,875,447	49,674	218	2,008,473	33,149
Communal Plots	88	1,157,866	28,878	81	1,117,159	18,563
GUSTAVO DÍAZ ORDAZ, 1965–70						
Ejidal Actions	3,912	23,055,619	374,520	2,769	14,139,560	240,695
Endowments	3,028	14,031,826	220,193	2,339	7,225,144	160,183
Extensions	—	—	—	—	—	—
Restitutions	—	—	—	—	—	—
New Centers of Population	532	4,162,690	46,579	235	3,796,582	26,657
Communal Plots	352	4,861,103	107,748	195	3,117,834	53,855
LUIS ECHEVERRÍA, 1970–76						
Ejidal Actions	2,208	12,243,317	223,250	2,202	13,328,852	206,452
Endowments	1,315	4,032,557	97,085	1,578	7,304,985	112,309
Endowments	—	—	—	—	—	—

Extensions	—	—	—	—	—	—
Restitutions	—	—	—	—	—	—
New Centers of Population	542	4,796,828	41,620	409	2,986,155	30,838
Communal Plots	351	3,413,932	84,545	215	3,037,712	63,305
JOSÉ LÓPEZ PORTILLO, 1977–80						
Ejidal Actions	1,432	2,924,610	104,218	852	3,139,803	72,270
Endowments	1,128	1,979,987	65,766	856	1,798,898	43,372
Extensions	—	—	—	—	—	—
Restitutions	—	—	—	—	—	—
New Centers of Population	157	419,696	11,705	133	1,035,132	12,181
Communal Plots	151	524,927	26,747	63	305,773	16,717
TOTAL, 1915–80						
Ejidal Actions	34,496	95,882,649	3,161,616	31,912	83,318,766	2,905,517
Endowments	31,372	68,981,197	2,686,302	29,851	62,830,291	2,597,167
Extensions	—	—	—	—	—	—
Restitutions	—	—	—	—	—	—
New Centers of Population	1,635	12,464,655	165,017	1,074	9,961,706	112,516
Communal Plots	1,489	14,436,797	310,297	987	10,526,769	195,834

SOURCE: Dirección General de Información Agraria, S.R.A., 1981.

Appendix I.
Population Growth in Selected Cities, 1960–70

City	State	Population	Rate of Growth (%)
Aguascalientes	Aguascalientes	181,277	3.80
Tijuana	Baja California	277,306	6.41
Mexicali	Baja California	263,498	4.36
La Paz	Baja California Sur	46,001	6.87
Villa Constitución	Baja California Sur	10,548	19.29
Campeche	Campeche	69,506	4.89
Cd. Del Carmen	Campeche	34,656	5.25
Saltillo	Coahuila	161,114	5.19
Colima	Colima	58,450	3.10
Tuxtla Gutuiérrez	Chiapas	66,851	5.14
Ciudad Juárez	Chihuahua	407,370	4.68
Chihuahua	Chihuahua	257,027	5.71
Durango	Durango	150,541	4.60
León	Guanajuato	364,990	5.91
Irapuato	Guanajuato	116,651	3.50
Chilpancingo	Guerrero	36,193	7.50
Acapulco	Guerrero	174,378	14.04
Pachuca	Hidalgo	83,892	2.75
Sahagún	Hidalgo	12,327	7.58
Guadalajara	Jalisco	1,193,601	5.13
Puerto Vallarta	Jalisco	24,155	12.92
Tlanepantla	México	45,575	6.05
Sta. Ma. Tulpetlac	México	17,144	18.24
Toluca	México	114,079	4.14
Morelia	Michoacán	161,040	4.98
Uruapan	Michoacán	82,677	6.34
Cuernavaca	Morelos	134,117	14.25
Yautepec	Morelos	13,952	4.40
Tepic	Nayarit	87,540	5.13
Monterrey	Nuevo León	858,107	3.83
Garza García	Nuevo León	20,934	11.20
Oaxaca	Oaxaca	99,535	3.36
Juchitan	Oaxaca	30,218	4.48
Puebla	Puebla	401,603	3.47
Tehuacán	Puebla	47,497	4.22
Querétaro	Querétaro	112,993	5.46
Chetumal	Quintana Roo	23,685	6.40
San Luis Potosí	San Luis Potosí	230,039	3.84

Appendix I, *continued.*

Ciudad Valles	San Luis Potosí	47,587	7.44
Culiacán	Sinaloa	167,956	7.30
Los Mochis	Sinaloa	67,953	6.13
Ciudad Obregón	Sonora	176,596	6.53
Hermosillo	Sonora	114,407	5.55
Villa Hermosa	Tabasco	99,565	6.21
Heroica Cárdenas	Tabasco	15,643	13.58
Tampico	Tamaulipas	179,584	4.05
Nuevo Laredo	Tamaulipas	148,867	5.05
Tlaxcala	Tlaxcala	9,972	2.91
Villa Vicente Guerrero	Tlaxcala	18,280	5.73
Veracruz	Veracruz	214,072	4.15
Jalapa	Veracruz	122,377	6.56
Mérida	Yucatán	212,097	2.27
Valladolid	Yucatán	14,663	4.83
Zacatecas	Zacatecas	50,251	4.89
Guadalupe	Zacatecas	13,246	5.52
Distrito Federal		6,967,000	3.50
Urban Area	Mexico City	8,355,000	5.20
In the Federal District		6,690,000	3.50
Urban Area			
In the State of Mexico		1,665,000	15.10

SOURCE: JLP, A–EH, 1980, pp.730–734.

Appendix J.1.
Strikes in Mexico, 1935–74

Year	No. of Strikes	No. of Strikers	Cause			Sector				Resolution			
			Contracts	Salary	Other	Primary	Secondary	Tertiary	Other	Workers	Employers	Transactions	Unknown
1935	642	145,212	318	38	165					292	105	201	44
1936	647	113,785	308	211	124					511	84	34	45
1937	576	61,732	409	43	92					388	64	37	87
1938	319	13,435	194	33	92					115	41	48	105
1939	303	14,486	208	27	58	38	168	97		119	65	46	73
1940	357	19,784	239	71	47	14	226	117		141	75	126	15
1941	142	2,748	62	61	19	16	98	28		57	52	30	3
1942	98	13,143	55	24	19	23	42	30	3	31	32	39	6
1943	766	81,557	76	681	9	45	682	38	1	50	28	118	570
1944	887	165,744	93	761	33	26	881	28	2	40	35	804	8
1945	220	48,055	97	105	18	16	167	27	10	2	7	157	54
1946	207	10,202	89	54	64		125	68	14	22	69	54	62
1947	130	10,678	81	25	26		92	37	1	27	36	41	26
1948	88	26,424	49	35	4	1	65	18	4	19	37	28	4
1949	90	15,380	64	22	4		68	23	1	29	29	30	2
1950	82	31,116	69	8	5		48	27	7	29	29	23	1
1951	144	13,553	89	51	4		97	41	6	77	34	30	3
1952	113	18,298	105	6	2		83	30		28	42	33	3
1953	167	38,552	142	22	3	6	82	78	1	23	40	104	10
1954	93	25,759	71	22		4	52	34	3	24	37	32	

Year													
1955	135	10,710	118	17	3	1	71	62	1	8	25	101	11
1956	159	7,573	116	40	11	6	82	71		14	45	100	7
1957	193	7,137	161	21	8	3	96	87	7	27	22	144	11
1958	740	60,611	407	325	1	17	515	207	1	25	62	653	
1959	379	62,770	226	162	13	14	210	155		40	70	269	
1960	377	63,567	115	249	8	11	208	158		11	19	347	
1961	373	37,184	197	168	20	7	167	199		127	23	212	
1962	725	80,980	641	69	50	5	523	197		21	25	672	
1963	504	26,035	5	1	1	269	185	126		126	28	339	
1964	62				1	19	27	15					
1965	67				1	29	33	4					
1966	91				1	43	41	6					
1967	78				2	30	35	11					
1968	157				16	80	50	11					
1969	144				5	80	42	17					
1970	206	14,329			2	136	68						
1971	204	9,299			2	130	71	1					
1972	30					30							
1973	57					33	70	4					
1974	452					416	33	3					

Appendix J.2.
Strikes in Mexico, 1935–76 (in percent)

Year	No. of Strikes	No. of Strikers	Cause Contracts	Salary	Other	Sector (%) Primary	Secondary	Tertiary	Other	Resolution (%) Workers	Employers	Transactions	Unknown
1935	642	145,212	49.5	5.9	24.1					45.4	16.3	31.3	6.8
1936	647	113,785	45.6	31.3	18.3					75.8	12.4	5.0	6.6
1937	576	61,732	71.0	7.4	15.9					67.3	11.1	6.4	15.1
1938	319	13,435	60.8	10.3	28.8					36.0	12.8	15.0	32.4
1939	303	14,486	68.6	8.9	19.1	12.5	55.4	32.0	—	39.2	21.4	15.1	24.0
1940	357	19,786	66.9	19.8	13.1	3.9	63.3	32.7	—	39.4	21.0	35.2	4.2
1941	142	2,748	43.6	42.9	13.3	11.2	69.0	19.7	—	40.1	36.6	21.1	2.1
1942	98	13,143	56.1	24.4	19.3	23.4	42.8	30.6	3.1	31.0	22.4	39.7	6.1
1943	766	81,557	9.9	88.9	1.1	5.8	89.0	4.9	0.1	6.5	3.6	15.4	74.4
1944	887	167,744	10.48	85.7	3.7	2.9	93.6	3.1	0.2	4.5	3.9	90.6	0.9
1945	220	48,055	44.1	47.7	8.1	7.2	75.9	12.2	4.5	0.9	3.1	71.3	24.5
1946	207	10,202	42.9	26.1	30.9	—	60.3	35.8	6.7	10.6	33.3	26.0	29.9
1947	130	10,678	62.3	19.2	0.2	—	70.7	28.4	0.7	20.7	27.6	31.5	0.2
1948	88	26,424	55.6	39.7	4.5	1.1	73.8	20.4	4.5	21.5	42.0	31.8	4.5
1949	90	15,380	71.1	24.4	4.4	—	75.5	25.5	1.1	32.2	32.2	33.3	2.2
1950	82	31,166	84.1	9.7	6.1	—	58.5	32.9	8.5	35.3	35.3	28.0	1.2
1951	144	13,553	61.8	35.4	2.7	—	67.3	28.4	4.1	53.4	23.6	20.8	2.0
1952	113	18,298	92.9	5.3	1.7	—	73.4	26.5	—	24.7	37.1	29.2	8.8
1953	167	38,552	85.0	13.1	1.7	5.5	49.1	46.7	0.5	13.7	23.9	62.2	—
1954	93	25,759	76.3	23.6	—	4.3	55.9	36.5	3.2	25.8	39.7	34.4	—

Year													
1955	135	10,710	87.4	12.5	—	0.7	52.5	45.9	0.7	5.9	18.5	74.8	—
1956	159	7,573	72.9	84.9	1.8	3.7	51.5	44.6	—	8.8	28.3	62.8	—
1957	193	7,137	83.4	10.8	5.6	1.5	49.7	45.0	3.6	13.9	11.3	74.6	
1958	740	60,611	55.0	43.9	1.0	2.2	69.5	27.9	0.1	3.3	8.3	88.2	
1959	379	62,770	59.6	40.1	0.2					10.5	18.4	70.9	
1960	377	63,567	30.5	66.0	3.4	2.9	55.1	41.9		2.9	5	92.0	
1961	373	37,184	52.8	45.0	2.1	1.8	47.7	53.3		32.2	6.1	58.8	2.9
1962	725	80,980	88.4	8.8	2.7	6.6	73.3	27.1		2.8	3.4	92.0	0.9
1963	504	26,035	98.8	0.9	0.1	9.6	51.7	35.5		24.2	5.3	65.1	2.1
1964	62					1.6	30.6	43.5	24.1				
1965	67					1.4	43.2	49.2	5.9				
1966	91					1.0	47.2	44.0	6.5				
1967	78					2.5	38.4	44.8	14.1				
1968	157					10.1	50.9	31.8	7.0				
1969	144					3.4	55.5	29.1	11.8				
1970	206					0.9	66.0	33.0					
1971	204					0.9	63.7	34.8	0.4				
1972	30						100						
1973	57						57.8	35.0	7.0				
1974	452						92.0	7.3	0.6				
1975	104					75.9	22.1	2.8					
1976	102						102						

NOTE: The data were gathered by students in my political research workshop at UNAM, from the archives of the Department of Labor, during 1978. The deficiencies in the data stem from the way in which the information was obtained. As a general sample of what we are trying to do, however, the data are valid and useful.

Appendix K.
Cotton Production, 1965–76

Year	Cultivated Area (ha)	Yield (Kg/Hectare)	Production (Metric Tons)	Cotton Seeds (Metric Tons)
1965	793	1,974	1,565	667
1966	701	1,913	1,341	550
1967	689	1,739	1,198	655
1968	723	2,028	1,466	679
1969	524	1,996	1,046	572
1970	403	2,139	862	724
1971	459	2,237	1,027	998
1972	500	2,130	1,065	855
1973	421	2,134	898	764
1974	567	2,358	1,337	846
1975	227	2,397	544	345
1976	235	2,480	583	369

SOURCE: FAO, *Production Yearbook* (1974, 1975, 1976, 1977).

Appendix L.
Jokes about Echeverría

Translator's note: The reader should keep in mind that humor loses much when it is translated and perhaps even more when it is explained. The Spanish and English versions are given here to allow the reader to see both the originals and their translations.

Although some of these jokes were included in the Spanish version of this book, others and their translations are taken from my unpublished manuscript *Humor and Politics*. I am grateful to Gustavo Segade of San Diego State University for his assistance in the translation of the jokes.

The humor against Echeverría concentrated on his alleged *pendejismo*, that is, his doltishness:

1. Iba Echeverría bajando las escaleras de Los Pinos vestido de Frak y cuando le preguntaron a donde iba respondió: "Voy a la graduación de mis lentes."

President Echeverría was leaving Los Pinos dressed in a tuxedo. When asked where he was going, he answered, "To see my eyeglasses graduated." (The play on words here is between the Spanish root concept *graduar*, "to grade or measure," or "to graduate," which is used to denote both a prescription for corrective lenses and the conferring of a degree. The president doltishly thinks he has to get dressed up to attend the prescription [*graduación*] for his glasses.)

2. Entra un mexicano al cielo y le muestran unos relojes que marcan las pendejadas que hacen los presidentes. Ve el de López Mateos, Alemán, etc., que avanzan a una velocidad moderada. Cuando pregunta por el de Echeverría le dicen: "Está como ventilador en la sala de juegos."

A Mexican gets to heaven and they show him the clocks that mark the times that the presidents were guilty of a *pendejada*. He sees those of López Mateos, Alemán, etc., which move at a moderate pace. When he asks for Echeverría's, they tell him, "It's being used as a fan in the gambling room."

3. Se encontraba Echeverría buscando un traje de buzo en el camarote de un marinero. Entra el marinero y sorprendido le pregunta: "Que hace usted aquí Sr. Presidente?"

"Estoy buscando un traje de buzo."

"Por que?"

"Porque el capitán me dijo que en el fondo no soy tan pendejo."

Echeverría was searching for a diving suit in a sailor's cabin. The sailor comes in and asks, "Mr. President, what are you doing here?"

"Looking for a diving suit."

"Why?"

"Because the captain told me that down deep I'm not such a *pendejo*.

The jokes that mocked him as a fool also made fun of his ignorance:

4. Le regalan una camioneta automática a Echeverría. Al día siguiente Echeverría se queja de que la camioneta no sirve. Cuándo le piden que se explique el dice: "Iba yo en la carretera en la "D" de despacio cuando un carro me rebasó, yo lo trate de alcanzar, puse la "R" de rapidísimo y el coche se rompió.

Echeverría is given a station wagon with an automatic shift, and the next day he complains that the car is no good. When they ask him what happened, he explains, "I was going down the road, with the gear shift on "D" for *despacio* ("slow"), when a car passed me, so I put it in "R" for *rapidisimo* ("fastest"), and the car broke down."

5. Estaba Echeverría escarbando en la base de un árbol y sus ayudantes le preguntan que es lo que hace, y este responde: "Estoy buscando la raíz cuadrada."

Echeverría's aides see him digging at the base of a tree, and they ask, "What are you doing, Mr. President?"

"I'm looking for square root."

6. A López Portillo le dicen el Kotex, porque está en el mejor lugar en el peor momento.

López Portillo is called the Kotex. He was in the best possible place but at the worst possible time.

Corruption was also included in the jokes:

7. Echeverría llega al cielo y San Pedro le dice: "¿Qué quieres hijo mío?"

"La Paz."

"¿Qué no te alcanzó con Can Cun?"

Echeverría gets to heaven, and St. Peter says to him, "What do you want, my son?"

"La paz."

"What, wasn't Can Cun enough for you?" (The pun is on *la paz*, or "peace," and the resort city of La Paz in Baja California).

8. Cuál es el perro de Echeverría? El Can Cun.

What is Echeverría's dog's name? The *Can*ine, *Cun*.

The jokes about Echeverría also included references to the allegation that his wife wore the pants in his family. This is an important criticism in a country like Mexico, where the macho mentality is still in effect:

9. A Los Pinos le dicen la casa de los sustos, porque hay una mujer con huevos y un hombre sin cabeza.

They call Los Pinos the haunted house because there is a woman there who has balls and a man with no head.

10. Echeverría le pregunta a Henry Kissinger como es que tiene tanta suerte con las mujeres. Kissinger le contesta: "Mira, yo llego a la casa, tiro la puerta, rompo los muebles y les demuestro quien es el que manda."

"Echeverría llega a su casa, tira la puerta, empieza a romper los muebles y cuando ya casi destruyo Los Pinos, se oye la voz de su esposa desde el otro cuarto: "Eres tu Henry?"

Echeverría asks Henry Kissinger how he has such success with women. Kissinger responds: "I go to their house, pound on the door, kick the furniture, and show them that I'm the boss."

Echeverría arrives at his house, pounds on the door, destroys the furniture, and just about finishes off the presidential mansion. A voice from the other room asks: "Is that you, Henry?"

Manifesto of the Latin American Labor Committees
September 3, 1974

The Terrorism of Echeverría/Rockefeller

The terrorist acts such as that involving José Guadalupe Zuno demonstrate, for anyone who wants to see, that the CIA (controlled by Rockefeller) has been active in Mexico through supposedly revolutionary or openly counterrevolutionary groups. As we shall show, the CIA is carrying out the fascist economic policy of Rockefeller through its chief agent, Luis Echeverría.

The fact that in Guadalajara, the second most heavily patrolled city by the army and the police, a kidnapping occurs of such magnitude cannot be explained except as an operation perfectly planned and carried out by those who do *not* have an interest in overthrowing the regime of Luis Echeverría. Rather, the opposite; whoever did this has an interest in using such provocative actions to encourage military-fascist control of the economy mainly from Guerrero to Jalisco [the central part of the country].

The strategy is obvious. As a provocation, the kidnappings operate at crucial political moments, such as the elections in Guerrero, the fourth presidential State of the Union address, etc., and bring as a consequence a police and military mobilization of such magnitude that, in addition to the indiscriminate repression against leftist democratic groups and the population in general, it creates a situation of general terror that necessarily affects all of life, not only political but also economic. That is the real nature of the provocation in the region where they have decided to strike.

Kidnapping as a terrorist practice has as a consequence the fascist control of the population. The CIA understands that from the experiences it has had for many years, especially its observation of the British methods of colonial domination, which taught it that a small occupying force can count on the psychological factor for maintaining its economic domination.

The process of "fascistization" from above consists of counterinsurgency operations localized in "laboratory zones," such as in Guerrero for the past several years on the model designed by Lucio Cabañas. These are zones of strategic importance as far as the economy is concerned, like those targeted in other countries in Latin America, especially Argentina. There the terrorist groups have been used to open a gap in the police-military control of the principal economic zones of the country (Buenos Aires, Tucumán, Santa Fe, Quebec, Catamarca, Mendoza, Paraná, etc.).

The implementation of fascism, as we well know, is the *only* way out of capitalist depression. For that reason, the population is prepared by methods of manipulation and control through the creation of a climate of terror and political instability which makes the masses call for order. But this order is martial, "the peace of the graveyard," the plundering, illegal imprisonment, kidnappings by police, torture, a fascist orgy accompanied by nationalistic hymns (the way Mussolini began), calls for unity and cooperation against the "dark forces" (which Echeverría never identified) that threaten the "holy interests of the fatherland." The political elite threatens the population by all the means of diffusion (press, radio, TV, leaflets thrown from helicopters, etc.) and calls for the people to participate in massive actions against the so-called murderers. But these mobilizations can, in the future, be used against the working class itself.

The fascist bands that previously went around the city killing at the very doors of the barracks and in full public view have given way to bands of peasants armed and manipulated into going around the cities in class confrontations of the characteristic fascist type.

The working class not only plays the role of victim of capitalist exploitation and dies of hunger in the slave labor camps. In addition, the fascism of Echeverría, designed by Rockefeller and manipulated by the CIA, has assigned the role of being its own hangman to the well-intentioned traitor of all the Mexican left. The atomization of the working class, the systematic destruction of its organizations, takes on its true image: the direction by the state of those masses toward fascism, toward the fratricidal struggle, of police spies, all in the name of "nationalism," of revolutionary chauvinism, of the verbal and abstract anti-imperialism of Echeverría, which conceals the true pillaging and genocide of the working class throughout the world.

The way in which the CIA's counterinsurgency methods have operated in Mexico must be understood as part of a worldwide process. Their most concrete forms have occurred in Vietnam, Northern Ireland, Chile, Brazil. . . . The massive manipulation and control of the population, of the puppet governments such as that of Echeverría, that on the one hand appear as the conciliator, as a democratic opening, while on the other hand and simultaneously, they are creating the fascist infrastructure of the Schat type [Schat was Hitler's minister of economy], in order to exploit and to exterminate, perfecting the methods of repression and control of the working class and of the entire population. Ultimately, this is the only way that fascism can be imposed from above.

The true problem facing Mexico today, as in the entire world, is how to impose an ever-greater austerity on the working class, including the unemployed. Austerity is the only way in which Echeverría can "pay as you go" the external debt, which will inevitably continue to grow. In fact, the debt itself cannot be paid, but merely the interest on it. Capitalist crises are always resolved solely by the plundering of nature and the working class. And LEA [Echeverría] understands that perfectly (and we assume his ministers understand it also). He also understands that the proposed increase in wages will not resolve the problem but will merely lead to the bankruptcy of small and middle-sized firms. Thus the state is taking over many of these, as is common in the early stages of fascism. These bankruptcies bring about a very high rate of unemployment, which in turn will lead to great political conflict. It is at this point that terrorism, in the form that provokes repression and generates fear in the population, is a counterrevolutionary fact. The virtual state of siege of Guerrero and now of Jalisco is a prime example of this phenomenon.

It could not be otherwise when we understand that for the rural and urban guerrilla movement, terrorism is only a political method, but it is militarily wrong. Such a movement has never been victorious against a regular army. One reason is that such movements are usually infiltrated (when they have not actually been created from the beginning) by agents of the CIA.

For anyone who has been following attentively and with a minimum of intelligence or memory, it is obvious that the terrorist groups that have been operating in Mexico in recent years, especially in Guadalajara (a very controlled atmosphere), are easily confused with groups and elements that are openly gangsteristic. This is especially true of groups such as FER and the September 23rd League. Another element of counterinsurgency, which also has taken place in Guadalajara, is that other terrorist groups have been pushed to action in response to the atmosphere of provocation created by groups such as that of Carlos Morales, "El Pelacuas," and others.

The role played by a band such as that of Carlos Morales, "El Pelacuas," shows clearly that the state uses such groups for repressive political ends. The group was "legalized" as members of the FEG, as "confidants" of the XV Military Zone, and as "cooperators" with the local police (apart from their own initiatives). This was shown by the timing of their arrest and the way in which they were arrested, as well as the immediate consequences that followed, such as the fall of the attorney general, the assistant attorney general, and the chief of the local police. Also, as has been made known, various North American members of the gang were suppliers of arms and experts in security installations.

Who is behind this state that behaves in such a way, impelled by the economic crisis and the necessity of fascism to resolve the crisis? The methods are clearly those used in counterinsurgency by the CIA: political groups with a cover of radical leftism infiltrated and prompted into action that is provocative, bands of gangsters that also carry out provocative actions and acts of counterinsurgency against authentic groups of the left that "do not compromise the official repressive bodies," in order to create a situation of chaos in which police and military control of the entire population becomes necessary. All this lays the base for the fascist regime in the ultimate stage of capitalism.

Appendix M.
Monetary Reserves, Less Gold

Year	Reserves
1971	752
1972	976
1973	1,160
1974	1,238
1975	1,384
1976	1,188

SOURCE: International Monetary Fund, *International Financial Statistics Year-book*, (New York, 1980), pp. 295–296.

Appendix N.
Mexico and Other Countries in the U.S. Press, 1972–78

Country	1972	1973	1974	1975	1976	1977	1978	Total
			Number of Mentions in the *New York Times*					
USSR	978	1,288	1,242	869	940	899	653	6,869
People's Republic of China	826	437	334	407	598	364	377	3,348
Great Britain	163	225	462	399	373	256	162	2,040
Rhodesia	160	118	67	187	521	482	325	1,860
Israel	194	212	321	300	257	225	99	1,608
South Africa	118	85	141	167	372	441	251	1,575
Italy	168	95	219	187	365	148	232	1,414
Japan	263	188	267	218	238	129	110	1,413
Chile	212	404	206	175	150	138	125	1,410
Spain	67	76	130	405	366	168	107	1,319
Egypt	145	60	259	300	233	190	103	1,290
France	126	132	339	162	214	185	132	1,290
Canada	201	161	187	130	224	261	121	1,285
South Korea	148	173	228	231	161	198	104	1,243
Argentina	151	208	180	248	244	150	57	1,238
Angola	17	7	162	371	490	60	32	1,139
Cuba	143	106	201	217	196	199	57	1,119
Greece	145	279	301	159	83	67	27	1,061
Philippines	167	143	94	138	109	115	84	850
Iran	24	51	90	111	149	100	249	774
Taiwan	184	70	36	102	101	98	122	713

Appendix N, *continued.*

Mexico	51	77	136	87	135	144	81	711
Total of 50 Countries	5,918	5,632	7,142	7,338	7,968	6,747	4,486	45,231

Number of Mentions in the *Washington Post*

USSR	1,118	1,244	928	1,027	924	1,141	1,161	7,541
Israel	240	753	313	605	570	852	965	4,298
People's Republic of China	615	557	293	334	429	337	425	2,990
Great Britain	377	503	295	273	541	457	285	2,731
Egypt	198	332	225	399	172	425	644	2,395
France	166	382	271	250	226	214	176	1,685
Japan	279	147	213	213	201	245	245	1,543
South Africa	98	130	71	133	375	394	261	1,462
West Germany	237	336	150	147	170	212	190	1,442
Rhodesia	92	109	59	91	303	262	295	1,211
South Korea	67	139	121	141	144	318	243	1,173
Chile	187	254	141	116	150	100	110	1,058
Cuba	90	93	112	141	163	230	211	1,040
Canada	142	271	85	101	154	180	88	1,021
Italy	96	127	75	108	261	104	136	907
India	175	180	126	73	129	133	86	902
Iran	23	84	80	131	124	149	285	876
Angola	11	10	20	219	453	76	59	848
Syria	25	121	93	113	257	94	112	815
Spain	53	92	87	222	183	126	33	796
Argentina	96	211	100	53	103	73	27	663
Greece	73	180	127	77	63	58	34	612
Mexico	55	86	75	68	127	135	67	603
Total of 50 Countries	5,336	7,899	4,174	6,150	7,252	7,401	7,040	45,952

Number of Mentions in the *Chicago Tribune*

USSR	610	578	433	585	521	599	649	3,973
Israel	126	303	107	310	233	442	533	2,054
Great Britain	278	214	236	208	326	281	183	1,726
People's Republic of China	296	176	108	127	84	124	174	1,089
Egypt	67	27	57	197	63	216	425	1,052
Japan	170	166	141	112	96	122	123	930
Canada	118	144	91	58	100	121	95	727
France	67	142	128	66	85	83	88	659

Appendix N, *continued.*

Country	1972	1973	1974	1975	1976	1977	1978	Total
West Germany	132	127	71	61	51	113	102	657
Cuba	40	45	57	66	92	125	108	533
Italy	43	51	48	44	103	59	144	492
South Korea	39	20	31	29	63	165	113	460
Rhodesia	38	15	7	12	76	143	157	448
Mexico	34	39	62	52	91	117	49	444
South Africa	14	25	18	19	137	151	80	444
Total of 50 Countries	2,574	3,025	2,136	2,747	2,877	3,706	3,848	20,913
Number of Mentions in the *Los Angeles Times*								
USSR	853	1,062	914	739	635	864	770	5,837
Great Britain	325	475	454	346	485	387	214	2,686
People's Republic of China	357	404	235	231	274	208	226	1,935
Japan	319	287	297	207	248	299	274	1,931
Egypt	109	206	159	273	44	293	515	1,599
France	147	309	243	119	182	186	177	1,363
West Germany	216	257	208	104	133	159	166	1,243
Mexico	135	147	181	145	190	292	128	1,218
Total of 50 Countries	4,153	6,085	4,971	4,648	4,961	5,589	5,430	35,857

SOURCE: T. Laichas, *Mexico in the U.S. Press.* Tables 3600–3603.

Appendix O.
Mexican Army Promotions, 1971–76

Year	Retirements	General (Brigada)	General (Ala)	General (Brigadier)	General (Grupo)	Colonel	Lieutenant Colonel	Major	1st Captain	2nd Captain	Lieutenant	2nd Lieutenant
1971	410	10		29	3	49	70	118	143	278	493	293
1972	169	8		29	3	50	64	109	126	219	901	100
1973	234	1		13	2	51	63	77	88	100	183	91
1974	264	2	1	12	2	44	67	82	102	165	268	71
1975	203	15	1	16	6	50	86	92	129	260	316	38
1976	239	6	2	29	2	57	79	95	140	236	437	36

SOURCE: JLP A-EH, 1979, pp. 959–969.

NOTES TO THE CHAPTERS

ACKNOWLEDGMENTS

1. Samuel Schmidt, *La autonomía relativa del estado* (México, D.F.: Ed: Qunito Sol, 1988) originally published as "El estado y su autonomía," in *Problemas del Desarrollo*, 40 (November 1979–January 1980).

EDITOR'S INTRODUCTION

I would like to thank the Organized Research Committee and Dean Henry Hooper of Northern Arizona University for financial support for this project. I would also like to thank Cheryl Cole Cothran, Frank Cordova, Magdaleno Manzanárez, Kim Vivier, and Kay Rogers for help in various stages of the translation. Of course, I am responsible for any deficiencies that remain.

1. Lawrence Koslow, ed., *The Future of Mexico* (Tempe, Ariz.: Center for Latin American Studies, Arizona State University, 1977); Roderic Camp, ed., *Mexico's Political Stability: The Next Five Years* (Boulder: Westview Press, 1986); Susan Kaufman Purcell, ed., *Mexico in Transition: Implications for U.S. Policy* (New York: Council on Foreign Relations, 1988); Miguel D. Ramirez, *Mexico's Economic Crisis: Its Origins and Consequences* (New York: Praeger, 1989).

2. Juan Miguel de Mora, *Esto nos dió López Portillo* (México, D.F.: Anaya Editores, 1982); Julio Scherer García, *Los presidentes* (México, D.F.: Ed. Grijalbo, 1986).

3. Luis Javier Garrido, "The Crisis of Presidencialismo," in Cornelius et al., eds., *Mexico's Alternative Political Futures*, 421.

4. Thomas C. Wright, "The Rise and Fall of the Cuban Revolution as a Factor in Latin American Politics" (paper presented at the Rocky Mountain Council on Latin American Studies, Flagstaff, Ariz., February 21–23, 1991).

5. Judith Teichman, *Policymaking in Mexico: From Boom to Crisis* (Boston: Allen and Unwin, 1988), 52.

6. John J. Bailey, *Governing Mexico: The Statecraft of Crisis Management* (New York: St. Martin's Press, 1988), 126–27.

7. Ramírez, *Mexico's Economic Crisis*; Clark Reynolds, "Growth, Distribution, and Structural Change in Mexico," in Koslow, ed., *Future of Mexico*, 19–33.

8. James M. Malloy, "The Politics of Transition in Latin America," in J.

Malloy and M. Seligson, eds., *Authoritarians and Democrats: Regime Transition in Latin America* (Pittsburgh: University of Pittsburgh Press, 1987), 235–58.

9. James Buchanan, Robert Tollison, and Gordon Tullock, eds., *Toward a Theory of the Rent-Seeking Society* (College Station, Tex.: Texas A&M University Press, 1980). Some argue that Latin American politics in general are characterized by the pursuit of special privilege, rather than the establishment of universal principles by which all receive similar benefits. See Malloy, "Politics of Transition."

10. Nora Hamilton, *The Limits of State Autonomy: Post-Revolutionary Mexico* (Princeton: Princeton University Press, 1982), 30.

11. Judith Adler Hellman, *Mexico in Crisis*, 2D ed. (New York: Holmes and Meier, 1983), 227–28, 214.

12. See the literature on the emergence of the welfare state, such as Peter Flora and Arnold Heidenheimer, eds., *The Development of Welfare States in Europe and America* (New Brunswick, N. J.: Transaction Books, 1981).

13. Roderic Camp, *Entrepreneurs and Politics in Twentieth-Century Mexico* (New York: Oxford University Press, 1989), 8.

14. José Luis Reyna, "Redefining the Authoritarian Regime," in José Luis Reyna and Richard Weinart, eds, *Authoritarianism in Mexico* (Philadelphia: Institute for the Study of Human Issues, 1977), 158.

15. Kevin J. Middlebrook, *Political Liberalization in an Authoritarian Regime: The Case of Mexico*, Center for U.S.-Mexican Studies, Research Report Series 41 (San Diego: University of California, 1985), 7.

16. Luis Rubio and Roberto Blum, "Recent Scholarship on the Mexican Political and Economic System," *Latin American Research Review* 25 (1) (1990): 181.

17. For an analysis of the powers of the Mexican president, see Jorge Carpizo, *El presidencialismo mexicano* (México, D.F.: Ed. Siglo XXI, 1986). For an argument that presidentialism *ought* to decline, see Scott Mainwaring, "Presidentialism in Latin America," *Latin American Research Review* 25 (1) (1990): 157–79.

AUTHOR'S INTRODUCTION

1. See James Wilkie, *La revolución mexicana: Gasto federal y cambio social* (México, D.F.: Fondo de Cultura Económica, 1978), in which the governments since the Revolution are analyzed through data about government spending. [This is an updated and expanded Spanish-language version of Wilkie's *The Mexican Revolution: Federal Expenditures and Social Change since* 1910, 2D ed. (Berkeley: University of California Press, 1970). Ed.

2. For a more elaborate version of the theoretical and methodological framework used in this work, see S. Schmidt, *La autonomía relativa del estado* (México, D.F.: Ed. Quinto Sol, 1988), and "El estado y su autonomía," *Problemas del Desarrollo* 40 (November 1979–January 1980). Also see Antonio Gramsci, *Antología* (Madrid: Siglo XXI, 1974).

3. For a good identification of the forces active in one system at a particular

time, see Mao Tse-tung, "Análisis de las clases de la sociedad China," in *Obras escogidas* (Pekin: Ediciones en Lenguas Extranjeras, 1968).

4. Failure to take account of all social forces and their legitimate interests helps to explain, for example, why anticommunism plays such an important role in the United States. North American policy makers, supported by scholarly analyses, see Latin America as a continent in turmoil because of the outside agitation of Communists, while they ignore the domestic forces at work in the various countries.

5. See the analysis of the French Revolution by Karl Marx, "El 18 Brumario de Luis Bonaparte," in *Obras escogidas* (Moscow: Ed. Progreso, 1969).

6. Vincent, Padgett, *The Mexican Political System* (Atlanta: Houghton Mifflin, 1976).

7. Daniel Cosío Villegas, *El estilo personal de gobernar* (México, D.F.: Ed. Joaquín Mortiz, 1974). He believes that Echeverría imposed his particular style on government, characterized by its extension into the bureaucracy and political habits. This is not exactly true; what Echeverría imprinted were certain personal flourishes.

8. Lawrence Peter, *El Principio de Peter* (Barcelona: Ed. Plaza & Janes, S.A., 1977), 41–42.

9. Luis Suárez, *Echeverría rompe el silencio* (México, D.F.: Ed. Grijalbo, 1979), 108.

10. Miguel Osorio Marban, *Revolución y política*, vol. 3 (México: D.F., n.p., n.d.) and Roderic Camp, *Mexican Political Biographies, 1935–1981* (Tucson: University of Arizona Press, 1982).

11. Judith Adler Hellman, *Mexico in Crisis* (New York: Holmes and Meier, 1978), 148.

12. Thomas Skidmore and Peter Smith, *Modern Latin America* (New York: Oxford University Press, 1984).

13. Lorenzo Meyer, "Desarrollo político y dependencia externa," in W. Glade and S. Ross, eds., *Críticas constructivas del sistema político mexicano* (Austin: University of Texas, Institute of Latin American Studies, 1973), 38: "The economic crisis of 1938 and 1939 sharpened the opposition of the enemies of the Cardenista policies, producing a wave of unrest that prompted the president to designate as his successor a moderate conservative—Avila Camacho—who would be able to neutralize General Juan Almazán, candidate of the right wing (both official and nonofficial). Thus Cárdenas did not support the candidacy of General Francisco Múgica, who was committed to preserving and extending the Cardenista program. This move to the right in 1938, as in 1928, was linked to foreign pressure." The important point here is that simplistic periodization is seldom possible. For a review of different views on presidential succession, see Samuel Schmidt and Jorge Gil, "Mexico: The Network behind Power," *Review of Latin American Studies*, forthcoming.

14. Suárez, *Echeverría rompe el silencio*, 109.

15. Ibid., 186.

16. Cosío Villegas, *El estilo personal.*

17. Shmuel Eisenstadt, *Ensayos sobre el cambio social y la modernización* (Madrid: Ed. Tecnos, 1970).

18. It is interesting to note that Carlos Salinas de Gortari's administration began in 1988 with a call for rapid modernization.

19. See Yehezkel Dror, *Estudios del futuro para la planeación estratégica* (México, D.F.: Programa Universitario de Cómputo, UNAM, 1984), and *Enfrentando el futuro* (México, D.F.: Fondo de Cultura Económica, 1990).

20. I am finishing a book on Mexican political humor entitled *Humor and Politics*. See also Samuel Schmidt, "Elitelore: Political Humor and the Mexican Presidents," *Journal of Latin American Lore* 16 (Summer 1990).

21. The U.S. press is full of biases and self-censorship, and the Mexican press is corrupt, so press information is only a general indication of reality and may not contain all the information that one needs for analysis.

22. Peter Smith, *Labyrinths of Power* (Princeton: Princeton University Press, 1979), and Roderic Camp, *Mexico's Leaders: Their Education and Recruitment* (Tucson: University of Arizona Press, 1980), have amply demonstrated this path.

23. In 1970 the average salary for an associate professor at UNAM was around U.S. $1,000 a month; by 1989 it had plummeted to under U.S. $400 a month.

24. After reading this book, one of my professors at UNAM, who was president of IEPES, the PRI Institute of Social, Economic, and Political Research, asked me: "Samuel, have you received a job offer yet?"

25. Octavio Paz, *El laberinto de la soledad* (México, D.F.: Fondo de Cultura Económica, 1986); Antonio Salgado, *Humor negro a la mexicana* (México, D.F.: Libra, 1986).

26. Juan Miguel de Mora, *The Principle of Opposites in Sanskrit Texts* (New Delhi: Pandit Rampratap Shastri Charitable Trust, 1982); *El Rig Veda* (México, D.F.: UNAM, 1980); and his translation of Bhavabhuti's *El último lance de Rama* (México, D.F.: UNAM, 1984).

27. Recently, he was asked to write the foreword to the *International Encyclopaedia of Indian Literature* (New Delhi: Daystar, 1988), edited by Ganga Ram Garg.

28. Juan Miguel de Mora, *T 68* (México, D.F.:EDAMEX, 1st ed., 1973; 2nd ed., 1989).

29. *Por la gracia del señor presidente* (México, D.F.: Ed. Asociados, 1975), *Esto nos dió López Portillo* (México, D.F.: Anaya Editores, 1982), *No, sr. presidente* (México, D.F.: Anaya Editores, 1983), *Ni renovación, ni moral* (México, D.F.: Anaya Editores, 1985), *Elecciones en México* (México, D.F.: EDAMEX, 1988).

30. In 1988 a Mexican soldier asked for political asylum in Canada. In his request he admitted his involvement in the killing of civilians in Mexico. He acknowledged killing sixty persons and knowing of another one hundred killed.

31. Maybe the attempts have been warning signals to make him understand that his life is in danger if he does not keep silent. He chooses not to interpret these incidents in this way and therefore does not remain silent.

32. Some of his political books include *Confesiones de un gobernador* (México, D.F.: Ed. Grijalbo, 1978), *Los últimos 91 días* (México, D.F.: Ed. Grijalbo, 1978), and *El juicio* (México: Grijalbo, 1984).

33. His last name is Muñoz, and the *Los Angeles Times* published it as *Munoz*. I later discovered that he is my sister-in-law's cousin, but I refused to convert the

affair into a family conflict. However, the connection does illustrate what a small world this is.

34. I include here the revised version for *Zeta* and not the original one prepared for *La Opinión*; the differences between the two versions are very slight.

35. To speak of a "political system" in itself implies something beyond an individualist conception of causation.

36. For an excellent example of how different explanations of the same events are possible when different policy makers have different information, see Graham Allison, *Essence of Decision: Explaining the Cuban Missile Crisis* (Boston: Little, Brown, 1971).

37. Jean-Francois Lyotard, "Pequeña perspectiva de la decadencia y de algunos combates minoritarios por entablar allí," in Dominique Grisoni, *Políticas de la filosofía* (México, D.F.: Breviarios del Fondo de Cultura Económica, 1982), 143.

38. Stefan Zweig, *La lucha contra el demonio* (México, D.F.: Ed. Tor, 1945).

CHAPTER 1. PROBLEMS FACING MEXICO AT
THE BEGINNING OF THE 1970s

1. Among the critics are: Alonso Aguilar and Ferando Carmona, *Mexico: Riqueza y miseria* (México, D.F.: Ed. Nuestro Tiempo, 1972); Varios, *El milagro mexicano* (México, D.F.: Ed. Nuestro Tiempo, 1971); Varios, *Neolatifundismo y explotación* (México, D.F.: Ed. Nuestro Tiempo, 1973).
Among the official versions are NAFINSA, *La economía mexicana en cifras* (México, D.F., 1981); Banco Nacional de Comercio Exterior, *La política económica para 1972* (México, D.F., 1972).

2. In this sense a book that stood out was Jorge Martínez Rios, ed., *El perfil de México en 1980* (México, D.F.: Ed. Siglo XXI, 1972), in which a large number of Mexican social scientists agreed that by 1980 the general situation in Mexico would be rather difficult. Reality beat them by several years.

3. For income distribution, see Pablo González Casanova, *La democracia en México* (México, D.F.: Ed. ERA, 1969); the essay by Ifigenia Martínez de Navarrete in Martínez Rios, ed., *El perfil de México en 1980*; Rolando Cordera, "Los límites del reformismo: La crisis del capitalismo en México," in *Cuadernos Políticos* 2 (México, D.F.: Ed. ERA, 1974); and Wilkie, *La revolución mexicana*.

4. See the socioeconomic diagnosis of the *Plan global de desarrollo* of the Mexican government. The data are valid for 1970.

5. C. Pereyra, "Mexico: Los límites del reformismo," in *Cuadernos Políticos* 1 (México, D.F.: Ed. ERA, 1974), 56.

6. J. L. Martin, "Labor's Real Wages in Latin America since 1940," in James Wilkie and Peter Reich, eds., *Statistical Abstract of Latin America*, vol. 18 (Los Angeles: UCLA Latin America Center Publications, 1978).

7. James Wilkie and Peter Reich, eds., *Statistical Abstract of Latin America*, vol. 20 (Los Angeles: UCLA Latin America Center Publications, 1980).

8. Martin, "Labor's Real Wages."

9. *Reseña Laboral*, vol. 1, no. 7 (México, D.F.: November 1973), 19. In addition

to differing a great deal from one source to another, the data on unemployment are dubious and noncomparable. These data, however, can be considered official since they come from the Department of Labor. The publication *Latin America* (New York: Facts on File, 1973), p. 1980, reported an investigation by an unspecified person at UNAM which claimed that of the 24 million working-age people, 9.6 million were unemployed.

10. *Revista Expansión* (México, D.F., July 1976), 14.

11. Casio Luiselli, *El sistema alimentario mexicano (SAM): Elementos de un programa de producción acelerada de alimentos básicos en México* (Working Papers in U.S.-Mexican Studies 22 (San Diego: University of California), 22.

12. "The limited internal market represents perhaps only one-half of the 50 million inhabitants of the country," according to M. Wionczek, "El desarrollo económico y el sistema político mexicano," in Glade and Ross, eds., *Críticas constructivas*, 110. Even this figure may be optimistic when one considers that the poorest 6 or 7 percent of the population earn incomes that barely allow them to subsist.

13. Although a godfather, sponsor, or patron is an integral component of Mexican politics, it is certainly not exclusive to Mexico. Peter, in *El Principio de Peter*, recommends the selection of a patron as an important factor in a successful career.

14. Arnaldo Córdova, *La formación del poder político en México* (México, D.F.: Ed. ERA, 1972). In his later works he maintains the same thesis.

15. S. Schmidt, *La política de industrialización de Miguel Alemán* (México, D.F.: UNAM, CELA, FCPS, 1977).

16. F. J. Alejo, "La política fiscal en el desarrollo de México," in *¿Crecimiento o desarrollo económico?* (México, D.F.: Ed. Sepsetentas, 1971), 104.

17. Benjamin Retchkiman, *Política fiscal mexicana* (México, D.F.: UNAM, 1980).

18. Wilkie, *La revolución mexicana*, 275.

19. Rosario Green, *El endeudamiento público externo en México, 1940–1973* (México, D.F.: El Colegio de México, 1976); "Mexico's Public Foreign Debt, 1965–1976," *Comercio Exterior de México* 24 (January 1978); and S. Schmidt, "Las distintas caras de la deuda del sector público mexicano," in J. Wilkie and S. Haber, eds., *Statistical Abstract of Latin America*, vol. 22 (Los Angeles: UCLA Latin America Center Publications, 1982).

20. Benito Rey Romay, *La ofensiva empresarial contra la intervención del estado* (México, D.F.: Ed. Siglo XXI, 1984), defends the state firms and adds some arguments to the ones mentioned here.

21. E. V. K. Fitzgerald, "The State and Capital Accumulation in Mexico," *Journal of Latin American Studies* 10 (1978): 269.

22. Luiselli, *El sistema alimentario*, 3.

23. See note 1.

24. See Carlos Fuentes's description of the death of Jacinto López in *Tiempo mexicano* (México, D.F.: Cuadernos de Joaquín Mortíz, 1972).

25. For the attainment of autonomy, see Consuelo García Stahl, *Un anhelo de libertad* (México, D.F.: UNAM, 1968).

26. See Luis Molina Piñeiro and Arturo Sánchez Vázquez, *Descripción de un conflicto* (México, D.F.: UNAM, 1980).

27. R. Ramírez, *El movimiento estudiantil en México* (México, D.F.: Ed. ERA, 1969), has a good description of the conflict.

28. Rosenstein Rodán responds to Muñoz Ledo in Glade and Ross, eds., *Críticas constructivas*.

29. Kenneth Johnson, *Mexican Democracy: A Critical View* (Boston: Allyn and Bacon, 1971), 70.

30. Manuel Velázquez Carmona, "Dinámica de las clases medias," *Revista Línea*, 14 (March–April 1975): 81.

31. Jorge Pinto Mazal, "Las clases medias en México," *Revista Línea* 14 (March–April 1975): 106.

32. Carlos Schaffer, "El capitalismo monopolista de estado," *Problemas del Desarrollo* 5 (20) (México, D.F.: Instituto de Investigaciones Económicas, UNAM, 1975), 73.

33. N. A. Smith, "Government vs. Trade Unions in Britain," *Political Quarterly* 46 (1975), argues that technological advance strengthens certain areas and, when the state does not permit the closing of firms to avoid unemployment, it strengthens the workers. In addition, when these firms become state property, the workers gain a doubling of strength because of the strategic importance of the firms and the impossibility of their closing.

34. Antonio Alonso, *El movimiento ferrocarrillero en México, 1958–1959* (México, D.F.: Ed. ERA, 1972).

35. Sergio Reyes Osorio et al., *Estructura agraria y desarrollo agrícola en México* (México, D.F.: Fondo de Cultura Económica, 1974).

36. Armando Bartra, *Notas sobre la cuestión campesina* (México, D.F.: Ed. Macehual, 1979).

37. Daniel Cosío Villegas, *La sucesión: Desenlace y perspectivas* (México, D.F.: Cuadernos de Joaquín Mortiz, 1976), 59–60.

38. S. Schmidt, *Democracia mexicana: La reforma política de López Portillo* (México, D.F.: CELA, FCPS, UNAM, 1981), and "Votación en la frontera Mexico-Estados Unidos, 1961–1982," in S. Schmidt, J. Wilkie, and M. Esparza, eds., *Estudios cuantitativos sobre la historia de México* (México, D.F.: UNAM, 1988).

39. See also Samuel Schmidt, "Las elecciones en la frontera México-Estados Unidos: Revisión de las tendencias," *Estudios Fronterizos* 21 (1990).

40. Luis Echeverría, "Discurso de toma de posesión como candidato del PRI," in *Caminos y voces* (México, D.F.: Government of Mexico, July 1971), 11.

CHAPTER 2. MANAGEMENT OF THE ECONOMY

1. Fitzgerald, "The State and Capital," 269.

2. Rosario Green, "Endeudamiento exterior y debilidad estatal: El caso de México," *Foro Internacional* 20 (July–September 1979): 85.

3. Porfirio Muñoz Ledo, "Apertura política para el desarrollo," in Glade and Ross, eds., *Críticas constructivas*, 224.

4. In the methodology of Wilkie, *La revolución mexicana*, the *economic* area includes communications and transport, natural resources, industry and com-

merce; the *social* includes education and culture, health and public assistance, welfare and social security; *administrative* includes defense, general administration, and public debt (see p. 257).

5. Wilkie, *La revolución mexicana*, 346.

6. P. Villarreal and Rocío P. de Villarreal, "Las empresas públicas como instrumento de política," *El Trimestre Económico* 45 (April–June 1978): 217. Also see Alejandro Carrillo, *La reforma administrativa en México* (México, D.F.: Miguel Angel Porrua Ed., 1980).

7. Tello, *La política económica*, 190. As with other data, there is no consensus on state employment. Lawrence Whitehead, "La política económica del sexenio de Echeverría," *Foro International* 22 (January–March 1980), accepts and cites the figures of Tello (p. 189) of 826,000 employees in 1970 and 1,315,000 in 1976. For M. Grindle, the number of bureaucrats was 1,150,000 in 1970: *Bureaucrats, Politicians, and Peasants in Mexico* (Los Angeles: University of California Press, 1977), 46.

Samuel I. del Villar, "Estado y petróleo en Mexico: Experiencias y perspectivas," in *Foro Internacional* 22 (July–September 1979), approaches the problem from another perspective. He mentions the rapid and unproductive growth of bureaucratic services, whose cost went from 6.2 percent to 9.6 percent of GNP between 1970 and 1976 (156). In the same period Whitehead says that "the deficit of the public sector (under budgetary control) increased from 2.5 percent of GNP in 1971 to 9.3 percent in 1976" ("La Política Económica," 497).

8. "Public expenditure certainly fed back into the inflationary process, not because of its magnitude, but because its traditional orientation had not fundamentally changed and because it was done largely by increasing the money supply. Its impact on total demand surpassed its impact on the total supply of goods that could be generated in the short run." Luis Angeles, *Crisis y coyuntura de la económica mexicana* (México, D.F.: Ed. El Caballito, 1979), 78.

9. Whitehead, "La política económica," 439–94. It is obvious that the problem was not the technocrats. López Portillo was selected to be secretary of the treasury because he had dedicated himself to planning since 1965 and had continued to be involved in planning when he was undersecretary of the presidency at the beginning of Echeverría's term. See Carrillo, *La Reforma Administrativa* and the additional explanation in Chapter 8.

10. Whitehead, "La política económica," 508.

11. Green, "Endeudamiento externo," 84. She believes that the weakness was a result of the reduction in loans, but the picture was much more complex.

12. See José López Portillo, *Cuarto informe de gobierno, Anexo estadístico histórico* (México, D.F.: Government of Mexico, 1980). From this point, the citation will be JLP A-EH, with the corresponding year.

13. Tello, *La política económica*, 106.

14. Angeles, *Crisis y coyuntura*, 88.

15. For the monetary policy, see Tello, *La política económica*, 127–37 and 144–45.

16. See Table 2.7.

17. See L. Solís, "External Equilibrium and Fuller Uses of Productive Resources in Mexico," in L. Koslow, ed., *The Future of Mexico* (Tempe: Center for

Latin American Studies, Arizona State University, 1977), 37–38, and Tello, *La política económica*, 202–3.

18. The problem of the devaluation is discussed in chapter 3, because it is more relevant to the reasons for the confrontation between state and bourgeoisie than to economic policy.

19. *Revista Expansión* (México, D.F., September 1, 1976), 9–13.

20. Villarreal and Villarreal, "Las empresas públicas," 226–27.

21. Suárez, *Echeverría rompe el silencio*, 209.

22. Angeles, *Crisis y coyuntura*, 89.

23. Grindle, *Bureaucrats*, 12.

24. Tello, *La política económica*, 220.

25. See Camp, *Mexican Leaders*.

26. Peter, *El Principio de Peter*.

27. Bartra, *Notas sobre la cuestión*, 11.

28. Tello, *La política económica*, 106. Businessmen never tired of saying that prices rose because of increases in wages. The president of CANACINTRA made this claim and also said that CONASUPO was guilty of disloyal competition (*Journal of Commerce*, April 7, 1972). In another measure, the wheel industry intended to put producers in direct contact with consumers, which would put intermediaries out of business, reducing speculation and lowering prices.

29. In 1973 Mexico ordered 9 million bushels of wheat, which increased to 16 million bushels in ten days (*Los Angeles Times*, April 16, 1973). Mexico imported 500,000 tons of wheat in 1973 and 150,000 tons of soybeans in 1974 (*Los Angeles Times*, April 28, 1973).

30. Angeles, *Crisis y coyuntura*, 171.

31. Bartra, *Notas sobre la cuestión*, 35.

32. *New York Times*, March 30, 1973.

33. Tello, *La política económica*, 55.

34. If it were possible to calculate the inflationary impact of corruption, this case would be a good example to use. It should be pointed out, however, that the percentages paid to facilitate transactions or to favor certain vendors vary by sector of the economy, by level of supply and demand, and by the risk involved in the particular service. When it involves something illegal, the amount depends on the punishment, fine, or type of infraction.

35. On February 3, 1972, the *Journal of Commerce* reported that Mexican industrialists protested the 12 percent increase in the minimum wage. On January 2, 1976, the *Miami Herald* reported that seventy-four Mexicans had bought condominiums in San Diego that were worth between $60,000 and $150,000 each. On August 11, 1976, the *Miami Herald* said that the banking system along the border reported an increase in deposits and investments over the preceding two years. An official of the Pan American Bank, commenting on the investments on South Padre Island, Texas, said: "We're calling it South Padre Island, Nuevo León," and added, "I don't think they are afraid of the peso, but of the president, of this administration." Or could it be fear of falling profits? Possibly, the problem was paranoia.

Finally, in November of 1976, seven of the eight banks in Mexico City reported being out of dollars. The eighth limited its sales to one thousand dollars per person

(*Los Angeles Times*, November 20, 1976). If profits were low, how could businessmen retire cash from their businesses, especially if they were preparing for the Christmas season? Were they merely speculating on the peso?

36. See S. Schmidt, "El modelo de desarrollo nacional," *Revista Línea*, 6 (November–December 1973).

37. Grindle, *Bureaucrats*, 138, 153.

38. Tello, *La política económica*, 102.

39. Ibid., 99.

40. Ibid.

41. Ibid.

42. Ibid., 102.

43. C. Arriola, "Los grupos empresariales frente al estado (1973–1975)," in *Foro Internacional*, 16 (April–June 1976): 458 passim, cited by Tello, *La política económica*, 64.

44. Tello, *La política económica*, 172. See Appendix F, the index of prices of exports from the U.S., for the effects of inflation in Mexico's principal supplier.

45. Since the Mexican economy is so closely related to that of the U.S., the peso should rise or fall along with the dollar. Nonetheless, its parity was maintained, which eventually cost the country dearly. In a puzzling statement Echeverría supposedly declared, "The devaluation of the dollar neither helps us nor hurts us, but completely the opposite."

46. Grindle, *Bureaucrats*, 10–15. This work is useful for analyzing a public firm, but it quickly loses sight of the general context.

47. Johnson, *Mexican Democracy*, 104.

48. Grindle, *Bureaucrats*, 75.

49. Ibid., 107.

50. "Mexico Warns Shopkeepers," *Miami Herald*, January 5, 1974. With respect to the problem of steroids, see the conflict over barbasco in Chapter 5.

51. See Grindle, *Bureaucrats*, esp. the chapter entitled "The Politics of Policy."

52. Whitehead, "La política económica," 506.

CHAPTER 3. MANAGEMENT OF POLITICS

1. *Los Angeles Times*, May 13, 1971.

2. *Miami Herald*, December 9, 1973.

3. *Miami Herald*, January 5, 1974; *Journal of Commerce*, June 27, 1974; *Miami Herald*, October 8, 1974. *Latin America* (New York: Facts on File, 1974).

4. *Washington Post*, August 28, 1971.

5. *Latin America* (1974). It was on May 26, 1972; see *Miami Herald, April* 16, 1974; *Los Angeles Times*, April 7, 1974.

6. Soledad Loaeza, "La política del rumor: México, noviembre–diciembre 1976," *Foro Internacional* 17 (April–June 1977): 563. Also see Carlos Fuentes, *Tiempo Mexicano*.

7. For rumors and their political context, see Chapter 4.

8. Sergio Reyes Osorio, et al., *Estructura agrícola agraria y desarrollo agrícola en México* (México, D.F.: Fondo de Cultura Económica, 1974), 942–43.

9. These are the declarations of José Luis Zaragoza, director of the National Center of Agrarian Research, in *El Heraldo de Mexico*, April 5, 1981. In 1982 Zaragoza was director general of planning and evaluation of the Department of Agrarian Reform.

10. Of the 2,732 resolutions executed during the sexenio of Echeverria, 55 percent were initially filed thirty or more years previously: S. Barchfield, *Power, Politics and Agrarian Structure* (Los Angeles: Department of Economics, University of Southern California, 1978), 19. Barchfield's figure is inflated because Echeverría executed only 2,202 resolutions. See Appendix H.

11. This information, supplied by the Department of Agrarian Reform, disagrees with Zaragoza's information (see note 9), but neither source explains why.

12. Even if the published presidential resolution really means that a determination has been made about the land, before the actual execution much technical work must still be done by the Department of Agrarian Reform. In addition, there can be legal protests (*amparos*) by the landowners and endowed peasants against the published resolution or disagreement by the peasants affected. Any of these procedures can effect a long delay in the delivery of the land to the peasants.

13. Wilkie, *La revolucion mexicana*. See his Epilogue I, in which he maintains an optimistic position about the achievements of Mexico in this respect.

14. Reyes Osorio, *Estructura agrícola agraria*, 970.

15. Mario Huacuja and José Woldenberg, *Estado y lucha política en el México actual* (México, D.F.: Ed. El Caballito, 1978).

16. For an excellent description of the electricity workers' conflict, see Jacobo Ostroski, "La tendencia democrática del SUTERM durante el período del Presidente Echeverría" (Tesis de licenciatura, UNAM, 1979).

17. Leopoldo Alafita, "Sindicalismo independiente en México: Algunos indicadores, 1971–1976," *Memoria del Primer Coloquio Regional de Historia Obrera* (México, D.F.: CEHSMO, 1977).

18. Suárez, *Echeverría rompe el silencio*, 199–200.

19. Huacuja and Woldenberg, *Estado y lucha*, 67.

20. *New York Times*, February 18, 1973.

21. *Los Angeles Times*, March 20, 1973.

22. *Miami Herald*, January 6, 9, 12, 17, 1973.

23. *Miami Herald*, September 22, 1974.

24. *Latin America* (New York: Facts on File, 1973). According to the *Washington Star Journal*, October 8, 1973, there were 1,230 strikes.

25. *Miami Herald*, October 3, 1973.

26. See *Washington Star Journal*, August 20, 1974, and *New York Times*, August 21, 1974. To strike legally in Mexico, the strikers must first give warning (*emplazar*) in order to allow the parties to negotiate. If the negotiation fails, the union can strike, which means that it can close the facility.

27. Green, "Endeudamiento externo," 114–16.

28. Possibly, the electrical workers' conflict was the most violent, and here the state demonstrated that it was the great arbiter. See Ostroski, "La tendencia democrática."

29. Johnson, *Mexican Democracy*.

30. *Miami Herald*, November 1, 1972.

31. Laws, regulations, decrees, and agreements of the federal government, 1970–1976, vol. 3, p. 1933.

32. Huacuja and Woldenberg, *Estado y lucha*, p. 138.

33. Ibid., 140.

34. The versions of the rescue of Figueroa range all the way from the claim that it was simulated to the assertion that the army heroically liberated him. But the version that says that 20 million pesos were paid for the rescue seems believable (Arturo Martínez Nateras, *El secuestro de Lucio Cabañas* [Madrid: Altalena, 1986]). In any case one consequence was the closing and destruction of the magazine *Por Qué?*, because it was going to publish a communiqué from Lucio Cabanas in which he would assert that a ransom was paid to liberate Figueroa. It is interesting to note that the intellectuals did not protest this attack on freedom of expression, as they later did after the political conflict over *Excélsior*.

35. Suárez, *Echeverría rompe el silencio*, 79. Echeverría asserted that the kidnapping was real. It is clear that the kidnapping was manipulated outside of the usual guerrilla dynamic, because there were no concrete demands and Zuno was freed without anything being given as ransom. His family says that he was freed because of his health. The first question that must be asked is, Since kidnapping a person of this importance is not easy, why did the guerrillas let him go without getting anything in return? Of course, it is always possible that secret negotiations were conducted.

36. Marlise Simons, "CIA Issue in Mexican Campaign," *Washington Post*, March 18, 1975.

37. *Miami Herald*, May 12, 1975.

38. Information from *Los Angeles Times*, August 22, 1973, and *Miami Herald*, May 12, 1975.

39. For a good account of the repression during the sexenio, see Juan Miguel de Mora, *Por la gracia del señor presidente: México, la gran mentira* (México, D.F.: Ed. Asociados, 1979).

40. Dana Markiewicz, *Ejido Organization in Mexico* (Los Angeles: UCLA Latin America Center Publications, 1980), 879, says: "The programs of rural organization developed between 1972 and 1976 never intended to radically transform economic relations in favor of the peasants; instead they helped to maintain people in rural areas by improving their conditions.

41. "The lack of technicians is the greatest failing of Latin American countries at the present time . . . . Without technicians, an effective agrarian reform cannot be achieved. Without technicians, they cannot achieve any of the stages of industrialization, and tax reform, educational reform, administrative reform are all frustrated." Rafael Caldera, *Democracia cristiana y desarrollo* (Caracas, Venezuela: IFEDEC, Colección Desarrollo y Libertad, No. 2, 1964).

42. Camp, in *Mexico's Leaders*, demonstrates that UNAM is a significant component in the promotion of officials. Some important cases of officials in González Casanova's university administration who moved on to federal positions are Félix Barra García, from secretary for student services to secretary of agrarian reform (1976); Gustavo Carvajal Moreno, from head of the Department of

Information and Public Relations to secretary and president of PRI and later secretary of agrarian reform (in the sexenio of López Portillo); Enrique Velasco Ibarra, from auxiliary secretary general to private secretary for López Portillo and later governor of Guanajuato, etc. See Cuauhtémoc Ochoa, "La reforma educativa en la UNAM," *Cuadernos Políticos* 9 (July–September 1976).

43. See Carlos Fuentes, *La muerte de Artemio Cruz* (México, D.F.: Fondo de Cultura Económica, 1970).

44. Víctor Flores Olea, *Marxismo y democracia socialista* (México, D.F.: UNAM, FCPS, 1968); *La rebelión estudiantil y la sociedad contemporánea* (México, D.F.: UNAM, FCPS, 1973); *Política y dialéctica* (México, D.F.: UNAM, Escuela de Ciencias Políticas y Sociales, 1964).

45. Loaeza, "La política del rumor," 564.

46. "To mitigate the negative implications of this domination [of the PRI], electoral reforms were enacted in 1963 that guaranteed greater representation in the Congress, specifically the Chamber of Deputies, to those registered national parties that achieved 2.5 percent of the national vote. These reforms were extended in 1973 to give representation to those parties that gain only 1.5 percent of the national vote." Koslow and Mumme, "The Evolution of the Mexican Political System," in Koslow, ed., *The Future of Mexico*, 59.

47. For the political platforms of this party and those of the opposition during the period, see Fátima Fernández Christlieb, "Cuatro partidos políticos sin registro electoral: PCM, PDM, PMT, PST," *Estudios Políticos*, 3–4 (September–December 1975).

48. "Primer pleno nacional," *Punto Crítico*, Year 2, No. 23 (December 1973).

49. *Washington Post*, September 23, 1971, and *New York Times*, September 24, 1971.

50. Johnson, *Mexican Democracy*, 111.

51. See an excellent analysis of the PMT in Rosa Ma. García Téllez, "El Partido Mexicano de los Trabajadores" (Tesis de licenciatura, UNAM, 1979).

52. *Los Angeles Times*, February 11, 1971.

53. Octavio Paz, *El ogro filantrópico* (México, D.F.: Ed. Joaquín Mortiz, 1979), 115–16.

54. Francisco Paoli, "Primer fracaso de la reforma política," *Revista Proceso*, No. 142 (July 23, 1979): 32–33.

55. The Political Constitution of the United States of Mexico, in Article 89, Section VI, regarding the powers and obligations of the president of the republic, says: "To dispose permanently of the totality of the armed forces, that is, the land army, navy, and air force, for the internal security and external defense of the Federation.

Thus only Díaz Ordaz could have given the order for mobilizing the army and massacring those attending the meeting of October 2. The secretary of national defense never would have accepted such an order from the secretary of government.

To speculate about whether Echeverría recommended such a measure or not is to lose oneself in the tangle of personal responsibilities and implies the loss of perspective of a very specific state policy at a particular point in time.

56. Echeverría said: "The acts [of October 2] were grave, painful, and

regrettable for everyone and should never be repeated." For that reason, "immediately on becoming president, I initiated a policy of dialogue in order to heal the wounds." This was not "an expiation or an escape valve, but a necessity if Mexicans were to coexist and to confront the issues that divided them. At times these issues were introduced or intermixed with external factors to better carry out imperialist penetration and to prepare the conditions for domination." Suárez, *Echeverría rompe el silencio*, 135–36.

57. Huacuja and Woldenberg, *Estado y lucha*, 96. Also see Loret de Mola, *Los últimos 91 días*. The latter blames Echeverría for everything that happened in Mexico. By reproducing intimate conversations of the president without mentioning the sources, he attempts to make us believe that his word is sufficient proof of what in fact is a simplistic treatment of serious charges.

58. Huacuja and Woldenberg, *Estado y lucha*, 99.

59. Suárez, *Echeverría rompe el silencio*, 136. When a high Mexican public official is fired, the public knows that he has resigned. Thus he has to accept the full responsibility for what happened under his authority.

60. M. Guerra Leal, *La grilla* (México, D.F.: Ed. Diana, 1979). This book provides a good example of how the opposition survives in Mexico, thanks to economic and political benefits from the regime. As a high official of PARM, the author tells how he personally and the party received money from the government.

61. See Huacuja and Woldenberg, *Estado y lucha*, 119–20 and Loret de Mola, *Los últimos 91 días*, 151–55.

62. Loret de Mola, *Los últimos 91 días*, 169–78.

63. Huacuja and Woldenberg, *Estado y lucha*, 111–13.

64. Luis Encinas, *La alternativa de México* (México, D.F.: Ed. SONOT, 1969), 13, 103.

65. Suárez, *Echeverría rompe el silencio*, 139–40.

66. Ibid., 133.

67. Pinto Mazal, "Las clases medias de México."

68. Loret de Mola, *Los últimos 91 días*, 105–224.

69. Bartra, *Notas sobre la cuestión*, 39.

70. *Los Angeles Times*, August 29, 1976.

71. Ibid., November 22, 1976.

72. See a description of the conflict in the series of thirteen articles that Jesús Blancornelas published in *Excélsior* beginning October 17, 1978; also see S. Schmidt, "La intervención del estado en la sociedad civil: El caso de Sonora, México, en 1976" (Paper presented to the Seventh Seminar on the History of Sonora, November 1981).

73. Loret de Mola, *Los últimos 91 días*, 70.

74. From an interview with Jesús Blancornelas in Tijuana, March 6, 1989. Blancornelas was one of the closest journalists to Biebrich; today he is the editor of the Tijuana weekly, *Zeta*.

75. Johnson, *Mexican Democracy*, 117.

76. *Los Angeles Times*, August 19, 1976.

77. *Miami Herald*, November 15, 1976.

78. *Washington Post*, November 30, 1976.

79. This practice was not new. In 1957 a group directed by Jacinto López

applied to the UGOCM. But even though it carried out the land invasions that resulted in expropriation and distribution, only one-third of the 853 beneficiaries were from this new organization.

80. S. Schmidt, "Sonora y Sinaloa: Un nuevo engaño," *Diorama de Excélsior*, February 14, 1977.

81. *Latifundistas* are frequently found in the legislature. See the list of legislators in M. Corbalá Acuña, *Sonora y sus constituciones* (México, D.F.: Author's edition, 1972).

CHAPTER 4. BUSINESS OPPOSES THE PRESIDENT

1. The theme of the electoral campaign also was attacked, by changing the slogan *"arriba y adelante"* (upward and onward) to *"atras y abajo"* (backward and downward) and *"abajo y al carajo"* (downward and to hell).

2. According to Manuel de la Isla (cited in Johnson, *Mexican Democracy*, 185), the PRI required bankers to attend the campaign. Thus Agustín Legorreta, Ladislao López Negrete (Banco Nacional de México) and Carlos Truyet attended homages to Echeverría to avoid economic reprisals.

3. Frederick C. Turner, "Mexican Politics: The Direction of Development," in Glade and Ross, eds., *Críticas constructivas*, 168–69.

4. *El Día*, December 17, 1970.

5. Declarations cited in Green, "Endeudamiento externo y debilidad estatal," 92–95. It should be noted that the 10 percent tax was levied on makeup and toilet articles of popular use. It is possible that those who implemented the law were confused, or the measure was to confuse the propagandists of business, or it really was a measure intended to raise revenues.

6. Ibid., 94.

7. Suárez, *Echeverría rompe el silencio*, 125.

8. Huacuja and Woldenberg, *Estado y lucha*, 221–22.

9. In 1973 I had the opportunity to see a computerized report from the Department of the Treasury which analyzed the five thousand most important firms in the country, by sales, number of employees, social capital, payment of taxes, etc. It contained a column that calculated the percentage of evasion, and the transnational firms had the lowest figure, 40 percent. The evasion of some domestic firms reached 80 percent of their taxes.

10. Suárez, *Echeverría rompe el silencio*, 195.

11. Whitehead, "La política económica," 499–500.

12. Tello, *La política económica*, 200. See also C. Gribomont and M. Rimez, "La política económica del gobierno de Luis Echeverría (1971–1976): Un primer ensayo de interpretación," *El Trimestre Económico* 44 (October–December 1977).

13. Suárez, *Echeverría rompe de silencio*, 196.

14. Johnson, *Opposition Politics*, 109.

15. Gustavo de Anda, *Hacia donde lleva Echeverría a México* (México, D.F.: Author's edition, 1973).

16. "As the sexenio 1970–1976 progressed, the leftist image of Luis Echeverría and of his collaborators greatly exceeded the reality. This distortion was funda-

mentally a consequence of the fears of the conservative groups that refused to accept even the most minimum of reforms." Loaeza, "La política del rumor," 566. The same author recognizes that during those years the government had "verbal revolutionaryism" (p. 584).

17. Hellman, *Mexico in Crisis*, 38–39.

18. *New York Times*, January 18, 1975.

19. Ibid.; see also the article by Stanley Meisler, in the *Miami Herald*, January 17, 1975.

20. Suárez, *Echeverría rompe de silencio*, 211.

21. Ibid., 220.

22. Loaeza, "La política del rumor," 576.

23. Ibid., passim, and Tello, *La política económica*, 134–54.

24. *Siempre*, August 8, 1975, cited in Whitehead, "La política económica," 504.

25. Loaeza, "La política del rumor," 583.

26. Karl Deutsch, *The Nerves of Government* (New York: Free Press, 1967), measures social cohesion by the velocity at which information is transmitted.

27. Whitehead, "La política económica," 501.

28. Tello, *La política económica*, 62.

29. As can be seen in Table 4.2, the figure that *Excélsior* gave on January 7, 1977 (see Loaeza, "La política del rumor," 583), with respect to the 4 billion pesos that returned before and after the first devaluation (more than 50 percent) was probably not far off. Suárez (*Echeverría rompe el silencio*, 201) claims that 4 billion pesos fled after the devaluation, "proof that large profits had been generated during the period." The figures of Angeles (*Crisis y coyuntura*, 107) are fairly credible, considering they are extremely difficult to ascertain. But one must consider that the capital that fled to European countries and others with banking confidentiality is usually not included in such figures.

30. Tello, *La política económica*, 159.

31. The supposed comment of Echeverría was famous: "Devaluation of the dollar neither hurts us nor helps us, but the opposite."

When Suárez interviewed him, he said: "It is evident that the peso was being devalued during the years of so-called stabilizing development, but it is also very evident that there was a conspiracy of great foreign interests and some oligarchic Mexican interests to extract a great deal of capital from Mexico, as a reprisal for the labor and agrarian policies of my administration and also to push us toward a financial and commercial disequilibrium that could be corrected only by funds coming from petroleum exports. This was intimately related to the low petroleum reserves of the United States.

"The devaluation was due to that exaggerated and perfectly planned flight of capital, and there was no other solution. The Mexican treasury authorities recommended it. I did not determine it; the peso was floated on the recommendation of the Bank of Mexico and the secretary of the treasury, and it was essentially due to international pressures." (Suárez, *Echeverría rompe de silencio*, 242–43.

On the exchange rate, Carlos Bazdresch wrote: "The fact that the exchange rate for the peso in relation to the dollar had not changed in twenty years . . .

conformed to the key role that this relation played as a signal for business and for the rest of society of the will of the government not to vary, to any significant degree, the distribution of resources between the government and the private sector." ("La deuda externa y el desarrollo estabilizador," mimeograph, 1974.) See the analysis of James Wilkie on the real value of the dollar, in the introduction to *Statistical Abstract of Latin America*, vol. 22 (Los Angeles: UCLA Latin America Center Publications, 1982).

CHAPTER 5. ECHEVERRÍA AS ANTI-IMPERIALIST

1. Jean-Jacques Servan-Shreiber, *The World Challenge* (New York: Simon and Schuster, 1980).

2. Gary Gereffi, "Los oligopolios internacionales. El estado y el desarrollo industrial en México: El caso de la industria de hormonas esteroides," *Foro Internacional* 17 (April–June 1977): 526.

3. Green, "Endeudamiento externo y debilidad estatal."

4. Whitehead, "La política económica," 495.

5. The United States, Britain, West Germany, Belgium, Denmark, and Luxembourg voted against the resolution.

6. Victor Urquidi, "La carta de derechos y deberes económicos de los estados: la cuestión de su aplicación," *Foro Internacional* 20 (October–December 1979): 182.

7. Ibid., 184–90.

8. Suárez, *Echeverría rompe el silencio*, 147.

9. T. M. Laichas, "Mexico in the U.S. Press: A Quantitative Study, 1972–1976," in J. Wilkie amd P. Reich, eds., *Statistical Abstract of Latin America*, vol. 20 (Los Angeles: UCLA Latin America Center Publications, 1980), 593.

10. During the term of López Portillo, Guillermo Rosell de la Lama, secretary of national patrimony, declared: "There seemed to have been a press campaign against the nation. I like to think that it was a matter of lack of information." Ibid.

11. See the excellent works of Ariel Dorfman and Armand Mattelart, *Para leer el Pato Donald* [Reading Donald Duck] (México, D.F.: Ed. Siglo, XXI, 1973), and A. Mattelart, *La cultura como empresa multinacional* (México, D.F.: Ed. ERA, 1979).

12. The Cinematographic Bank reached the point of providing up to 90 percent of the financing of three state firms that displaced private producers. Production declined from eighty-five to sixty films a year, and in the new system the employees gained participation in profits, although it appears that profit figures do not exist. The state also controlled two distribution companies, five hundred movie theaters, two studios, and a film school. *Los Angeles Times*, March 24, 1976.

13. Rumors or anecdotes about this particular matter are very interesting. One anecdote refers to Colonel García Valseca, owner of the newspaper chain *El Sol de México*, one of the most important in the country. The chain would generally not pay PIPSA, and at the end of each sexenio, the colonel would go to the PRI's presidential candidate, who would forgive the debt. (It should be pointed out that

one rarely found criticism of the government in the *Sol* newspapers.) When the colonel went before Echeverría, the latter, in keeping with tradition, told him not to worry, that the debt would be forgiven. But when he returned to his offices, he found auditors of the Treasury Department. The debt that *El Sol* then had to pay was so great that the owners had no choice but to sell the chain to SOMEX, which in turn sold it to Vázquez Raña, who became the new president of the chain and who bought it with Echeverría. For those who repeated this version of the rumor, the fact that Mario Moya Palencia, former secretary of government, became the new director of the newspaper was sufficient proof.

14. For the problem of the two hundred-mile limit, see A. Székely, "La reclamación mexicana sobre un mar patrimonial de doscientas millas," *Boletín Mexicano de Derecho Comparado* 9 (Nos. 25–26) (January–August 1976).

15. Americans stopped going to Tijuana to get divorced and began to go to Haiti, which thereby gained such tourists.

16. According to the Bank of Mexico, the rate of increase in tourism declined by 4.7 percent. Data cited by Conrad Manley, "Mexico Weighs Reduction in Tourism Tax," *Journal of Commerce*, May 15, 1975.

17. Schmidt, "Las distintas caras."

18. *Washington Post*, November 28, 1975.

19. *New York Times*, November 30, 1975. According to the *Miami Herald* (December 23, 1975) it was 50 percent.

20. *Los Angeles Times*, December 14, 1975.

21. *Christian Science Monitor*, December 30, 1975.

22. S. Schmidt, "Sionismo y política," *Diorama de Excélsior*, December 5, 1976.

23. *Journal of Commerce*, September 20, 1976.

24. *Miami Herald*, September 10, 1976.

25. Cited in S. Schmidt, "México ante el conflicto Arabe-Israeli," (Paper presented at the International Colloquium on the Arab-Israeli Conflict, Center for Studies of the Third World, México, D.F., November 1983).

26. Susan Kaufman Purcell, "Mexico's Policy toward Central America," LASA Forum 14 (Summer 1983), suggests that the Mexican government did something similar with Cuba in the 1960s to isolate "Guevarism" and to persuade Cuba to abstain from aiding Mexican guerrillas. In return, Cuba got Mexico's support against the U.S. blockade.

27. S. Schmidt, "Las inversiones extranjeras y el desarrollo nacional: Un análisis preliminar" (Tesis de licenciatura, UNAM, 1973). Also see B. Sepúlveda and F. Chumacero, *La inversión extranjera en México* (México, D.F.: Fondo de Cultura Económica, 1973), and F. Fajnzylber and T. Martínez Tarrago, *Las empresas extranjeras, expansión a nivel mundial y proyección en la industria mexicana* (México, D.F.: Fondo de Cultura Económica, 1976).

28. Gereffi, "Los oligopolios internacionales," 491. This article is a good treatment of the barbasco conflict. All the citations with respect to this problem are from this work.

29. The same conclusion is reached by Schmidt, "Las inversiones extranjeras"; R. Tancer, "Regulating Foreign Investment in the Seventies: The Mexican Approach," in Koslow, ed., *The Future of Mexico*; and Meyer, "Desarrollo político y dependencia externa."

30. *Miami Herald*, January 15, 1976.

31. Armando Bartra, *Notas sobre la cuestión*, 42.

32. No one knows for sure how many Mexicans there are in the United States, just as no one knows how many of those deported have been deported before. But the former figure is the most confused and the one that is the most manipulated for political purposes. According to Manuel García y Griego, in *Indocumentados, mitos y realidades* (México, D.F.: El Colegio de México, 1979), in the polemic over the volume of immigration to the U.S., the estimates that are made by the U.S. Immigration and Naturalization Service are virtually impossible if they are considered by age groups and federal entity of origin.

There are some data that can be accepted, however. According to Hellman, in *Mexico in Crisis*, 87, the *bracero* program brought 12 million Mexicans to work in the U.S. between 1942 and 1964; after this program was ended, only 100,000 a year were allowed to enter. These figures seem reasonable. It should be recalled that the "12 million" were almost certainly not 12 million different people, but 12 million different visits by an unknown number of different people. It is also not known how many stayed in the U.S. or returned as illegals.

33. Hellman, *Mexico in Crisis*, 87, calculates that $1 billion of funds entered Mexico during the last six years of the *bracero* program.

34. Whitehead, "La política económica," 493.

35. Tomás Peñaloza, "Mecanismos de la dependencia: El caso de México, 1970–1975," *Foro Internacional*, 17 (July–September 1976): 22.

36. See ibid., 15–16; Huacuja and Woldenberg, *Estado y lucha*, 199; and Whitehead, "La política económica," 496, all of which claim that this law was the reason that Mexico did not join OPEC. Also see Shoshana Baron Tancer, "Introduction to the International Dimension," in Koslow, ed., *The Future of Mexico*, 187–88.

37. Notice with what ease militant students were converted into Soviet agents.

38. A direct reference to asylum in Mexico for the politically persecuted, especially the wave of Chileans who came after Pinochet's coup. What would these gentlemen have said if they had known that Hernando Pacheco, a Spanish refugee, was a presidential adviser?

39. Certainly the biggest annoyance was the approach to China.

40. Reference to the changes in agrarian legislation.

41. These senators appeared not to know that free textbooks had a long history in Mexico. The reference seems to be directed at the fact that under Echeverría, revisions that the bourgeoisie considered pernicious were made in textbooks.

42. Allusion to government attempts to organize the peasants collectively to make them more suitable for credit.

43. *New York Times*, August 16, 1976.

44. *Miami Herald*, August 17, 1976.

CHAPTER 6. END OF THE SEXENIO: COUP D'ETAT?

1. The total figure is from José López Portillo, *Tercer informe de gobierno, Anexo estadístico histórico* (México, D.F.: Government of Mexico, 1979), but it is

aggregated. The other figure is from Alan Riding, "Mexican Army, amid Rumors, Insists It Steers Clear of Politics," *New York Times*, February 5, 1974.

2. R. Camp, "Mexican Military Leadership in Statistical Perspective since the 1930s," in J. Wilkie and P. Reich, eds., *Statistical Abstract of Latin America*, vol. 20 (Los Angeles: UCLA Latin America Center Publications, 1980), 599.

3. Riding, "Mexican Army." One must remember that because of corruption and smuggling, a customs post is a source of privileged income and one of the most coveted spoils for a certain type of politician.

4. Meyer, "Desarrollo político," 13.

5. This is the version of Loret de Mola, *Los últimos 91 días.*

6. SOMEX was the most important financial instrument for managing bankrupt or fiscally ailing firms that were nationalized.

7. "Mexico's Election: The American Connection," in the *Washington Post*, January 27, 1976.

8. Joaquín Cisneros, Díaz Ordaz's private secretary, said in an interview with *Proceso*, October 13, 1980, that Echeverría asked Díaz Ordaz to fire Ortiz Mena, secretary of the treasury, and Gil Preciado, secretary of agriculture, so that they would not disturb him in the campaign, which the president did.

In the case in question Reyes Heroles was not eligible because of the constitutional provision that for one to be a presidential candidate, both of one's parents must be Mexican by birth; in his case they were Spaniards. This change possibly had some other political connotations.

9. Loaeza, "La política del rumor," 583.

10. *Excélsior*, March 2, 1977.

CHAPTER 7. CONCLUSION

1. Kenneth Godwin, "Mexican Population Policy: Problems Posed by Participatory Demography in a Paternalistic Political System," in Koslow, ed., *The Future of Mexico*, 146, 157.

POSTSCRIPT, 1990

1. The commercial balance was in surplus for only a short time. See John Pool and Steve Stamos, *The ABC's of International Finance* (Lexington, Mass.: Lexington Books, 1987).

2. I disagree somewhat with the concept of "technocrat" for two reasons. First, many people identify as technocrats those who have studied, usually at a university. Thus the term is conceived so broadly as to be almost meaningless. It is true that recent presidents have pursued university and graduate studies, but de la Madrid and Salinas did so while they were high officials. This practice makes one wonder either how necessary the degree was to bureaucratic and political success or whether the system of Mexican degrees is too generous. It is clear that Mexican presidents since Alemán have achieved the highest academic degree that was in style in the country at the time. Recently, the country is coming to expect a graduate degree

of its leaders. Second, people identify as a technocrat whoever prefers technical solutions for political problems. Recent presidents have generally preferred bureaucratic solutions to political problems.

3. For networks and their structure, see Ronald S. Burt, *Toward a Structural Theory of Action* (New York: Academic Press, 1982).

4. Echeverría said that López Portillo was selected as the presidential candidate because he had the fewest "attachments," he had not reached any secret agreements, and he had devoted himself to the service of the country without engaging in política barata ("cheap politics"). *Excélsior*, November 13, 1975. Cited by Smith, *Labyrinths of Power*, 288–89. See also Chapter 3 in this book, especially the section called "The Governors."

5. The biographical data on the presidents are taken from Camp, *Mexican Political Biographies*.

6. Frank Brandenburg, *The Making of Modern Mexico* (Englewood Cliffs, N.J.: Prentice-Hall, 1967).

7. Manuel Bartlett (secretary of government), Miguel González Avelar (secretary of public education), Carlos Salinas de Gortari (secretary of planning and budgeting), Ramón Aguirre (chief of the Department of the Federal District), Alfredo del Mazo (secretary of energy, mines and parastatal industries), Sergio García Ramírez (federal attorney general of justice).

8. In the presidential election of 1988 the five candidates were assigned the following percentages of the popular vote:

Carlos Salinas (PRI): 50.36 percent
Cuauhtémoc Cárdenas (National Democratic Front, FDN): 31.12 percent
[The FDN included the Authentic Party of the Mexican Revolution (PARM), the Party of the Cardenista Front for National Reconstruction (PCFRN), the Mexican Socialist Party (PMS), and the Popular Socialist Party (PPS).]
Manuel J. Clouthier (National Action Party, PAN): 17.07 percent
Rosario Ibarra (Revolutionary Party of the Workers, PRT): 0.42 percent
Gumersindo Magaña (Mexican Democratic Party, PDM): 1.04 percent
(Data taken from Fundación Arturo Rosenblueth, *Geografía de las elecciones presidenciales de México*, 1988 [México, D.F., 1988].)

9. Ernest Becker, *La lucha contra el mal* (México, D.F.: Fondo de Cultura Económica, 1980), does a magnificent analysis of the role of wars in the search for spiritual nourishment of the victorious people, who feed themselves spiritually with the death of the vanquished.

10. See the material relevant to this point in Chapter 3, especially the section entitled "The Governors."

11. It is interesting to note that the resignation of Carlos Tello as secretary of planning and budgeting and of Julio Rodolfo Moctezuma as secretary of the treasury in 1977 were attributable to a serious disagreement between them in the heart of the economic cabinet of José López Portillo.

12. Most academics are in agreement with this image of the pyramid of power; see a graphic description in Padgett, *The Mexican Political System.*

13. Complaints of corruption abound regarding the peasant and agrarian question, complaints that previously would have been diverted by the hope for more land. See the case of the Laguna region, where Salinas was poorly received as a candidate and where he did not return as president until late 1990.

BIBLIOGRAPHY

Aguilar M., Rubén. "Participación de la banca privada mexicana en el desarrollo socio-económico del país." *Temas de negocios*, Vol. 2, No. 8. México, D.F., 1972.

Aguilar, Alonso, and Fernando Carmona. *México: Riqueza y miseria.* México. D.F.: Editorial Nuestro Tiempo, 1972.

Alafita, Leopoldo. "Sindicalismo independiente en México: Algunos indicadores, 1971–1976." *Memoria del Primer Coloquio Regional de Historia Obrera.* México, D.F.: CEHSMO, 1977.

Alejo, F.J. "La política fiscal en el desarrollo de México." In *¿Crecimiento o desarrollo económico?* México, D.F.: Ed. Sepsetentas, 1971.

Allison, Graham. *Essence of Decision: Explaining the Cuban Missile Crisis.* Boston: Little, Brown, 1971.

Alonso, Antonio. *El movimiento ferrocarrillero en México, 1958–1959.* México, D.F.: Ed. ERA, 1972.

Angeles, Luis. *Crisis y coyuntura de la economía mexicana.* México, D.F.: Ed. El Caballito, 1979.

Arriola, C. "Los grupos empresariales frente al estado (1973–75)." *Foro Internacional* 16 (April–June, 1976).

―――――. "La crisis del Partido Acción Nacional (1975–76)." *Foro Internacional* 17 (April–June 1977).

Banco Nacional de Comercio Exterior. *La política económica para 1972.* México, D.F., 1972.

Barchfield, S. *Power, Politics and Agrarian Structure.* Research Papers in Economics, Department of Economics, University of Southern California, 1978.

Bartra, Armando. *Notas sobre la cuestión campesina.* México, D.F.: Ed. Macehual, 1979.

Basañez, Miguel. *La lucha por la hegemonía en México, 1968–1980.* México, D.F.: Ed. Siglo XXI, 1985.

Bazdresch, Carlos. "La deuda externa y el desarrollo estabilizador." Mimeograph, 1974.

Becker, Ernest. *La lucha contra el mal.* México, D.F.: Fondo de Cultura Económica, 1980.

Brandenburg, Frank. *The Making of Modern Mexico.* Englewood Cliffs, N.J.: Prentice-Hall, 1967.

Burt, Ronald S. *Toward a Structural Theory of Action.* New York: Academic Press, 1982.

Caldera, Rafael. *Democracia cristiana y desarrollo.* Caracas, Venezuela: IFEDEC, Colección Desarrollo y Libertad, No. 2, 1964.

Camp, Roderic. "Mexican Military Leadership in Statistical Perspective since the 1930s." In J. Wilkie and P. Reich, eds., *Statistical Abstract of Latin America,* vol. 20. Los Angeles: UCLA Latin America Center Publications, 1980.

——. *Mexico's Leaders: Their Education and Recruitment.* Tucson: University of Arizona Press, 1980.

——. *Mexican Political Biographies, 1935–81.* Tucson: University of Arizona Press, 1982.

Carrillo, Alejandro. *La reforma administrativa en México.* México, D.F.: Miguel Angel Porrua Ed., 1980.

Corbalá Acuña, M. *Sonora y sus constituciones.* México, D.F.: Author's edition, 1972.

Cordera, Rolando. "Crisis nacional y política económica." *Revista Mexicana de Ciencia Política* 21, (No. 80) (April–June 1975).

——. "Los límites del reformismo: La crisis del capitalismo en México." *Cuadernos Políticos* 2. México, D.F.: Ed. ERA, 1974.

Córdova, Arnaldo. *La formación del poder político en México.* México, D.F.: Ed. ERA, 1972.

Cosío Villegas, Daniel. *El estilo personal de gobernar.* México, D.F.: Ed. Joaquín Mortiz, 1974.

——. *La sucesión: Desenlace y perspectivas.* México, D.F.: Cuadernos de Joaquín Mortiz, 1976.

Cothran, Dan, and Cheryl Cole Cothran. "Mexican Presidents and Budgetary Secrecy." *International Journal of Public Administration* 11 (3) (1988).

De Anda, Gustavo. *Hacia dónde lleva Echeverría a México.* México, D.F.: Author's edition, 1973.

de Kay, John. *Mexico: The Problem and the Solution.* México, D.F.: S.E., 1927.

De Mora, Juan Miguel. *T 68.* México, D.F.: EDAMEX, 1ST ed. 1973; 22D ed. 1989.

——. *Por la gracia del señor presidente: México, la gran mentira.* México, D.F.: Ed. Asociados, 1979.

——. *El Rig Veda.* México, D.F.: UNAM, 1980.

——. *Esto nos dió López Portillo.* México, D.F.: Anaya Editores, 1982.

——. *The Principle of Opposites in Sanskrit Texts.* India: Pandit Rampratap Shastri Charitable Trust, 1982.

——. *No, sr. presidente.* México, D.F.: Anaya Editores, 1983.

——. trans. Bhavabhuti's *El ultimo lance de Rama.* México, D.F.: UNAM, 1984.

——. *Ni renovación, ni moral.* México, D.F.: Anaya Editores, 1985.

——. *Elecciones en México.* México, D.F.: EDAMEX, 1988.

"Defenderemos el derecho de huelga con la huelga misma." Solidaridad, Nos. 164–65 (July 1976).

Del Villar, Samuel. "Estado y petróleo en México: Experiencias y perspectivas." *Foro Internacional* 22 (July–September 1979).

Deutsch, Karl. *The Nerves of Government.* New York: Free Press, 1967.

Dorfman, Ariel, and Armand Mattelart. *Para leer el Pato Donald.* México, D.F.: Ed. Siglo XXI, 1973.

Dror, Yehezkel. *Estudios del futuro para la planeación estratégica.* México, D.F.: Programa Universitario de Cómputo, UNAM, 1984.

_____ . *Enfrentando el futuro.* México, D.F.: Fondo de Cultura Económica, 1990.

Echeverría, Luis. *Caminos y voces.* México, D.F.: Government of Mexico, S.E., July 1971.

Echeverría, Rodolfo. "Las clases medias explotadas." *Revista Línea* 2 (February–March 1973).

Eisenstadt, Shmuel. *Ensayos sobre el cambio social y la modernización.* Madrid: Ed. Tecnos, 1970.

Encinas, Luis. *La alternativa de México.* México, D.F.: Ed. SONOT, 1969.

Fajnzylber, F., and Martínez Tarrago, T. *Las empresas extranjeras, expansión a nivel mundial y proyección en la industria mexicana.* México, D.F.: Fondo de Cultura Económica, 1976.

Fernández Christlieb, Fátima. "Cuatro partidos políticos sin registro electoral: PCM, PDM, PMT, PST." *Estudios Políticos* 3–4 (September–December 1975).

Fitzgerald, E. V. K. "The State and Capital Accumulation in Mexico." *Journal of Latin American Studies* 10 (1978).

Flores Olea, Victor. *Política y dialéctica.* México, D.F.: UNAM, 1964.

_____ . *Marxismo y democracia socialista.* México, D.F.: UNAM, 1968.

_____ . *La rebelión estudiantil y la sociedad contemporánea.* México, D.F.: UNAM, 1973.

Fuentes, Carlos. *La muerte de Artemio Cruz.* México, D.F.: Fondo de Cultura Económica, 1970.

_____ . *Tiempo mexicano.* México, D.F.: Cuadernos de Joaquín Mortíz, 1972.

Fundación Arturo Rosenblueth. *Geografía de las elecciones presidenciales de Mexico, 1988.* México, D.F., 1988.

García Stahl, Consuelo. *Un anhelo de libertad.* México, D.F.: UNAM, 1968.

García Téllez, Rosa Maria. "El Partido Mexicano de los Trabajadores." Tesis de licenciatura, UNAM, 1979.

García y Griego, Manual. *Indocumentados, mitos y realidades.* México, D.F.: El Colegio de México, 1979.

Gereffi, Gary, "Los oligopolios internacionales. El estado y el desarrollo industrial en México: El caso de la industria de hormonas esteroides." *Foro Internacional,* 17 (April–June 1977).

Glade, William, and Stanley Ross, eds. *Críticas constructivas del sistema político mexicano.* Austin: Institute of Latin American Studies, University of Texas, 1973.

González Casanova, Pablo. *La democracia en México.* México, D.F.: Ed. ERA, 1969.

Gramsci, Antonio. *Antología.* Madrid: Ed. Siglo XXI, 1974.

Green, Rosario. *El endeudamiento público externo en México, 1940–1973.* México, D.F.: El Colegio de México, 1976.

_____ . "Mexico's Public Foreign Debt, 1965–76." *Comercio Exterior de México* 24 (January 1978).

_____ . "Endeudamiento externo y debilidad estatal: El caso de México." *Foro Internacional* 20 (July–September 1979).

Gribomont, C., and Rimez, M. "La política económica del gobierno de Luis Echeverría (1971–76): Un primer ensayo de interpretación." *El trimestre económico* 44 (October–December 1977).

Grindle, Merilee. *Bureaucrats, Politicians and Peasants in Mexico.* Los Angeles: University of California Press, 1977.

_____ . *Official Interpretations of Rural Underdevelopment: Mexico in the* 1970s. Working Papers in U.S.-Mexican Studies, 20. San Diego: University of California, 1981.

Guerra Leal, M. *La grilla.* México, D.F.: Ed. Diana, 1979.

Hellman, Judith. *Mexico in Crisis.* New York: Holmes and Meier, 1978.

Huacuja, Mario, and José Woldenberg. *Estado y lucha política en el México actual.* México, D.F.: Ed. El Caballito, 1978.

Johnson, Kenneth. *Mexican Democracy: A Critical View.* Boston: Allyn and Bacon, 1971. Rev. ed. New York: Praeger, 1978.

Koslow, Lawrence, ed. *The Future of Mexico.* Tempe: Center for Latin American Studies, Arizona State University, 1977.

Laichas, T. "Mexico in the U.S. Press: A Quantitative Study, 1972–1976." In J. Wilkie and P. Reich, eds., *Statistical Abstract of Latin America,* vol. 20. Los Angeles: UCLA Latin American Center Publications, 1980.

Loaeza, Soledad. "La política del rumor: México, noviembre–diciembre de 1976." *Foro Internacional* 17 (April–June 1977).

López Cámara, Francisco. "El dilemma político de las clases medias en México." *Revista Línea* 14 (March–April 1975).

López Portillo, José. *Tercer informe de gobierno.* México, D.F., 1979.

_____ . *Cuarto informe de gobierno.* México, D.F., 1980.

Loret de Mola, Carlos. *Confesiones de un gobernador.* México, D.F.: Ed. Grijalbo, 1978.

_____ . *Los últimos 91 días.* México, D.F.: Ed. Grijalbo, 1978.

_____ . *El juicio.* México, D.F.: Ed. Grijalbo, 1984.

Luiselli, Casio. *El sistema alimentario mexicano (SAM): Elementos de un programa de producción acelerada de alimentos básicos en México.* Working Papers in U.S.-Mexican Studies 22. San Diego: University of California, 1980.

Lyotard, J. "Pequeña perspectiva de la decadencia y de algunos combates minoritarios por entablar allí." In Dominique Grisoni, ed., *Políticas de la filosofía.* México, D.F.: Breviarios del Fondo de Cultura Económica, 1982.

Macotela, C. "El sindicalismo en el cine." *Otro Cine* 1 (No. 4) (October–December 1975).

Manley, Conrad. "México Weighs Reduction in Tourism Tax." *Journal of Commerce,* May 15, 1975.

Mao Tse-tung. "Análisis de las clases de la sociedad China." In *Obras escogidas.* Pekin: Ediciones en Lenguas Extranjeras, 1968.

Markiewicz, Dana. *Ejido Organization in Mexico, 1934–763.* Los Angeles: UCLA Latin America Center Publications, 1980.

Martin, J. L. "Labor's Real Wages in Latin America since 1940." In James W.

Wilkie and Peter Reich, eds. *Statistical Abstract of Latin America*, vol. 18. Los Angeles: UCLA Latin American Center Publications, 1978.

Martínez Nateras, Arturo. *El secuestro de Lucio Cabañas*. Madrid: Altalena, 1986.

Martínez Rios, Jorge, ed. *El perfil de México en 1980*. México, D.F.: Ed. Siglo XXI: 1972.

Marx, Karl. "El 18 Brumario de Luis Bonaparte." In *Obras Escogidas*. Moscow: Ed. Progreso, 1969.

Mattelart, Armand. *Agresión desde el espacio*. Buenos Aires: Siglo XXI, 1973.

————. *La cultura como empresa multinacional*. México, D.F.: Ed. ERA, 1979.

Melgarejo, José Luis. "Devenir de la clase media en México." *Revista Línea* 14 (March–April 1975).

Memoria del Primer Coloquio Nacional Regional de Historia Obrera. México, D.F.: CEHSMO, 1977.

Meyer, Lorenzo. "Desarrollo político y dependencia externa: México en el siglo XX." In William Glade and Stanley Ross, eds., *Críticas constructivas del sistema político mexicano* Austin: University of Texas, Institute of Latin American Studies, 1973.

Molina Piñeiro, Luis, and Arturo Sánchez Vázquez. *Descripción de un conflicto*. México, D.F.: UNAM, 1980.

Monson, Robert. "Political Stability in Mexico: The Changing Role of Traditional Rightists." *Journal of Politics* 35 (August 1973).

Muñoz Ledo, Porfirio. "Política laboral y desarrollo nacional." *Reseña Laboral* 1 (May 1972).

Ochoa, Cuauhtémoc. "La reforma educativa en la UNAM." *Cuadernos Políticos* 9 (July–September, 1976).

Osorio Marban, Miguel. *Revolución y política*. México, D.F.: n.p., n.d.

Ostroski, Jacobo. "La tendencia democrática del SUTERM durante el período del Presidente Echeverría." Tesis de licenciatura, UNAM, 1979.

Padgett, Vincent. *The Mexican Political System*. Atlanta: Houghton Mifflin, 1976.

Paoli, Francisco. "Primer fracaso de la reforma política." *Revista Proceso* 142 (July 23, 1979).

Paz, Octavio. *El ogro filantrópico*. México, D.F.: Ed. Joaquín Mortiz, 1979.

————. *El laberinto de la soledad*. México, D.F.: Fondo de Cultura Económica, 1986.

Pellicer de Brody, Olga. "Las relaciones comerciales de México: Una prueba para la nueva política exterior." *Foro Internacional* 17 (July–September 1976).

Peñaloza, Tomás. "Mecanismos de la dependencia: El caso de México, 1970–1975." *Foro Internacional* 17 (July–September 1976).

Pereyra, C. "México: Los límites del reformismo." *Cuadernos Políticos* 1 México, D.F.: Ed. ERA, 1974.

Peter, Lawrence J. *El Principio de Peter*. Barcelona: Ed. Plaza & Janes, S.A., 1977.

Pinto Mazal, Jorge. "Las clases medias en México." *Revista Línea* 14 (March–April 1975).

Pool, John, and Steve Stamos. *The ABC's of International Finance*. Lexington, Mass.: Lexington Books, 1987.

Portes Gil, Emilio. "La Confederación Nacional Campesina." *Revista del México Agrario*, 5 (3) (1972).

Purcell, Susan Kaufman. "Mexico's Policy toward Central America." *LASA Forum* 14 (Summer 1983).

Ramírez, R. *El movimiento estudiantil en México*. México, D.F.: Ed. ERA, 1969.

Retchkiman, Benjamin. *Política fiscal mexicana*. México, D.F.: UNAM, 1980.

Rey Romay, Benito. *La ofensiva empresarial contra la intervención del estado*. México, D.F.: Ed. Siglo XXI, 1984.

Reyes Osorio, Sergio, et al. *Estructura agrícola agraria y desarrollo agrícola en México*. México, D.F.: Fondo de Cultura Económica, 1974.

Reyna, José Luis. "The Mexican Authoritarian Regime: Is It Still Consolidating?" México, D.F.: El Colegio de México, mimeograph, n.d.

Riding, Alan. "Mexican Army, Amid Rumors, Insists It Steers Clear of Politics." *New York Times*, February 5, 1974.

Saldivar, Americo. *Ideología y política del estado mexicano, 1970–1976*. México, D.F.: Ed. Siglo XXI, 1981.

Salgado, Antonio. *Humor negro a la mexicana*. México, D.F.: Libra, 1986.

Sanderson, Susan W. "Agrarian Policy, Political Stability and Modernization in Mexico." Mimeograph, 1980.

Schaffer, Carlos. "El capitalismo monopolista de estado y los sindicatos en México." *Problemas del Desarrollo* 5 (20). México, D.F.: Instituto de Investigaciones Económicas, UNAM, 1975.

Schmidt, Samuel. "Las inversiones extranjeras y el desarrollo nacional: Un análisis preliminar." Tesis de licenciatura, UNAM, 1973.

_____ . "El modelo de desarrollo nacional." *Revista Línea* 8 (November–December 1973).

_____ . "Sionismo y política." *Diorama Excélsior*, December 5, 1976.

_____ . *La política de industrialización de Miguel Alemán*. México, D.F.: UNAM, CELA, FCPS, 1977.

_____ . "Sonora y Sinaloa: Un nuevo engaño." *Diorama de Excélsior*, February 14, 1977.

_____ . "El estado y su autonomía." *Problemas del Desarrollo* 40 (November 1979–January 1980).

_____ . *Democracia mexicana: La reforma política de López Portillo*. México, D.F.: UNAM, CELA, FCPS, 1981.

_____ . "La intervención del estado en la sociedad civil: El caso de Sonora, México, en 1976." Paper presented to the Seventh Seminar on the History of Sonora, November 1981.

_____ . "Las distintas caras de la deuda del sector público mexicano, 1970–1976." In James W. Wilkie and Stephen Haber, eds., *Statistical Abstract of Latin America*, vol. 22. Los Angeles: UCLA Latin American Center Publications, 1982.

_____ . "México ante el conflicto Arabe-Israeli." Paper presented at the International Colloquium on the Arab-Israeli Conflict, Center for Studies of the Third World, México, D.F., November 1983.

_____ . *La autonomía relativa del estado*. México, D.F.: Quinto Sol, 1988.

_____ . "Votación en la frontera México-Estados Unidos, 1961–1982," In S.

Schmidt, J. Wilkie, and M. Esparza, eds., *Estudios cuantitativos sobre la historia de Mexico*. México, D.F.: UNAM, 1988.

———. "Elitelore: Political Humor and the Mexican Presidents." *Journal of Latin American Lore* 16 (Summer 1990).

Schmidt, Samuel, and Jorge Gil. "Mexico: The Network behind Power." *Review of Latin American Studies*, forthcoming.

Sepúlveda, B., and Chumacero, F. *La inversión extranjera en México*. México, D.F.: Fondo de Cultura Económica, 1973.

Servan-Shreiber, Jean-Jacques. *The World Challenge*. New York: Simon and Schuster, 1980.

Skidmore, Thomas, and Peter Smith. *Modern Latin America*. New York: Oxford University Press, 1984.

Smith, N. A. "Government vs. Trade Unions in Britain." *Political Quarterly* 46 (1975).

Smith, Peter. *Labyrinths of Power: Political Recruitment in Twentieth-Century Mexico*. Princeton: Princeton University Press, 1979.

———. *Los laberintos del poder*. México, D.F.: El Colegio de México, 1982.

Suárez, Luis. *Echeverría rompe el silencio*. México, D.F.: Ed. Grijalbo, 1979.

Székely, A. "La reclamación mexicana sobre el mar patrimonial de doscientas millas." *Boletín Mexicano de Derecho Comparado*, 9 (Nos. 25–26) (January–August, 1976).

Tello, Carlos. *La política económica en México, 1970–1976*. México, D.F.: Ed. Siglo XXI, 1980.

Tyler, Michael. "The Mexican 'Legal Revolution' and Economic Nationalism, 1970–1974." Los Angeles: UCLA, Department of History, mimeograph, n.d.

Urquidi, Víctor. "La carta de derechos y deberes económicos de los estados: La cuestión de su aplicación." *Foro Internacional* 20 (October–December 1979).

Varios. *El milagro mexicano*. México, D.F.: Ed. Nuestro Tiempo, 1971.

———. *Neolatifundismo y explotación*. México, D.F.: Ed. Nuestro Tiempo, 1973.

Velázquez Carmona, Manuel. "Dinámica de las clases medias." *Revista Línea* 14 (March–April 1975).

Villarreal, P. and Rocío P. de Villarreal. "Las empresas públicas como instrumento de política." *El Trimestre Económico* 45 (April–June 1978).

Whitehead, L. "La política económica del sexenio de Echeverría: Qué salió mal y por qué?" *Foro Internacional* 22 (January–March 1980).

Wilkie, James. *The Mexican Revolution: Federal Expenditures and Social Change since 1910*. 2D ed. Berkeley: University of California Press, 1970.

———. *La revolución mexicana: Gasto federal y cambio social*. México, D.F.: Fondo de Cultura Económica, 1978.

Wilkie, James and Stephen Haber, eds. *Statistical Abstract of Latin America*, vols. 21 and 22. Los Angeles: UCLA Latin America Center Publications, 1980.

Wilkie, James and Peter Reich, eds. *Statistical Abstract of Latin America*, vols. 18 and 20. Los Angeles: UCLA Latin America Center Publications, 1978 and 1980.

Zermeño, Felipe, "Sonora: La lucha por la tierra." *Boletín de Crítica Económica* 3 (May–June 1976). México, D.F.: Escuela Nacional de Economía, UNAM.

Zweig, Stefan. *La lucha contra el demonio*. México, D.F.: Ed. Tor, 1945.

MAGAZINES

Latin America (New York: Facts on File)
Proceso
Punto Crítico
Reseña Laboral

NEWSPAPERS

Excélsior
El Heraldo de México
Journal of Commerce
Los Angeles Times
Miami Herald
New York Times
Washington Post

INDEX

ABOUT THE AUTHOR

Samuel Schmidt has taught at the University of California at Los Angeles, San Diego State University, and the University of San Diego. He is an associate professor at the Universidad de Guadalajara and the Universidad Autónoma de Nuevo León. His Ph.D. in political science was earned at the National Autonomous University of Mexico, his M.A. at the Hebrew University of Jerusalem. He was a postdoctoral fellow at UCLA's Department of History. Professor Schmidt has lectured not only at universities in the United States and Mexico but also in Spain, Israel, and Venezuela.

Among Professor Schmidt's publications are *La autonomía relativa del estado* (1986) and *Estudios cuantitativos sobre la historia de México* (1988). He has also published articles on Mexican political humor, economic policy, politics, and elections. He is editor of *Nuestra Economía*, a journal published by the School of Economics of the Universidad Autónoma de Baja California in Tijuana.

ABOUT THE TRANSLATOR

Dan A. Cothran, Associate Professor of Political Science at Northern Arizona University in Flagstaff, received his Ph.D. in 1979 from Cornell University. He taught in the Faculty of Commerce at the University of British Columbia and now teaches and does research in Latin American politics, comparative public policy, and government budgeting. The focus of his research has been budgetary uncontrollability and strategic uses of budgetary secrecy by Mexican presidents. He has published in such journals as *Western Political Quarterly, Mexican Studies, Public Budgeting and Finance, Policy Studies,* and *International Journal of Public Administration.*